HOW
LUCK
HAPPENS

Also by Janice Kaplan

The Gratitude Diaries

HOW
LUCK
HAPPENS

Using the New Science of Luck to Transform

Life, Love, and Work

JANICE KAPLAN
AND BARNABY MARSH

DUTTON

DUTTON

An imprint of Penguin Random House LLC
375 Hudson Street
New York, New York 10014

LIBRARY OF CONGRESS CATALOGING-IN-PUBLICATION DATA

Names: Kaplan, Janice, author. | Marsh, Barnaby, author.
Title: How luck happens : using the new science of luck to transform work, love, and life / Janice Kaplan, Barnaby Marsh.
Description: 1 Edition. | New York : Dutton, 2018.
Identifiers: LCCN 2017035996 (print) | LCCN 2017041723 (ebook) |
ISBN 9781101986400 (ebook) | ISBN 9781101986394 (hardback) |
ISBN 9781524743284 (export edition)
Subjects: LCSH: Self-actualization (Psychology) | Success. | BISAC: SELF-HELP
/ Personal Growth / Success. | MATHEMATICS / Probability & Statistics / General.
Classification: LCC BF637.S4 (ebook) | LCC BF637.S4 K33212 2018 (print) | DDC 158—dc23
LC record available at https://lccn.loc.gov/2017035996

Printed in the United States of America
1   3   5   7   9   10   8   6   4   2

Set in Fairfield LT Std Light
Designed by Cassandra Garruzzo

For our wonderful children . . .
and everybody who wants to make more luck in the world

Contents

Contents

HOW
LUCK
HAPPENS

Preface

You don't have to travel very far in Hollywood to encounter men and women driving Uber cars or doing chores for TaskRabbit as they wait for the lucky break that will catapult them to stardom. Many majored in drama in college or starred in a hometown production of *Rent*—and now they need someone else to notice their talent, too.

"You have to give yourself a chance to get lucky," said Cassie, a bright-eyed redhead I met one warm evening at a café on Sunset Boulevard. She was behind the bar, making her signature Moscow mule—vodka, lime, and ginger beer. (I ordered a Diet Coke.) But making the perfect drink wasn't what kept Cassie going. As we chatted, she told me she had recently graduated from college and had driven her beat-up Kia two thousand miles west to come to Hollywood. Now she was waiting for the lucky encounter that would make her a star.

"I just keep saying to myself, *Harrison Ford*," Cassie said.

Ah, yes, lucky Harrison. His early adventures are as legendary among acting aspirants as the exploits of Indiana Jones. When he first arrived in Los Angeles in the 1960s, Ford got so little attention for his acting prowess that he started working as a carpenter. A young director who was also starting out hired him to build some cabinets for his house. They got to know and like each other, and the director gave Ford a part in a small movie he was shooting on a minimal budget. It was turned down by six movie studios but eventually became an unexpectedly massive hit.

The movie was *American Graffiti*. The director was George Lucas. Perhaps you've heard of him? A few years later, Lucas got the go-ahead to make another movie the studios didn't really believe in—*Star Wars*—and he cast his new buddy Harrison Ford in it.

"You think you'll find your own George Lucas in the bar?" I asked Cassie when she came over to refill my drink.

"You bet," she said with a grin.

And why not? She had put herself in a place to get lucky, right here at the edge of the Hollywood Hills, where many producers and directors live. Maybe the next guy she served would be an executive at Paramount (or at least the Disney Channel) who would spot her potential.

For Harrison Ford, the chance encounter with Lucas led to the cascade of events that made him one of the biggest stars of his generation. If not for those cabinets, he might never have rocketed to international fame in *Star Wars*. A different actor would have been frozen in a large block of carbonite as the very cool Han Solo.

The idea that chance events can play such a huge role in a career is both encouraging ("It can happen to me!") and discouraging ("But what if it doesn't?"). Many people in Hollywood and elsewhere believe you make your own luck, which explains the would-be screenwriters who have their scripts with them at all times, ready to present to anyone with a friendly face.

Watching Cassie dash around the café with her big smile and lively chatter, I realized that it was possible I would see her on the big screen someday. But more than a single chance encounter would be at play. In moving to Hollywood, working at the bar, and talking to people (like me), she was creating her own opportunities. She had put all the pieces in place to make her own luck.

We chatted a little more until a friend of mine arrived, and

Cassie discovered that I had once been a TV producer with a fun and interesting career. At the end of the evening, when Cassie dropped the bill off at our table, she asked, "Any advice on how I can be one of the lucky ones?"

"You will be," I said encouragingly.

I left a big tip and walked out with an even bigger question spinning in my head.

What can any of us—including Cassie—do to make ourselves one of the lucky ones? Sure, random chance plays a role in life, but we can't just shrug our shoulders and leave it at that. We have to take the right steps and control what we can.

I thought of the poem by Emily Dickinson in which she wrote that luck isn't chance, it's hard work, and "Fortune's expensive smile / is earned—" I've always liked that phrase, and now, as I walked to my car in the warm Los Angeles night, I wondered what it takes to win fortune's expensive smile. How do we go about making our own luck?

I was still thinking about that question when I got back to New York and had afternoon tea with my friend Barnaby Marsh. Having gone to Oxford as a Rhodes Scholar, Barnaby still likes strong tea and scones, and I'm always happy to join him. Barnaby is in his early forties, with a quirky, original way of thinking, and he holds appointments at both the Institute for Advanced Study at Princeton and the Program for Evolutionary Dynamics at Harvard. In other words, he's the kind of guy you turn to when you're trying to figure something out.

So I told him about Cassie, and I presented the Harrison Ford conundrum: If the now-famous actor hadn't met George Lucas, would he still be making his living with a hammer and nails?

Barnaby sat very still for a minute or two, staring off into the distance, thinking about the problem.

"It's complicated," he said finally. "Unforeseen events—like that meeting with Lucas—can play a role. But if you put enough of the right elements in place, you can take some of the onus off its all being random chance."

Well, that sounded promising. I started thinking about what those right elements for creating luck might be. Talent was surely one of them. So was hard work.

"What advice would you give Cassie?" I asked him.

He broke off a piece of a scone and munched it thoughtfully. "I'd say that luck is all around us, waiting to be found. But most people walk right by it and don't realize that it's there for the taking. There's enough luck in the world for everyone if you know where to look."

So why do we so often miss it? Barnaby turned briefly scientific on me and pointed out that, biologically, the human attention span was set to screen out things that weren't necessary for survival. Now we needed to turn that instinct on its head and learn to screen things *in*.

"Opportunities are all around you, and you just have to learn to see them," he continued. "There are ways everyone can make themselves luckier."

Barnaby was convinced that whether you're Harrison Ford looking to be an actor, a millennial wanting to find true love, or a corporate executive plotting to be CEO, you have more control over the events in your life than you realize. We often don't recognize how many things we set in motion by our own actions. Sometimes the seed of opportunity that we plant doesn't blossom into luck until weeks or months or even years later. When it does, it looks to everyone else like random chance—but we've made it happen. Call it planned serendipity.

Barnaby told me that his research at Oxford had been on risk-taking, and he was working on theoretical concepts of luck at the Institute for Advanced Study. Through his academic work, he was in the process of developing a new science of luck.

"You could say I have a Luck Lab," he said with a smile.

It took only a couple of more scones to realize that we could be a great team, using his theoretical work as the basis for my more practical approach. Together, we would take the next year to explore all aspects of luck—in love and work and family and finance. Barnaby would be my guide, and we would meet weekly to try to answer Cassie's question about how she could be one of the lucky ones.

What we ultimately discovered surprised both of us. We found that it wasn't magic or serendipity or rubbing horseshoes that would make Cassie lucky—it was knowing the right steps to take. So come join us on our thrilling journey of discovery. The approaches we uncovered are almost guaranteed to bring luck to Cassie and Barnaby and me . . . and you.

PART ONE

UNDERSTANDING LUCK

Luck is what happens when preparation meets opportunity.

—*Seneca*

CHAPTER ONE

Prepare to Be Lucky

*Be open to opportunity. . . . Get the information you need. . . .
See what you're not seeing. . . . Drive to the intersection of
chance, talent, and hard work.*

Barnaby's Luck Lab at the Institute for Advanced Study was
tucked away amid the beautiful wooded fields of Princeton,
New Jersey—a perfect place for thinking big thoughts about the
science of making luck. As we took a walk together through the
peaceful grounds one morning, Barnaby told me that Albert Einstein wandered these same tree-lined paths while mulling over his
famous theories. Our new ideas might not disrupt the theory of
relativity, but we hoped they would change the way people thought
about luck—and the possibilities for their own futures.

It had rained hard the previous night, and the sun hadn't yet
dried out the wet ground. Scooting around a puddle, I told Barnaby
that writing my previous book *The Gratitude Diaries* had taught me
that we have more control over our own happiness than we sometimes realize. I was delighted that the book had inspired so many
people to lead happier lives, and I had a feeling that understanding
how to make yourself lucky—under any circumstances—could have
a similar effect.

Barnaby nodded. "If you're driven to make your life a little better
and wonder why things don't always go your way, our new approach
will let you claim the luck that should be yours."

We both agreed that luck isn't the same as random chance. If you flip a coin ten times to determine your future, you are relying on chance—and most people would agree that's pretty silly. If you talk to people, prepare yourself, look for opportunity, and then jump on the unexpected events that might (randomly) appear, you are making luck. And that's what we all need to do.

"Luck isn't a zero-sum game. There's plenty of luck for everyone if you know where and how to look for it," Barnaby said.

Barnaby thought the evidence was pretty clear that luck is not passive—it requires action, and many events that may seem like random chance are not so random after all. He was convinced that by understanding the underlying dynamics of luck, you can gain control over aspects of your life that once seemed to depend on chance, fate, or the phases of the moon. We would work together using insights and recent discoveries in psychology, behavioral economics, mathematics, and neuroscience to develop a new way of understanding luck.

"We're at the starting point of a brand-new field, and instead of finding the research, we're going to have to create it," he said.

The Luck Lab was the right place to do this, since the Institute for Advanced Study, where Barnaby has an academic appointment, is famous as a font for big ideas. Over the years, it has attracted geniuses from around the world—and it's fun to drive around local streets named after many of them. Along with Einstein, the great mathematician and philosopher Kurt Gödel was a professor there, and so was the early computer scientist and game theory pioneer John von Neumann. Renowned theoretical physicist J. Robert Oppenheimer, also known for his work building the first atomic bomb at Los Alamos National Laboratory, was a longtime director.

And Barnaby and I felt we were the right team to tackle the project. We had very different backgrounds and life experiences. I've had a successful career as a journalist, magazine editor, and TV producer in the New York City area and raised two terrific sons with my handsome doctor-husband. Barnaby grew up in Alaska and was homeschooled until he started college—at which point he launched into academic and career experiences that took him around the globe. He became a top executive at a major foundation that gives away $100 million a year. A quirky and original thinker, he knows more people than anybody I've ever met. He recently settled in New York City with his wife, Michelle, and their two very young and adorable daughters—though "settled" is never the right word for him.

We hoped our research in luck would be powerful and game-changing and give people a new view of their own lives and experiences. Barnaby had already been coming up with strategies about opportunity and risk and effort and how these affect your ability to transform your future. It was all very erudite and heady, and my job would be to bring it down to earth and see how the theories worked in everyday life.

As a practical schedule, Barnaby would escape to this ivoriest of towers every Monday and Tuesday to make conceptual models and try to develop theories of luck that worked across all contexts—whether you were trying to get a job, find a mate, or survive as a species in the evolutionary sweepstakes. On Wednesdays we would meet and talk them through. Along the way, I would find the academics, entrepreneurs, and celebrities who could illustrate the points and help us both see how people could wittingly or not make luck happen for themselves.

By the end of the year, we would know exactly what it takes to make yourself lucky. This new science of luck would have straightforward principles that would work to make things go better in all aspects of your life.

———————

"Beyond the theoretical work, it's important to understand the right actions to take so you can put yourself on the luck-making path and create the destiny you want for yourself," Barnaby said.

We were so engrossed in conversation that we hardly noticed how muddy we were getting as we slipped and slid along the (actual) path where we were walking. By the end, my canvas shoes were thoroughly soaked and caked with dirt.

"Luck may be like gratitude in that a lot depends on your perspective," I told Barnaby as we emerged from the woods. "I consider this a very lucky walk in that we have exciting ideas and a good plan. But someone else might see it as unlucky that I have to throw away my shoes."

He smiled. "Sacrifices are always made in the name of science."

I looked down at my muddy feet. Part of luck was about finding new opportunities. Compared to that, finding new shoes shouldn't be very hard.

A couple of days after we got back from Princeton, Barnaby suggested I take a first shot at seeing how our basic theory worked in practice. If we were right that you make your own luck, could I try to get lucky on one particular day?

For this experiment I didn't need a blackboard full of equations. I would simply try to create my own luck.

My day didn't look to be very exciting. I planned to do a few errands in the morning, then go to Penn Station and catch a train to visit my wonderful mother-in-law.

"Does any part of that sound lucky to you?" I asked Barnaby.

It also happened to be Friday, May 13th—not the obvious day to have beautiful opportunities fall from the sky.

But Barnaby asked me to set out on my day with a slightly different perspective than usual. He gave me some basic guidelines for luck: I should stay attentive to opportunities, be prepared for anything, and try the unexpected.

"And luck will just rain down on me?" I asked dubiously.

Since it was already storming outside, it would have been better for some sunshine to appear. But a challenge is a challenge, and I was intrigued.

My day started unremarkably with visits to the post office and drugstore, and then I headed to Penn Station. I had left plenty of time and arrived early (way too early) for my 10:15 A.M. train. Penn Station is grim and dreary, and hanging out there didn't feel very lucky at all.

But with the advice to be prepared, I had studied the train schedule and knew there was an earlier train at 9:46. I didn't think there was time to make it—but why not try?

When I ran to the gate, the escalator was (mysteriously) going up from the track, not down to it. I dashed over to a security guard hanging out nearby and asked what to do.

"You have to go all the way around to the other side and take the staircase," he said.

I felt momentarily defeated—the train was leaving in about one minute, and the corridor to the other side looked long. But I thought of a high school coach who used to cheer, "Go for it! Take a chance!" So I ran around the station to the staircase, galumphed down the steps, and got onto the train a moment before the doors closed.

What luck!

I felt a surge of triumph. It was a small victory, but I had made it happen.

Wait a minute. Was that the secret? I could control more than I realized?

A week earlier, I had been in almost the identical situation and hadn't hustled quite as much. The train door literally slammed in my face. That felt like an unlucky day, while this one suddenly felt much more positive.

With the train success in my mind, I felt a surge of confidence. I arrived at the other end earlier than planned, so I took a pleasant walk to my mother-in-law's apartment (the rain had even stopped) rather than taking a cab. We went out for lunch and chatted cheerfully with the waitress at the diner. I thanked her for making me a salad that wasn't on the menu and confided that I was trying to make lucky things happen all day. At dessert, the waitress brought over a chocolate cupcake with a candle in it.

"This one's on us. A lucky day is worth celebrating," the waitress said.

Catching an earlier train and getting a free chocolate cupcake weren't exactly earth-shattering events. But on a Friday the thirteenth, they definitely counted on the good side of luck.

When I reported this story to Barnaby the next day, I was somewhere between amazed and baffled. I was starting to agree that luck isn't a magical and mystical force that falls from the sky—it's something that we can (at least partly) create for ourselves. That's fairly stunning to realize, since most of us sit back and hope for good luck when we really should be taking the right steps to make it happen. The sharp-tongued Australian novelist Christina Stead noted in 1938 that "a self-made man is one who believes in luck and sends his son to Oxford." In other words, chance plays a role in life, but it's not everything. The foundations for luck are set by our own actions—what we try, whom we talk to, how fast we decide to run for the train.

If luck is all around us, waiting to be found, then we have to stop walking right by it or whizzing past in our SUVs. Lucky occurrences usually aren't as haphazard as they may first appear. It's true that fortune is not fairly distributed and some options are beyond your control. I had been born in the United States to middle-class parents who wanted me to advance, and in the history of the world, that counted as an enormous, unbelievable privilege. But no matter how you start out or where you hope to land, knowing the dynamics of chance changes . . . well, your chances.

"You can uncover the luck, grab it for yourself, and share it with friends!" Barnaby told me now.

To make good luck, you need the right information so you can prepare for the right actions. Knowing the possible steps keeps you from being buffeted by forces you can't control and gives you power over more aspects of your life. We often have greater control over our future than we realize. It was exciting to think that I didn't have to wait for lucky days—I could make them.

Barnaby and I decided to launch our project with a national survey on luck—and we put it together carefully to make sure it would be wide-ranging and statistically significant. When the results started coming in, we were surprised—and also delighted. Fully 82 percent of people believed that they had some or great influence over the luck in their lives. Only 5 percent thought that no matter what they did, they couldn't change their luck. So our belief that you could make luck happen fit in with an overall American attitude that random events may occur, but that doesn't mean life is out of your control. You just have to learn the right approaches.

Finding those right approaches was our big challenge—because luck is in the details. The great scientist Louis Pasteur once pointed out that "Luck favors the prepared mind." A wise thought—but he never said what the preparation looks like. So we would try to fill in the blanks and uncover the step-by-step process for preparing to be lucky.

When I mentioned to my friend Liz that I was learning how to create luck for myself, she immediately asked if I was buying a lottery ticket. But a lottery is not a good model for luck in the rest of life. Even though it's been around since the days of the Roman Empire and ropes in millions of buyers (and dreamers), a lottery is just a game that raises money and hopes. You buy a ticket, and then everything else is left to chance. There are crazy odds against you and nothing you can do about them. (Some Australians found one thing they could do to win. But we'll get to that later.)

In the big matters that make us seem truly fortunate in life—a good job, a happy family, and a feeling of success—life isn't a lottery at all. Random chance does play a part in our lives and serendipitous events occur that you can't easily explain, but chance is just one element of the luck picture. If you think about luck as strictly random events, you're missing the bigger point. To get lucky, you need to put aside what you can't control and focus on the other elements that *are* completely under your control.

When I visited Barnaby at the Luck Lab the next time, he took me over to the math library, where he liked to work. Library stacks are often dark, but he had a favorite table by a bay window where light poured in—and the office where Albert Einstein had worked was just below us.

"We probably have a better view than he did," Barnaby said cheerfully.

Inspired by the ghost of genius past, we talked about successful people we knew and tried to tease out the elements that made them lucky. Certain traits—like smarts, determination, energy, and original thinking—got repeated over and over. Chance sometimes played a role—good timing and all that—but it never stood alone.

In addition to our national survey, Barnaby had sent questions about luck to several hundred Rhodes scholars, and we started looking over the answers. Many people described an unexpected event that had influenced their life—a trip abroad that resulted in a job, a foundation that offered a grant, an investor they sat next to at a dinner who helped them start a company.

"Serendipity!!!" one person wrote (with far too many exclamation marks).

But what seemed like serendipity often had an identifiable basis if you followed it back a few steps. The person who met the investor at dinner, for example, had an exciting idea and talked about it to everybody who would listen. A colleague who was impressed by his concept had invited him to the dinner. Lucky? Yes. Random chance? Not really. I started to see the role people had in making their own luck, and a simple formulation suddenly became clear to me.

"Real luck occurs at the intersection of chance, talent, and hard work," I said.

Barnaby nodded thoughtfully. "Nice. Chance, talent, and hard work." Then with a little smile, he added, "A little poetic, but nice."

Before we could add science to the poetry, we needed to define each of the elements. For the moment, we would put chance aside and focus on the other two.

Hard work is open to everyone, and so, surprisingly, is talent. You don't have to be able to sing like Beyoncé or act like Meryl Streep to be lucky (though it doesn't hurt), since talent also involves elements that all of us can develop—an openness to opportunity, a willingness to take risks, an ability to think differently from others, and even a dose of optimism. With the right approach, you can make the lucky combination of chance, talent, and hard work happen for yourself—and get luckier in every part of life.

My lucky Friday the thirteenth showed me the power of these basic principles. Careful preparation and a willingness to try (*I will run for that earlier train!*) both fit into the hard-work element of luck. My decision to take a positive approach by talking to the waitress, thanking her, and being friendly was one of the skills that helps lead to luck (and cupcakes).

I started to think of the three elements of luck as being like one of those old-fashioned slot machines where you pull the handle and three items have to line up in a row. People get addicted to waiting for the three cherries, for example, to appear next to one another. Psychologists call it "variable ratio reinforcement"—you don't know when you'll get the reward, so you keep trying, expecting it to appear at the next pull of the handle. I'm much too logical to find any appeal in slot machines—but I might be won over if I knew I could line up two of the cherries myself.

And that's what happens in real life. If you want a payoff of any kind—a new job, a new love—you don't have to wait for completely random luck to get those cherries lined up. The talent and hard-work cherries are under your control. You can learn how to put them directly in the slots—and then you're two-thirds on your way to a lucky life.

You could say that in knowing how to make luck, you turn life into a bowl of cherries.

CHAPTER TWO

Some People Have All the Luck—And You Can Be One of Them

Get the right information. . . . Believe that you're lucky. . . . Learn a lesson from Vanna White. . . . Decide to find a four-leaf clover (and don't quit until you do).

At our next meeting, Barnaby and I began to talk about people's preconceptions about luck. A surprisingly small percentage thought it was totally random, as our national survey showed. Some 67 percent of respondents said that working hard had contributed to lucky outcomes in their own life, and 64 percent said they got lucky by being curious and seeking new opportunities.

Recognizing the nuances of making luck can be complicated. For millennia, philosophers and theologians have danced around discussions of luck. Back in 293 BC, the Romans dedicated one of the first temples (many more would follow) to Fortuna, the goddess of fortune and luck. She was widely worshipped for the bounty she could potentially distribute and the prosperity she might offer. Medieval artists portrayed the capriciousness of the fate she doled out by having her stand on a ball or next to a wheel of fortune. When the Roman poet Ovid was sent into exile, he glumly pointed out that Fortuna "admits by her unsteady wheel her own fickleness; she always has its apex beneath her swaying foot." Ah, the fickle foot of fate. The equivalent Greek deity was Tyche, who was sometimes depicted in a blindfold. If the goddess who controls your destiny is blind, you're not so surprised when unexpected things happen.

You have to travel pretty far (and across a couple of millennia) to get from Fortuna to Vanna White, who flips the letters on the endlessly popular TV show *Wheel of Fortune*. It is the longest-running syndicated game show ever and has been on the air in one form or another since 1975. On the TV show, you start with an element of random luck—spinning a real-life wheel with twenty-four slots to determine how much money you are playing for, maybe $300 or $1,000. You can also land on a slot where you lose everything—which means Ovid was right about the fickleness of fate.

But after that casino-style spin, you leave Fortuna behind and the real work begins. To actually win, you have to put in some effort, fill in the blanks, and have the skill to guess the answer before your competitor figures it out. That combination of chance, talent, and hard work is a pretty good definition of what creates good fortune—whether on a TV show or in everyday life. With apologies to the admirable Fortuna, Vanna and her game may offer a better example of what modern luck is really all about—since it puts you solidly at the intersection of hard work, talent, and chance.

Some people seem naturally lucky—but it could be that they're just adept at weaving the strands of skill and effort and opportunity to their advantage. I had the feeling that anybody could learn the same techniques. I decided to look around and see what I could find.

A few days later, I went to a local park to watch a seven-year-old I know play softball. It was a low-key game, and when one of the little girls got tired of standing in the outfield, she shouted that she was going to look for four-leaf clovers. Several others quickly followed. After a while, most of the seekers gave up—they drifted back to the game or did some lackadaisical cartwheels. But one little girl in a yellow T-shirt and cutoffs (I'll call her Sunny) kept going in her search and finally jumped up in excitement. She'd found it! She ran back to her friends to show off her good luck charm.

"You're so lucky, and now you'll be even luckier!" said one of the friends who clustered around her.

Yes, Sunny was lucky—but not in any mystical way. She'd had the persistence to keep looking after the others gave up and an ability to spot patterns or differences that most would have missed. She didn't mind lots of disappointments and had the resilience to keep going. Since three-leaf clovers are more common than four-leaf clovers by almost ten thousand to one, she'd had to face a lot of failures before finding the winner. But she liked the challenge and always expected to find what she wanted—and she probably had fun looking, too.

The little friend who announced that Sunny would go from lucky to luckier was probably right (and not because Sunny now has a four-leaf clover). The qualities that let Sunny find that four-leafer in the first place—persistence, focus, and attentiveness to possibility— will give her a huge boost in creating her own luck in life. When you say someone is lucky, what you really mean is that all three of the key elements—chance, talent, and hard work—converged for a great result. Even if the end point seems as wondrous and magical as finding a four-leaf clover, her actions led to it in one way or another. Even if she didn't realize it.

Thinking of herself as a lucky person, and having others see her that way, will only add to Sunny's advantages. Luck comes in cascades. When you start on a lucky path, you tend to stay there. I pictured some of those sweet seven-year-olds going home and complaining at dinner about their friend's good luck. *How come she found the four-leaf clover? She's always sooo lucky. How come I didn't find it?* An appeasing parent might promise, "You'll get lucky and find it next time." But while that may make dinner calmer, it won't do anything to assure that the child really *does* improve her luck. Whether you're seven or seventy, if you see yourself as buffeted by forces over which you have no control, you tend to give up and lament your fate. Better to remind the young seeker of four-leaf clovers that she can change her luck with focus and effort.

In his play *A Streetcar Named Desire*, playwright Tennessee Williams gave tough guy Stanley Kowalski the great line "You know what luck is? Luck is believing you're lucky, that's all." Stanley—played by Marlon Brando in the movie—might not have been the brightest (or nicest) guy around, but he looked great in a T-shirt, and he was definitely right about luck. "To hold a front position in this rat race, you've got to believe you are lucky," he said.[1] Rat race or not, the observation makes sense. You have to believe you're lucky to take the action that will make you lucky.

The unexpected happens in life, and how you respond to it (or don't) determines whether you set yourself up to be one of the lucky ones. You can probably look back at the twists and turns that your own life has taken and marvel at the serendipitous moments that brought you to your current spot. Maybe your friend dragged you to a party you didn't plan to go to, and that's where you met the love of your life. Or you ran into the CEO in the elevator, and a chance conversation led to your current job. What if you had stayed home

---

1. Brando's other memorable moment in *Streetcar* is when he hollers, "Stella! Hey, *Stella!*"—which doesn't have quite the larger significance of his insight into luck.

from the party or taken a different elevator? You shake your head and marvel at how lucky you were.

It's true that things we haven't planned can have an extraordinary influence on all that comes after. But far more important than what objectively occurs is *what you do with each event*. You could have stood in that elevator and been too intimidated to talk to the CEO— in which case it wasn't a lucky ride at all. Or you could have had a few too many tequila shots at the party and been too blurry-eyed to notice the handsome spouse-to-be lurking by the guacamole. Similarly, George Lucas hiring Harrison Ford to build his cabinets was a (more or less) random event that didn't guarantee any outcome beyond a nice place to store the pasta and ketchup. Ford became successful because of the actions he took afterward.

Happenstance plays a role in all our lives—but it's not as deterministic as we sometimes think. My terrific literary agent, Alice Martell, started her career as an attorney at a major law firm and quickly decided she'd made a mistake. She just didn't love law. One of her clients happened to be a bestselling author, and after she and Alice became friends, Alice helped her negotiate a big book contract. The publisher on the other side of the desk was so impressed that he asked Alice if she'd ever thought of becoming an agent. Until that moment, she never had.

"But once he said it, I went to work in publishing and eventually started my own agency," Alice told me one day as we were chatting about life and luck in her pretty office. "I love what I do, and I'm always amazed at how lucky I was. If the publisher hadn't made that comment, I'd probably still be practicing law—and unhappy every day!"

There's a certain romantic charm to the idea that your career was launched by simple serendipity. But luck rarely appears from nowhere. Lucky seeds have to land on fertile ground, and chance events need to merge with intent and direction for anything to happen. I suggested to Alice that since she had been moderately miserable as a lawyer, her eyes were probably open for other opportunities. Having the bestselling author as a client presented one lucky path, but if that opportunity hadn't happened, she would have been alert for another.

"Your next client might have been an actor, and you would have negotiated his contract and followed *that* path. In that case, you could be in Hollywood running a movie studio now!" I said, only half joking.

A couple of weeks after we had the conversation, Alice called me to say that she was still reeling at the new view of her own career. She'd always felt like forces beyond her control had determined her career—moving her from (unhappy) lawyer to (happy and successful) agent. Now she was willing to believe that her own determination and will had set the luck in motion.

"I've spent all these years fretting that if not for a few lucky events, I could still be suffering as a lawyer. You've completely changed my view!" she said. She was also a little wistful about the fact that she wasn't running that movie studio.

Like Alice, you've probably had those pivotal moments in life where everything changed. Looking back, you can see them clearly—the comment made, the job that was offered, the person who caught your eye across a crowded room. As you tell the story of your own life, those are the big events that you probably describe. But what did you put in place, maybe without realizing it, to make those moments happen? And equally important, how many other moments did you simply miss? (You too could be running a movie studio.) The real trick is to learn how to recognize those moments of luck moving forward.

The combination of chance, talent, and hard work that transforms the biggest events in your life like love and career also puts a mark on everyday occurrences. Many things that you attribute to random luck turn out not to be so random. So, for example, imagine that you're driving in a big American city and need to park your car. You're cruising slowly down the block (because there's a truck in front of you, no doubt) when a big SUV pulls out of a spot. You swoop in and, with the motor still running, check the sign—and discover the spot is even legal. Whoop-de-doo! You've just saved the $32.50 that it would have cost to park in a garage—and can put it toward ordering an extra drink and appetizer at dinner. (In some cities, you still have to feed the meter—but nothing is perfect.)

Landing that spot may strike you as nothing more than a classic example of being in the right place at the right time. You didn't seem to do anything special—you just drove by as someone else pulled out. Lucky you! But if spot-finding is truly random, everyone should be equally good at it, and that's not the case. A lot of people will tell you that they're simply lousy at street parking (count me among them) and would never even try it, while others, including my husband, Ron, are masterful. He drives to the theater or other evening events in Manhattan at least a couple of times a week, and he never, ever goes to a parking lot. He doesn't have a rabbit's foot hanging from his rearview mirror, but he does have a few talents. He's extremely observant and has sharp vision, so he'll notice someone getting into a parked car on a side street or the slight motion of an engine turning on, and he'll immediately head in that direction. He also relies on his great memory and head for numbers—different streets allow parking at different hours—to know exactly which street will be the best bet. With his combination of experience, preparation, knowledge, and observation, he simply makes himself lucky.

The bad-eyed and impatient among us will never be great at parking. But knowing your strengths and weaknesses means you can find the techniques necessary to improve your luck. (My technique is to let my husband drive.) Recognizing that there are factors other than random chance at work means you can change your approach and increase your luck. Anyone can learn the streets the way my husband has, arrive early to an area that opens for parking at six P.M.—and get one of those "lucky" spots. Even I have managed to do that on occasion.[2]

Once you see the elements that go into generating luck, you realize that luck isn't random if anyone can generate more and more of it. Lucky occurrences usually aren't as haphazard as they may first appear. Like meteors shooting across the sky, they can seem magical at first glance. But once you know the principles behind them, they are both predictable and explicable. People often talk about being in the right place at the right time, but that "rightness" often happens because you've taken all the necessary steps along the way.

The writer and filmmaker Jean Cocteau once wryly pointed out that he believed in luck because "how else can you explain the success of those you dislike?" I sympathize. It's comforting to conclude that the person who has her name in lights (or has found the parking

---

2. This comes with a caveat Barnaby learned when he optimistically grabbed a street spot without bothering to check the sign. When he came back, the car was gone. What seemed like good luck turned into a long afternoon at the towed-car lot.

spot) was simply luckier than you—rather than that she had more talent, drive, or smarts. And maybe she didn't. Certainly there are a lot of people with fancy cars and huge followings on Instagram who don't seem completely . . . deserving. But instead of dismissing them as unfathomably lucky, you might try to figure out how they got where they did. The good news is that luck isn't a zero-sum game. You don't have to knock somebody else off his perch in order to increase your own luck. There's plenty of luck to go around if you know how to look for it. The question is, How do you make luck happen for yourself?

Sometimes, luck is all about getting the right information—you ask one more question and suddenly seem like the luckiest person in the room! As an example, Barnaby offered a thought experiment. You have to decide whether you want to walk down a dark tunnel that has a big prize at the end. You're told that one in a hundred people who go into the tunnel fall into a deep hole and can't get out. Would you go?

"Probably not," I said, proving that I'm not much of a risk taker.

Barnaby laughed. "Okay, you wouldn't, but a lot of people might decide that the odds aren't bad and try it. And what if you're told that fifty people fall into that hole?"

"Then I'd stay away from the tunnel. No prize at the end is worth those odds."

"I'd agree," Barnaby said. "But now I'll give you some extra information. All the people who made it to the end of the tunnel and got the big prize had flashlights."

Aha! Now the excursion doesn't seem quite as random or risky. You can go to your local Walmart, buy yourself the sturdiest LED flashlight you can find, and set off for the prize. You've figured out how to be lucky.

In real life, information is rarely so straightforward. But we're always walking down metaphoric dark tunnels, hoping for something special and rewarding at the end—a better job, greater success, a chance to meet Prince, or Princess, Charming. And there are indeed always pitfalls and potholes we can fall into. Being able to shed some light on the situation makes us luckier and better able to manage the risks and opportunities.

Once we have our flashlights in hand, we have to know where to shine them. We regularly miss lucky opportunities because we're looking in the wrong place or don't notice what's in front of us. Most of us think we're seeing the world as it is—but we're simply not.

The most important talent anyone who seems lucky possesses is a very basic one—the ability to pay attention and notice opportunities. A great example of how easy it is to miss something important comes from the psychologists Christopher Chabris and Daniel Simons, who met some twenty years ago at Harvard University and began doing research on attention and perception. They created a now-famous video in which six college-age men and women, half in black T-shirts and half in white ones, are moving around, and you're asked to count how many times the players wearing white shirts pass the basketball.[3] Okay, you can do this. You focus carefully on the players in white and watch the ball. At the end of the short video, the announcer's voice asks how many passes you counted. If you get the correct answer of fifteen, you probably pat yourself on the back. Good observing! But the next question may change your mind: "Did you see the gorilla?"

---

3. You can pull up "The Invisible Gorilla" video on YouTube. Try it. You'll be surprised.

Um . . . the gorilla? Halfway through the game, a person in a gorilla costume came to the middle of the screen, beat his chest, and walked off. Whoops. In experiments that have been done over and over with people of all ages and backgrounds (starting with Harvard students), at least half miss the gorilla. If you haven't seen the video, you're probably convinced that of course you would see the gorilla. Everybody thinks that. But you get so busy counting passes that you simply miss the other action that's happening right in front of you.

The video got so much attention when it first appeared that the researchers did an update. I found it online and tried it out. This time, I knew about the gorilla, so even as I was counting the passes, I noticed him coming in and felt pretty good about myself. (I can see everything!) But the researchers had another surprise at the end. Did you notice that one of the players walked off the court? Or that the color of the background curtain changed in the middle of the game from red to gold? If you're like most people, including me, the answers are no and no.

If you're overlooking a gorilla beating his chest and a background changing color, there's a good chance that you're missing a lot of things all around you—many that could turn into luck. So how do you change that? Barnaby and I were mulling that when we attended a conference in Chicago and happened to be seated one night with two neuroscientists who do research in the area of attention. Over dinner, where I definitely noticed the excellent grilled fish, I brought up the invisible gorilla and the problem of knowing where to look. Dr. Ed Hamlin, who has taught at Duke and the University of North Carolina and now runs the Center for the Advancement of Human Potential in Asheville, explained that good attention is flexible, allowing us to switch between narrow focus and open focus. In the gorilla video, you're narrowly focused on counting the passes, so you miss the bigger picture. If you allow yourself to watch the scene with a wider view, you see the gorilla, but you can't count the passes.

So where should you look to capture everything?

"Good attention is flexible," said Dr. Hamlin. "You always have to adjust to demands and circumstances." A baseball fan, he described the All-Star game he'd just watched in which the second baseman bobbled a ball hit his way. "He'd probably done that play hundreds of times in practice and never missed it. But this time he looked up to see where the runner was, and he lost his focus." The ability to switch from the narrow view to the wider one can be the key to a lucky play—or a mortifying miss.

Shifting your attention and recognizing the right place to look at the right moment isn't always easy. Dr. Hamlin admitted that even though he works with attention problems, his wife complains that he never knows when dinner is ready. He's so busy burrowing into the work in front of him that he misses other signals—like the fact that it's seven-thirty at night and the smell of roasted chicken is wafting from the kitchen.

Barnaby, who has a great ability to concentrate, pointed out that even though we were sitting in a noisy restaurant with the din of conversation all around us, if somebody on the other side of the room said his name, he would immediately hear it. Our other dinner companion, David Ziegler, a researcher in neuroscience at the University of California School of Medicine, San Francisco, described that as pop-out attention—the things that grab our notice no matter what. More important (and subtle) is top-down attention, the events and circumstances that we notice only when we focus.

All of us are bombarded each day with millions of bits of

information, and we get lucky when we know where we want to focus—or which possibilities we want to fire up. Estimates vary, but big-data analysts at IBM say we create some 2.5 quintillion bytes of data every day—which you can write out as 2,500,000,000,000,000,000, if that helps you see just how big a number we're talking about. Needless to say, we're not built to take in even the tiniest fraction of that. Possibilities abound in every direction, and if you wait for one of those bytes or possibilities or bits of stimulus to turn into luck, you're sure to miss it. As with the gorilla video, you have to know where you're looking—because it takes looking in the right place to get lucky.

When you think of luck, you tend to consider the pop-out kind. You win the lottery! You get to the intersection just as the light turns green! A tree falls down in a storm and misses your house! Those events announce themselves as being good luck—and they're hard not to notice. But most luck arrives in subtler form. You have to pay attention as it quietly swirls around you, ready to be snagged.

As Barnaby and I walked away from that dinner, we talked about the challenge of recognizing lucky opportunities and agreed that we would each make a focused effort to see more possibilities. However, that was just a general step and we were most excited to start analyzing and understanding the specific actions that contribute to luck—and develop the principles that could make you lucky in any aspect of your life.

We had just one more topic to discuss first. If luck is at the intersection of talent, hard work, and random chance, what influence can we have over chance itself?

CHAPTER THREE

Pick the Statistic You Want to Be

Understand the odds. . . . Don't confuse risk with luck. . . .
Wear Hawaiian shirts in Boston (once in a while).

In talking about the need to make your own luck, Barnaby and I often used the shorthand that luck doesn't fall from the sky—but we understood that if you want to be literal, even that truth isn't 100 percent accurate. A woman named Ann Hodges was at her home in Sylacauga, Alabama, one day in 1954, napping on the couch under a big quilt, when a hunk of black rock crashed through the ceiling and hit her on the thigh. With that (unlucky) burst from the sky, she became the only confirmed person in history to have been hit by a meteorite.

You probably shouldn't spend a lot of time worrying about meteorite strikes since "it's more likely you get hit by a tornado and a bolt of lightning and a hurricane all at the same time," Florida State College astronomer Michael Reynolds said about that remarkable hit. And yet we do worry. Scientists say an asteroid that smashed into the earth 66 million years ago led to a change in climate that caused the extinction of the dinosaurs. It was long ago and rare, but who knows—if there's an asteroid strike every 66 million years, another may be due tomorrow.[1]

---

1. In *Armageddon,* the highest-grossing movie of 1998, a bunch of oil drillers go into space to save the planet from the threat of an impending asteroid. The very survival of Earth turned out to depend on Bruce Willis.

Now that I was thinking of luck as a combination of chance, talent, and hard work, I had decided that the wisest approach was to put chance aside and focus on the other two—the ones you could control. But I also understood that the unpredicted and the unforeseen can seem overwhelming. If you're going to be hit by a meteorite, everything else seems kind of unimportant.

So before figuring out the principles of making luck, I wanted to get a little better perspective on randomness. We've all had situations that seem like crazy coincidence—you're traveling in a remote location and run into someone you know, or an old friend from college calls just as you're thinking about her. Your reaction is probably *Amazing! What are the odds?*

And it turns out the odds can be very different than you expect.

The random and unlikely keep us enthralled—at least in part because they can turn life and expectations so dramatically upside down. There are 7 billion people on the planet—so even if something is a million-in-one shot, it will happen to 7,000 of us. That's a lot of bolts from the blue.

Impossible odds don't mean something is impossible. In 2016, the English football club Leicester City was given a 5,000–1 chance of winning the championship of the Premier League. For some perspective, bookmakers gave the same odds to Bono becoming the next pope. Essentially those odds mean *Are you crazy? It's not going to happen.*

The Premier League is big and powerful, with no draft or salary caps, and the same four teams have won the championship for the previous twenty years. Little underfunded Leicester City had lost so many games the previous season that they barely escaped being tossed out of the league altogether. The closest they had come to a championship was finishing second in the 1928–29 season. They spent about a tenth as much on their players as the more popular teams like Manchester United and Arsenal.

But with all that, they won. One way to think of 5,000–1 odds is that if the teams in the Premier League played for five thousand years, Leicester City would win the title once. The BBC called it "one of the greatest sporting stories of all time." Closer to home, NBC Sports said, "It's not like anything we can comprehend in America." Others noted that during spring training in America, even the worst baseball teams are given 500–1 (or so) odds of winning the World Series. Leicester City was considered ten times worse than the worst.

But the funny thing is that after the win, various pundits had explanations for why it all happened. They praised the analytics the team used in recruiting and signing players, pointed to the surprising coach, and noted that the famous four top teams all sputtered. Had the players on Leicester City made their luck (as the first two explanations would suggest), or was it simply that year 5000 comes around if you wait long enough? I certainly don't know enough about English football to say—but it's definitely easier to explain an event after it occurs than before.

However you cast it, the Leicester City story is inspiring even to those who don't know that English football is really the same as American soccer. However long the odds, if you want to make luck happen, you don't quit. Something can happen. You can change the odds. You can surprise yourself and everyone else.

There's a parable about two rulers who are rolling the dice to see who will control the world. The first rolls, and each die lands with a six on its face—a total of twelve is as good as it can be.

"I win. You can give up," he tells his opponent.

But the other leader insists on his turn. When he rolls the dice, one lands on a six and the other breaks into two pieces—with half showing a six and the other half a one. So he got a thirteen. What are the odds? You don't actually know the best that can be done unless and until you keep trying to do it. You could end up being surprised by outcomes beyond what you originally considered.

Barnaby spent years of his academic career studying risk, and when I brought up the question of odds at our next Wednesday meeting, he pointed out that one way to beat the odds is to personalize them.

"Pick the statistic you want to be," he told me.

"What does that mean?" I asked.

We were having breakfast at a local café, and I glanced over at the banana bread on the table, trying to decide if I should have a piece. Barnaby caught my gaze and smiled as he picked his example.

"Think of it this way. Statistics now say that about a third of Americans are obese. But that doesn't mean every individual has a one-in-three chance of being too fat. You can decide what you're going to eat and how much you'll exercise, and that will affect your weight. You get to decide which statistic you're in."

"So I shouldn't have the banana bread," I said with a sigh.

Barnaby laughed. "It's not really a problem for you. And that's the point. Saying there's a 30 percent chance of being obese is one thing. Saying that *you*—whoever you are—have that probability is very different."

I ate the banana bread. And since the topic intrigued me, I did a little more research later and found out that Barnaby was completely right. Most studies show that genetic factors play only a small part in obesity, and lifestyle is more important than anything else. Research out of the Harvard School of Public Health shows that even if you have the genes associated with obesity, what you eat and how much you exercise will have a greater influence on your shape than your genetics. Where you live has a role in obesity, too. In some states (topped by Alabama), obesity is over 35 percent, while in Colorado, the perennially leanest state, it's more like 20 percent. But if you live in one of the fattest states and eat fruit and vegetables and go for daily runs, you'll easily beat the odds. In fact, the overall odds won't apply to you at all.

As we continued with our breakfast discussion of risk and statistics, Barnaby surprised me by telling me that when his first daughter, Mandarin, was born, he wanted her to share the bed with her parents. His wife, Michelle, thought it was a terrible idea. She told Barnaby that co-sleeping babies are five times more likely to die than those who are put safely in their own cribs. Some are crushed when parents roll over on them, and others suffocate in sheets and blankets or get wedged in the sides of beds. There is also a clear connection between the devastation of sudden infant death syndrome (SIDS) and co-sleeping. One comprehensive review showed that 69 percent of babies who died of SIDS slept in their parents' bed. The statistics were pretty clear—the safest place for a baby is in a crib.

"But babies all over the world have traditionally slept with their mothers, and I felt there would be benefits for nursing and other considerations. So I took another look at the statistics," Barnaby said.

He found that many of the risks of co-sleeping occurred when parents were intoxicated or obese or had lower education levels. Another key problem involved sleeping on a soft surface—a couch, waterbed, or squishy mattress—and having an excess number of blankets. None of those factors applied in the case of his family.

"So I calculated that the standard reference statistic being used of a one in a thousand risk was probably much lower for us," Barnaby said. "By changing or eliminating certain risk factors, you can shift the risk curve—and effectively change your chances, or luck."

Mandarin snuggled next to Mom and Dad for a year, and so did baby Jasmine when she arrived. Both girls are fine and beautiful and thriving. A lot of people might disagree with his decision on co-sleeping while others wildly support it—the topic remains controversial—but the bigger issue is an important one.

"We can't remove all risks, and life is always about trade-offs," Barnaby said. He pointed out that there are statistical risks involved with taking the kids out anytime in the car—but we do it anyway. "What's important is that you understand the reality of the risks you're taking."

Mark Twain popularized the expression "lies, damned lies, and statistics," and it's very easy to get swayed by experts tossing around numbers—or encouraging you to misinterpret them. If you hear a report (usually from a doctor on TV) that eating kale or running ten miles a day reduces your risk of a particular disease by half, it could be that your odds went from .002 to .001. In practical terms, that 50 percent decrease doesn't mean anything at all. If you like kale, go ahead and make a salad. But don't expect it to be a major source of luck. Similarly, you can theoretically know that an 80 percent chance of rain predicts what will happen eight out of ten times with the meteorological conditions as they are. But all you really care about is whether the baseball game this afternoon is going to be canceled.

If you understand the odds, you can play with them. So, for example, back in 1992, an Australian investor syndicate came up with a strategy for getting lucky in the lottery. Instead of buying just one (or two or three) tickets, they planned to win the Virginia Lottery by buying a ticket for every possible combination. At the time, each of the one-dollar tickets had six bubbles that could be filled with a number from 1 to 44, which meant there were some 7 million combinations. Filling out all those little forms would take a very long time, so they bought blocks of tickets through more than a hundred different retailers. It kept the stores humming. "No one wants to be in line behind anyone who's there for three or four days," said one disgruntled Virginian in a public hearing after the lottery fix. The syndicate managed to get only 5 million of the 7 million combinations before time ran out—but the odds were on their side, and they won the $27 million jackpot.

You probably don't want to try this at home. Even if you could borrow the money to buy all those tickets, most state lotteries are now dramatically harder to fix. (Having the number of choices go up to 49 instead of 44 may not sound like a big deal, but it doubles the possible combinations to 14 million.) And even if you win, you always run the risk of having to share the big bucks with other ticket holders who (randomly) picked the right combination. In major lotteries, like the national Mega Millions drawings, it would be impossible to print the necessary number of tickets, no matter how many retailers you had on your side. But the Australian investors were right in their general theory: If you increase your chances, you increase your odds.

When I first heard the story of the Virginia Lottery, my thought was *Yikes! The syndicate got only five million of the seven million— they could still lose!* Barnaby said his thought was—*Five out of seven—great odds!* That's the funny thing about statistics and odds—they are just numbers, and we give them our own emotional overlay. As you are making your luck (and living your life), you make very personal decisions on how much risk to take in everything from family to finance.

One young guy I know spent a lot of time in his twenties ice climbing. He was strong and careful and certain that he wouldn't make the kind of mistakes that, statistically, lead to a high rate of accidents in the sport. But once he was good enough to be climbing increasingly treacherous routes and spending more and more time on the slippery slopes, he realized he couldn't keep beating the odds. When you are climbing at a high level of difficulty, accidents happen that you can't predict. He put away his ropes.

Other climbers keep going—up rocks and mountains and in high-risk sports. One of the most famous Alpine climbers in the world, Ueli Steck, died in 2017 when he was preparing to race up a treacherous ridge of Mount Everest. He had set speed records on famous peaks like the Matterhorn, and he once charged up every big peak in the Alps at a record-breaking pace, climbing eighty-two mountains (each more than 4,000 meters) in sixty-two days. His death at age forty was sad, but Steck surely knew he was playing against tough odds. He made the choice that a life of thrills and adrenaline was worth the risk. You and I and my ice-climbing friend might have made a different choice—but in that way, we each get to define for ourselves what makes a lucky life.

The next time Barnaby and I visited the Luck Lab, we took another walk in the woods. (It was less muddy this time—no more shoes sacrificed to science.) I mentioned that in our national survey, some 66 percent of people thought you could make luck for yourself by being willing to take risks. Barnaby didn't completely agree with them.

"Everybody has a different view of risk, and it's not necessarily true that more risk equals more luck," he said.

Connecting risk and luck is deep in the American psyche. We used to revere the gutsy cowboy who rode across the plains to make his own luck and now we exalt the cowboy entrepreneur who tosses away the rules, takes audacious risks, and rides triumphantly to glory. It makes for good movies and folklore—but not so much for reality.

"The luckiest and most successful people often look like they're taking risks, but they always have a floor under them so they can't fall too far," Barnaby said. "I hear that again and again from people who have made fortunes. Instead of risking everything, they make their luck by seeing what others don't and capturing opportunity."

As we continued to walk, I noticed a long swooping bridge to one side of us made of wooden slats and wire. It spanned a pond, and while there didn't seem to be much on the other side, I asked Barnaby if he wanted to walk across.

"I heard the bridge was designed and built by Princeton engineering students," Barnaby said. He climbed up a couple of steps and then walked unhesitatingly out to the center as the bridge swayed.

"Should I join you?" I asked, staying on firm ground.

He looked around for a moment and then shook his head no and came back.

"This bridge is a great example that sometimes there is an asymmetry to luck. The amount of good luck you can make on this bridge is limited, but the bad luck is high if you fall off," he said. "Not all risks are worth taking."

We headed back inside to the Luck Lab, and Barnaby told me that early in his career, he advised for an oil company (the man has done everything!), which made him think a lot about different kinds of risk—and how they pay off. As Barnaby explained it, geologists typically go out with sounding equipment to look for pockets in the earth where there may be oil. After they collect extensive data and find possibilities (and it's never a certainty), the company has to decide which spots to pursue. Drilling is expensive, so they can't drill everywhere.

"To get the highest possible yield, you drill for medium-sized fields that will yield profitability for the company. But there's also the pressure for huge finds in unexpected places that are expensive to explore. It's hard to go after both, so you have to choose one or the other. And those different approaches attract different kinds of risk takers, whether they are engineers or executives," Barnaby said.

In our own lives, we regularly make the same kinds of decisions. Go after the small-percentage play that has a huge payoff? Or take the safer course that yields less dramatic but more constant results? In other words, should you encourage your child when he watches a basketball game and says all he wants in life is to play in the NBA? Unless he's six-foot-seven and never misses a three-point shot, possibly not. We love hearing about people who think huge, take on the impossible, and win, but you can have an equally good life on a surer path and a safer bet.

"Taking the heroic path isn't the only way to luck," Barnaby said. "Extraordinary outcomes are rare, and we do a disservice to ourselves if we think that's the only definition of making your luck."

Following up on his oil-drilling example, Barnaby pointed out that a petroleum engineer can decide to spend ten years freezing in the Arctic looking for that undiscovered gusher that will change everything. Or he can go to the warm spot in Houston with predictable fields that will generate a steady return. Movie studios face the same question. They can take on the safe and somewhat predictable theme (hello, *Batman—Part 18*), or try something off-the-wall and different that will probably flop but may be a megahit. A college senior thinking about his future makes a similar calculation. Go to dental school for a sure and secure future? Or become an entrepreneur and invest everything in your idea for a start-up selling ice-cream sandwiches by mail?

Living your life by statistics makes theoretical sense. You can see how many dentists go broke versus how many start-up entrepreneurs. You can check how many people like ice cream and how many competitors you would have. Calculate your chances of success and decide the luckiest path. But the "what are the odds?" approach is just not how most of us are wired. We make decisions based on popular information or what our friends have done or we follow our hearts (which leads to some very foolish risks). If your college roommate had a successful start-up, you're probably more likely to jump in and try one, too. We expect good outcomes even when they are highly unlikely, and we ignore potential downsides.

I was a big fan of the Caltech physicist Leonard Mlodinow, whose bestselling book *The Drunkard's Walk* had long been a favorite of mine. He had an appealing way of explaining statistical chance and once (somewhat whimsically) wondered how many people would enter a state lottery if the likely outcome was presented as one person would win a fortune, millions of others would get nothing, and one person would die a violent death. Because that's pretty much what happens. Pulling together statistics on car accidents and estimates of how many people make an extra trip to buy a ticket, he figured there's about one additional car fatality per major lottery. But who ever takes that into account when deciding whether or not to buy a lottery ticket?

Years ago, when I was the editor of a big magazine, we had a breakfast every month for everyone who worked at the company. Along with fruit platters and too many cream doughnuts, we served up sweepstakes tickets to everyone who attended. Then the CEO pulled numbers out of a hat to award the prizes—dinner for two at a restaurant, gift baskets, a designer scarf. As the winners rushed forward to claim their prizes, at least one of them would invariably shout, "I can't believe it! I've never won anything before!"

It's not a surprise, of course. Winning a sweepstakes or lottery of any kind means beating the odds. But Barnaby told me that his wife, Michelle, regularly entered the drawing at their local Trader Joe's for a week of free groceries. Thousands of people went to that very popular store—but she had won three times.

"It doesn't make sense," he said.

And yet unexpected events, good and bad, happen all the time. Mathematicians like to point out that there's a big difference between asking how likely it is that Michelle will win three times and how likely it is that *someone* will win three times. Think of it this way. If ten thousand people drop their entries into the bowl each week, you have a 1-in-10,000 chance of winning. But there's a 100 percent chance that someone will win—and the same person winning twice in a few months isn't as unusual as it may sound. Mathematicians refer to it as the law of big numbers, and it gives us a new way of thinking about odds. Some years ago a woman in New Jersey won the state lottery twice in four months. Even more amazing than Michelle's groceries, right? Reporters said she had beaten odds of 1 in 17 trillion. But then two statisticians at Purdue University, Drs. Stephen Samuels and George McCabe, begged to differ. They pointed out that those odds were based on a given person buying a single ticket for both lotteries and winning each time. But out of the millions and millions of people buying hundreds of millions of lottery tickets, the odds of a double winner somewhere in the country were dramatically different. One in 17 trillion? Nope—more like one in 30.

Another classic example is the birthday party problem. If you're going to a party that has 23 people, it's likely that two people in the room have the same birthday. But if you want to be in a room where it's likely that someone has *your* birthday, you'd need a much bigger crowd—something like 183 people. (If your head is spinning, we have all the math at the end.)

And sometimes it's important to remember that it's okay to toss probabilities out the window and decide that you're going to make your own luck. Barnaby thought that one guy who would know a lot about that was his acquaintance Doug Rauch, who spent many years running Trader Joe's nationally.

"So that's how Michelle won!" I said. "It was fixed!"

"Absolutely not! He's not even there anymore!" Barnaby insisted.

So we gave Rauch a call, and I was quickly convinced that he knew nothing about the mystery of Michelle and the free groceries. But he knew a lot of other stuff about making luck in the grocery business. One of the early employees of Trader Joe's when it was a small store in Los Angeles, he had some early successes—including fame as the guy who dreamed up All American Nut Butter. "Higher in protein than peanut butter and significantly less expensive—and we sold hundreds of thousands of pounds," he told us, still proud all these years later.

The peanut crop in America had failed one year, driving up the price of the lunchtime staple—and he had the idea to make a substitute out of cottonseed. The development was complicated, but mostly it taught him the important lesson that "luck comes when you tap into a more innovative mind-set. Instead of just looking at what exists, you start thinking about what doesn't exist and what *could* exist."

Turning cottonseed into peanuts (which sounds like magic) wasn't the only risk Rauch took. He came up with a plan to leapfrog the company three thousand miles away, expanding from California to the East Coast. Big risk? More like crazy stupid ridiculous risk. The owners and the CEO liked the idea, but the founder of the company, Joe Coulombe, who had since left, took him out to lunch to tell him not to sell his house in California when he moved to Boston. It couldn't work. He would be back.

"I thought, 'This is the founder of Trader Joe's! It's like God telling me that I'm going to fail,'" he said.

In case that divine message wasn't enough, the solid New Englander Tom Chappell, who had started the toothpaste company Tom's of Maine, took Rauch out to dinner and was equally dubious. Tom didn't think anything about the company would transfer well—including the employee uniforms.

"Tom said, 'You're not going to keep the Hawaiian shirts, are you? I mean, they make sense in California—the beach, the surfers—but you get up in Boston, you look like a bunch of idiots,'" Rauch recalled. Tom also thought the entire store model—with no counters or service or fresh deli—would fail. Boston was the capital of fresh fish—why would anybody buy frozen fish? "I came away from that dinner incredibly depressed. I even had our shirt supplier do a long-sleeved Hawaiian shirt to see what it would look like."

The long-sleeved Hawaiian shirt looked as ridiculous as it sounds. So Rauch decided to risk the long odds everyone predicted and come east with Hawaiian shirts and frozen fish. If the odds were against him, he would make his own odds—sticking with the model he believed in. "It was slow, it was hard. It was a slog and always a struggle," Rauch told us. "But that's the way businesses go, and life, too. It's not an overnight success many times. You can't change who you are to be something else. You have to believe in yourself and have the courage to keep going."

Rauch and his team stuck with the plan and kept expanding up and down the East Coast. Rauch eventually became president of Trader Joe's nationwide, and by the time he left in 2008, he had opened 104 stores.

Going against the odds won't always work. But the big success story is rarely the one people predict. The odds said that Trader Joe's would do better in Boston with the employees wearing nice embroidered shirts and selling fresh fish from behind counters. Rauch used his own instincts and research and insights into the food business to take a different approach.

Figuring out whether or not to gamble is a simple equation—or at least it is for mathematicians. You just multiply the odds of something occurring times the expected payoff. So, for example, if you have a 10 percent shot at winning $1000, you multiply 10 percent (0.1) by 1000 and get 100. Theoretically, you should be willing to put in up to a hundred bucks for the opportunity. But in real life, odds and potential payoffs aren't always so clear—and emotions come into play, too. I'd see this problem as presenting a 90 percent likelihood that I'm going to lose whatever I put in. So maybe I'd risk five bucks. (This explains why I don't have a career in private equity or venture capital.)

Did Doug Rauch have a 10 percent chance of succeeding when he moved Trader Joe's to Boston? Twenty percent? Five? Every action he took changed the odds—and ultimately that's what's important in making your own luck. Shortly after talking to Rauch, I got a call from an agent informing me that I was being considered to head up a very exciting project. A big list of potential people had been winnowed down—and she thought about ten names were still in the running.

I didn't get too excited. In fact, I immediately told myself that it wouldn't happen. A one-in-ten shot wasn't very good. The other people were very talented. I'd just ignore it and see what happened.

But wait a minute! Was there a way to change those odds? My natural instinct was to back away—if you expect nothing, you don't get disappointed. But you also don't get lucky. So I thought about what might set me apart. I called a few people. I sent a funny email. I whipped out a previous project I'd done that was similar and might make a difference. Maybe I didn't start as the obvious choice—but Hawaiian shirts in Boston weren't a shoo-in, either. Somebody had to make them lucky.

A week later, I got a call that the contenders had been narrowed to four, and the people making the decision could meet me the following Wednesday. As it happened, I was supposed to be flying to the Bahamas to give a speech. But . . . *Make your opportunities! Be the statistic you want to be!* I paid a big fee to change my flight to the next day (and still got there in time for the speech). I prepared for the meeting and gave it my all.

As I write this, I don't yet know whether I got the project—but it doesn't matter. I did everything I could to shift the odds in my favor. One way or another, I worked to make the luck happen. And when you look at your life, knowing you've pushed and believed and tried to change the odds is what makes you feel lucky.

I chatted about that with a woman named Christy Clark, who lives in Boulder, Colorado. Or she *used* to live in Boulder. When we spoke, she told me that the very next week, she and her husband and their first-grade daughter were moving full-time to Paris.

"How fabulous!" I said.

In terms of personal risk-taking, it was one of the bolder moves I've heard.

Intrigued by Paris since she was a kid in New Jersey, Christy married her high school sweetheart, Cliff, and they visited the beautiful city on their honeymoon and again with their baby daughter. They took vacations there and eventually bought and renovated a gorgeous apartment near St. Germain des Prés. It started to seem right to her to have a new adventure.

Moving to Paris with a young child when you don't speak French sounds pretty dicey. But Christy had done everything she could to make sure it would work.

"We have a wonderful life in Boulder, but my heart sings when I'm in Paris," she said.

As a psychotherapist in private practice, she regularly told couples to make luck (and love) by trying things they'd never done before. "Always ask yourself the question of why you're doing something," she said. "Am I doing it because it's familiar? Change is hard and scary, but think of all the luck you can make if you're willing to feel a little uncomfortable."

For days after I spoke to Christy, I couldn't stop thinking about her. I imagined her wandering through the Louvre and eating pain au chocolat and playing with her daughter in the Luxembourg Gardens. Had she increased her odds for a lucky life? Maybe some statistic shows how many people are happy in Boulder versus Paris, and no doubt some mathematician could work out the odds for marital bliss if you move to your dream city instead of staying put. But if so, I would respectfully tell Christy to ignore all of them. There are good days and bad ones in any life, and you make luck by trying to have more of one than the other. Maybe doing what makes your heart sing is one way to become the statistic you want to be.

PART TWO

HOW TO GET LUCKY

I have noticed that even those who assert that
everything is predestined and that we can
change nothing about it still look both ways
before they cross the street.

—*Stephen Hawking*

CHAPTER FOUR

Skate to Where the Puck Will Be

*Be in the place where opportunity can find you. . . . Know
that one thing leads to another. . . . It's okay to move away
from Mom. . . . Why Mother Teresa flew first class.*

After spending Mondays and Tuesdays at his Luck Lab in
Princeton, Barnaby would come to our weekly Wednesday
get-togethers full of new ideas and theories. The first question when
he came to New York was always where we would meet. I had one
or two favorite spots in the city, but now the range of my hangouts
expanded dramatically. A new restaurant in Columbus Circle, the
Loeb Boathouse in Central Park, a coffee bar on the West Side—
Barnaby was always looking for someplace better than where he'd
been before.

"Where you spend your time is important," Barnaby told me one
day as we sat down in one of those shared workspaces that have
been proliferating in big cities. "To get lucky, you have to be in a
place where opportunities are going to be around you."

He told me that in thinking about how place affects luck, he kept
coming back to hockey great Wayne Gretzky.

"He had an amazing insight about making luck," Barnaby said.

Gretzky was on four Stanley Cup–winning teams in the 1980s
and 1990s and set extraordinary scoring records that still stand.
When he was asked to explain how he scored so many goals, he
always had one answer: "I skate to where the puck will be."

I tried not to let my disappointment show. If Barnaby thought that was brilliant, maybe it was. But . . . really?

"Skate to where the puck will be?" I repeated.

Barnaby nodded. "It's really important in life—not just hockey—because lucky people put themselves in places where opportunity comes. Then they can wait calmly and capture the luck as it approaches."

"But doesn't everybody do that?" I asked.

Barnaby shook his head. "Most people stay home watching television."

I laughed. He was right. Recent statistics from Nielsen say that Americans spend about five hours a day watching TV in one form or another, plus another two hours or so consuming media on their phones and tablets. Seven hours a day is pretty much a full-time job. But unless you're prepping to be a judge on *Dancing with the Stars*, you're not going to get lucky by sitting home and watching television. Luck comes from being in a place where you can take advantage of the unexpected. Your couch is not one of those spots.

"We should make stickers to put on TVs that read LUCK KILLER!" Barnaby joked.

I reminded him that I used to be a television producer, but I got the point.

Gretzky's line about skating to where the puck would be was funny but also practical and true, because when the puck got to him, he was ready—and also often the only one there. You can score all sorts of (real and proverbial) goals by being in the right place for positive things to happen—whether you're looking for a job, a spouse, or a sports trophy. I'd already learned that lucky events aren't nearly as haphazard as they may appear. Being in the right place at the right time can be a matter of sheer chance, but just as often, some reasoned trajectory got you to that spot. If you're trying to get lucky, you have to think about where you're headed—and where the puck will be.

I thought of a story I'd heard about Oscar-winning actress Charlize Theron, who left her home country of South Africa after a string of bad events in an unusually dramatic childhood. Her mother shot and killed Theron's alcoholic father in self-defense (there were no charges), and Theron moved to Italy and then America, looking for better luck. It didn't happen immediately. She wanted to be a dancer, but her knees gave out. She was so depressed that her mother told her to come back home, but at age nineteen, she went to Los Angeles to give herself one last chance. It wasn't looking good—until she had a screaming fit in a bank when a teller refused to cash the check her mom had sent from South Africa.

If you're wondering where the luck part comes in, hang on. A man standing in the bank happened to be a talent agent. He saw this beautiful woman emoting dramatically and gave her his business card. That launched her career.

Now I'm not suggesting that exploding in rage is the way to get lucky. But by dragging herself to Los Angeles after all that had gone wrong, Theron put herself in a place where opportunities were most likely to happen. If she'd given up and gone back to South Africa, everyone at home would have understood and consoled her on her hard luck. Instead, she gave herself the chance to get lucky—and the 2004 Academy Award for Best Actress ended up on her mantel rather than someone else's.

Americans have a reputation for being always on the go, but it turns out that making big moves like Theron did is unusual here. According to an analysis in *The New York Times*, a scant 20 percent of Americans live more than a couple of hours' drive away from their moms, and half of all grown-ups in the country stay within eighteen miles of those moms.[1] I am a great fan of mothers, but they are not necessarily the source of all luck. Moving away from Mom can lead to new connections and better possibilities.

Grabbing at luck can be complicated because opportunities aren't always predictable. You can move to Los Angeles planning to audition for commercials, but instead you throw a tantrum in a bank, get an agent, take acting classes, and end up playing a serious role that wins you an Oscar. Each of those events (the tantrum in the bank, getting an agent . . .) could have numerous different outcomes, and one doesn't lead inexorably to the next. You have to see the possibility and grab it.

Barnaby was full of examples of people who had made luck by going where the opportunities would be. The Greek shipping magnate Aristotle Onassis didn't start out lucky—his family lost everything during the Greco-Turkish War, and he fled to Buenos Aires as a teenager. But even when Onassis was too broke to eat out, he would go to the most expensive hotel and order tea.

"He understood that if you want to be rich, you go where the rich people are!" Barnaby said.

Onassis broke a few rules along the way, like getting a job as a telephone engineer so that he could listen in on other people's business calls and figure out his own angles. He always put himself in a place where he could meet the people who would help him. It's probably excessive to say that this rule led him to be one of the richest men in the world, the lover of opera diva Maria Callas, and the husband to widowed Jacqueline Kennedy. But the determined effort to make

---

1. Since parents aren't always together, it's apparently more efficient to track moms than dads.

his own luck certainly helped him rebound, and his go-for-it principles still resonate.

I probably wouldn't use my last dime for tea in a fancy hotel, but
maybe that's why I'm not as rich as Onassis. To get lucky, you have
to be in a place where you can make opportunities. It's always easy
to find reasons and excuses not to do something, and a defeatist
attitude can sometimes even seem like the rational one. Maybe it is.
But it's not the one that will make you lucky.

"Fear and lack of confidence are great inhibitors of luck because
they keep you from going after what you want and making the connections that will get you there," Barnaby said.

You're not a good target for luck when you're sitting at home depressed or hiding under the covers in bed. (Unlike the tooth fairy,
luck doesn't sneak in while you sleep.) If you want to make luck, you
have to ratchet up your courage and try the unexpected.

Barnaby was convinced that the Gretzky principle of going where
the puck will be works for everyone—and the secret was just adapt-
ing it to your own objectives. Even the saintly need to make luck.

"It's why Mother Teresa flew first class!" Barnaby said. "She could
raise more money for her charities on a first-class flight from India
to London than almost any other place."

As soon as I got home, I checked that one out. For most of her
life, Mother Teresa lived in India and dedicated her life to the people she described as the unwanted, unloved, and uncared for in
society. She started a congregation called the Missionaries of Charity, which expanded rapidly over the years, and by the time she died
in 1997, it included thousands of nuns in more than a hundred
countries, all of them vowing to give "wholehearted free service to
the poorest of the poor."

Mother Teresa quickly figured out that you need a lot of money to take care of the poor and forgotten—and she was intent on gathering charitable donations. Though she believed that understanding the poor meant living among them, she often flew in the first-class cabin of airplanes. She got some criticism for that, but being in the front of the plane on her frequent travels ultimately brought luck that she could spread far. Talking to people on long flights from India to London (and elsewhere) gave her a captive fund-raising audience and generated some of her biggest contributions. She understood that the executive who could afford seat 1A was probably more able to contribute generously to her cause than the guy in the middle seat of the last row in economy. In person, this small and intent woman was hard to turn down. Her passion was her power.

Mother Teresa was canonized by the Catholic Church in 2016 as Saint Teresa of Calcutta. The canonization caused some controversy (though it didn't mention her travel arrangements), and even in her down-to-earth days, critics sometimes pointed out her many connections with dubious (albeit rich) executives and dictators. More positively, she did whatever was necessary to help fund her important activities and bring some luck to the neediest. Sometimes she found the people who could help in India and sometimes at international meetings and sometimes just walking to the bathroom in the first-class section of the airplane. She went where the donors would be.

An '80s new wave rock band called the Fixx had a hit song called "One Thing Leads to Another." Fans were probably more interested in the hot dance beat than the philosophical reasoning behind the words, but the title also hits on a simple truth—because in life and luck, one thing *does* lead to another. You set the stage for one positive result and others will follow from it—and often the luck gets bigger and bigger. As the writer E. B. White charmingly put it, "There's no limit to how complicated things can get, on account of one thing always leading to another."

People with big ambitions tend to cluster together with some implicit understanding that luck feeds luck. When Mark Zuckerberg was a Harvard undergraduate and started Facebook, he moved to Palo Alto for a summer to give his company the best chance of being lucky. He went where the luck would be. In that tech-focused environment, one thing definitely led to another—because one person led to another. Zuckerberg hired Sean Parker (who had started Napster) to be president of his budding company. Looking for investments, Parker went to Reid Hoffman, who headed the social networking site LinkedIn. Hoffman liked the idea but couldn't invest (he thought it was a conflict of interest), so he introduced Parker to Peter Thiel, whom he had worked with at PayPal—and Zuckerberg got his first $500,000 angel investment.[2] Zuckerberg profited (hugely, as it turned out) by being in a place where luck and support could flow his way. For Zuckerberg and Facebook, the luck happened when one person led to another—Parker to Hoffman to Thiel.

If you have a brilliant idea for a start-up that needs serious money to get under way, you've probably already thought about moving to Silicon Valley (or at least taking a trip there). You can splurge for lunch at the beautiful Madera restaurant on Sand Hill Road and take it as a tax write-off, since there's a pretty good chance that the

---

2. The half a million dollars gave Thiel more than 10 percent of the young company—ultimately one of the luckiest investments he ever made. After Facebook went public a few years later, Thiel sold his shares for more than a billion dollars. (Whether he has used the money well is not necessarily clear.)

person at the next table is someone who can help. You're not going to accost him while he's eating his tuna tartare, but the chance of making the right connection is better when you're in the midst of the action and a couple of blocks from the offices of the most powerful venture capitalists in the world. You've put yourself in the place where lucky opportunities are more likely to happen.

But before you buy your one-way plane ticket to San Francisco, it's worth remembering that the spots offering the biggest opportunities, like Silicon Valley or Hollywood, are also the places where you face the greatest competition. Barnaby told me that biologists have noticed this in the natural world for a long time and call it "ideal free distribution"—noting that more animals gather in the spots richest in resources. For a squirrel, a grassy area with lots of nuts and fruits scattered on the ground might seem like the perfect place to hang out. But if all the other squirrels are there too, and you're on the small side and don't have sharp claws, maybe you're better off on the less fertile land down the road. You may not get quite as many nuts and berries, but you can do just fine, thank you, and lead a perfectly nice life (even in the winter).

The same theory holds for human beings looking to get lucky in finding a job or a lover or a chance to get rich. You want to go to the places that have the best opportunities *and where you can compete.* If you're an entrepreneur with a small start-up and are barely making a go of it at home in rural Indiana, maybe you need to develop it a bit more before heading to Silicon Valley. On the other hand, if the company is soaring and you're doing a lot better than anyone else you know in town, you might want to take the leap to the coast. The bold move works to make you lucky only when you're ready to take it.

A couple of months earlier, I met a young woman named Alice Brooks when we were both in Cedar Rapids, Iowa, to speak at a women's leadership conference (a great place for lucky things to happen). I had given the keynote address and she led an afternoon seminar, but we connected in a car on the way back to the airport—and then couldn't stop talking. For once I was glad that we had a long wait for our planes.

Alice took advantage of being in the right place after she graduated from MIT in 2010 and went to Stanford to get a graduate degree in mechanical engineering. She was one of the few women in the program, and fired up by the entrepreneurial spirit encouraged at Stanford, she decided she wanted to create a toy for little girls that encouraged them to be as excited about engineering as she was. She imagined a toy where little girls could design a project and then build and wire it.

"When I was a little girl, I asked for a Barbie for Christmas, and my dad gave me a saw instead. So I built dolls and a dollhouse," she said with a laugh. "That's just the kind of experience girls need."

At Stanford, she began to design toys for girls with flashing lights and circuits and, along with her friend Bettina Chen, who was also in the engineering program, decided to start a company. A great idea—but then, everybody in Silicon Valley has a great idea. They worked every element in the luck chain to make the idea a success—finding the right contacts, crowdsourcing, getting mentors, being out in the marketplace where chance events could occur. Then they got themselves into a position where many entrepreneurs want to be—on the TV show *Shark Tank*.

If you've never watched that program, you have to trust me that it's a lot more entertaining than it might sound. The "sharks" are five hugely successful businesspeople ("titans of industry," the show calls them) who listen to pitches from entrepreneurs and decide if they want to invest money (their own) in the start-up companies. Produced by Mark Burnett, who launched into reality television years ago with the show *Survivor, Shark Tank* is a kind of *Survivor* for capitalists. The show has gotten so popular that the producers get some forty thousand applications every year from people who want to swim into the tank. But they also go out looking for entrepreneurs who would make good TV—and it didn't take them long to hear about two attractive Stanford engineers making a smart toy for girls.

Brooks told me she was flattered the first time the producers called, but she turned them down. She recognized that while the show was meant to be fun for viewers, the sharks were also shrewd businesspeople looking to invest with savvy entrepreneurs who had potentially profitable companies. She'd get one chance to impress them. Being in the right place doesn't help if you're not ready to take full advantage of the opportunity. She wanted her company to have bigger sales and a more impressive story before she went on the show.

Finally the company was in a position where she felt ready to say yes to the producers. "We were going to be the first episode on season six, so we watched the previous five seasons and took notes on every question that got asked," Alice said. "Then we divided up the questions so that when we were asked something, we could answer immediately and not have to look at each other."

Being on that TV show was definitely the right place—and their smooth presentation and quick answers impressed the group. The results were a great example of luck favoring the prepared. Billionaire Mark Cuban invested $250,000, for 2.5 percent of their company.[3] They already had sales of $1.7 million when they appeared on the show, and those soared to some $5 million the following year. A few years later, in January 2016, they sold out to a Wisconsin-based toy company—making Brooks very rich before her thirtieth birthday.

In trying to figure out how to skate to where the puck will be, it helps to listen to the full advice Gretzky got from his hockey-obsessed dad. Even though Gretzky was naturally talented from a young age, his dad drilled him on the essentials of the game. In his autobiography, Gretzky reported that their conversations would go like this:

> Dad: Where's the last place a guy looks before
> he passes it?
> Young Wayne: The guy he's passing to . . .
> Dad: Where do you skate?
> Young Wayne: To where the puck is going, not where
> it's been.

It's easy to understand that you want to skate to where the puck will be, but the second part of that sentence is equally important. You don't want to skate to where the puck has *already been*. In looking for luck or success, it's natural to go where others have already found it. You may find it there—scientists tell us that lightning

---

3. On the show, Cuban and fellow shark Lori Greiner of QVC fame were supposed to team up with equal shares, but Lori dropped out afterward. What you see on the air is not always what the entrepreneurs get.

absolutely does strike twice in the same spot—but it's also possible that the biggest luck opportunities will have moved on. Everybody else is clustering in the previously lucky area, so you might do well to try to figure out where that puck is going.

Young entrepreneurs like Alice are always trying different versions of their company and staying flexible enough to move toward an ever-changing future. She brought an early version of her building toys to families around town so she could watch how little girls played with them, and then she adapted the toy. Being willing to work hard and constantly change her plan increased her chances for success. Start-up companies are always talking about their beta version—which means they're still trying stuff out and looking for ways to improve. Or they say they're in Version 2.0—which means the first plan didn't work and they've moved on to another one. Both of these approaches are valuable for your own life, too. When the rules are changing (as they always are), the only way to stay ahead is . . . to stay ahead. Allow yourself to be in your own beta version or keep moving forward to Life 2.0. You're not guaranteed a multimillion-dollar payout, but being able to look forward rather than backward does improve your chances.

Young entrepreneurs aren't really much different from every other species that needs to evolve. Barnaby spent many years studying ornithology (did I mention he has eclectic interests?), and as we talked one day, he brought up a bird called the rock dove that used to live on the Mediterranean coast in Europe and North Africa. As cities grew, there were more chances to get lucky finding food away from the coast, and many of the doves moved inland. They continued to follow opportunities to be where the food would be. Rock doves are now called pigeons. Perhaps you've seen them in your favorite city?

Similarly, raptors were never city birds until a red-tailed hawk decided that the ornate molding of a very nice building on Fifth Avenue in Manhattan was a good place for his nest. Named Pale Male by a writer, he became a local celebrity when the wealthy residents of the building decided they didn't want him there—and dismantled the nest. Bird enthusiasts and the Audubon Society intervened, and eventually the nest was rebuilt with a reported $40,000 supporting platform beneath it (to keep any debris from falling on pedestrians below). Pale Male has now been at his penthouse perch more than twenty-five years, and with a succession of mates (eight, at last count) has sent many offspring into the world. There are now reports of other red-tailed hawks nesting all over the city, including on the Plaza Hotel.

The rock doves and Pale Male got lucky by moving away from the spots that had been right in the past and looking for future opportunities. Doing that can feel like a bit of a risk, but it's the kind that can pay off for animals of all varieties—including people.

Being in the right place to get lucky can sometimes be very literal. Back in the 1972 Olympics, American sprinters Rey Robinson and Eddie Hart were favorites to medal in the 100- and 200-meter races. But their coach had an outdated schedule for the qualifying rounds and they missed their quarter-final contests. There was no pleading the case—they were eliminated. That story resonates over the decades because it seems so outrageously unfair. Even those who never previously heard of Robinson and Hart know that they must have driven themselves and trained for years in order to make the Olympics in the first place. The coach took the fall and accepted all the blame[4]—but if you're not in the right place you can't get lucky.

---

4. It later turned out that the coach had checked with an official to make sure he had an updated schedule. (Maybe if it's the Olympics, you check twice.)

So that brings us back to Gretzky, always making sure he got to a place where he could become lucky. He had one other insight that works in life as well as hockey—"You miss 100 percent of the shots you don't take." In other words, you can't get lucky unless you put yourself on the line. And for that, it's necessary to pull yourself out of a comfort zone (and definitely out of bed) and meet the people who can make one thing lead to another. From the outside, it may look like you've been lucky, but you've really just skated to where the puck is going next.

CHAPTER FIVE

Connect to the Power of Other People

Identify new networks. . . . Talk to the guy next to you on the plane. . . . Give luck to get luck. . . . Rely on the strength of weak ties. . . . Go to every party.

Shortly after discussing an Elena Ferrante novel at my book club one evening, we all drifted over to the table, which had been set up for dessert. As we tucked into fruit and gelato (and chocolate cookies, let's admit), one of the women said she had an announcement. Her husband had a friend who used to work with a talented guy in the digital world who just got fired and needed a new job. Did anybody have any leads?

I took another strawberry. *What?* Her husband had a friend who used to work with . . . The connection sounded as baffling as trying to figure out who really wrote the Elena Ferrante novels.

The guy who needed the job was named Sree Sreenivasan—and I shouldn't have been surprised to find out that Barnaby knew him, since Sree clearly had a huge network. How else would an Indian journalist who was born in Tokyo end up being discussed by a bunch of women in an Upper East Side book group? When I checked out his story, Sree turned out to be the perfect example of Barnaby's next principle—that you make luck through other people.

Sree was already well-known in the social media world when he was hired as the first chief digital officer of the Metropolitan Museum of Art—a position created just for him. He considered it a dream job. But after three years, the Met decided to cut back top staff, and in June 2016, he was let go. He said later that his first reaction was panic, and he thought about retreating. Climbing into a hole is a natural reaction when you're down, but unless you're a badger, holes don't lead anywhere. So he decided to use his many friends and followers on social media for support. He announced his situation on Facebook and said that he usually walked for five miles every day—and now that he had more time, it would be ten miles. He invited people to sign up to walk and talk with him, and he put up a form that read: "If there's one thing Sree should consider doing next it is . . ." Some 1,300 people reached out to him in what he called a "global digital hug." He was apparently being discussed everywhere—including at my book club. By the end of the month, he had a new job as chief digital officer for the City of New York—a much bigger job than where he had been.

Sree's good luck revolved around using his connections—and his extended network—in a very public way. When his new position was announced, he posted, "I got this role because I was open and frank and asked for help. I think the more we are all clear about the help we need, the more that people can help us."

It's probably fair to say that more often than not, luck depends on other people. Harvard Law School professor Lawrence Lessig has argued that the more interconnected we are, the more creative and innovative we become.[1] Expanding on this idea, writer Steven Johnson points out in his book *Where Good Ideas Come From* that during the Renaissance, breakthroughs arose from "the inventive genius, the rogue visionary who somehow sees beyond the horizon that

---

1. He feels so strongly about this that he argues for more open copyright laws and has made his book *The Future of Ideas* available for free on the web.

limits his contemporaries—da Vinci, Copernicus, Galileo." But after 1800, there was a huge change, and now most innovation occurs in collaborative environments. Rather than sitting alone at a desk and hoping for a eureka moment, most creative people are sharing ideas and building on one another's work. Executives and investors are talking to one another about possibilities. In our more networked world, working with other people creates luck.

A simple secret of luck is to be with the people who can (and will) cause good things to happen for you. And it's not always who you think. Family and friends may be the bulwarks of support in most of your life, but the connections that propel you into the luck stratosphere are sometimes the most unexpected.

The much-admired sociologist Mark Granovetter, who has degrees from Princeton and Harvard and is now a chaired professor of sociology at Stanford, refers to this as "the strength of weak ties."[2] You have strong ties with people like close friends or colleagues whom you see at least once a week and weak ties with those you encounter less frequently. Interestingly, it's the weak ties that usually matter, whether you're looking to land a potential mate or a new job in digital media. You and your best friends already know most of the same people—you have "overlapping social circles," as the sociologists like to say. But those with whom you're more weakly tied—like Sree and the ladies at the book club—probably have an entirely different social network. Connecting with them opens up a whole new community of possibilities—and because each new

---

2. His 1973 paper by that title, published in the *American Journal of Sociology,* is one of the most cited papers in the social sciences.

person is connected to many others, your possibilities are suddenly vastly larger.

Granovetter's insight into the wonderfully oxymoronic strength of weak ties has inspired complex studies about networks and how information and luck spread. People who know how to play the networking game often end up looking like the luckiest ones around.

Barnaby told me about his friend Lara Galinsky, who regularly uses the power of networks at conferences she runs. A consultant to many nonprofit organizations, she organizes luck circles instead of the standard bonding exercises that many of us have come to dread (beach Olympics, anyone?). Barnaby and I met Lara at a local café for breakfast, and over oatmeal and iced tea, she explained that her goal is to help everyone increase their opportunities for lucky events and connections to occur. She starts by dividing people into random groups of five—the core luck circle. Each person tells the group one thing that he or she needs to get lucky—something that would make a real difference in life. Then the groups mingle, and people walk around talking to one another and seeing if they can spread luck.

"As you move around, you're carrying five people's dreams in your pocket," Lara told us as she sipped her tea. "It's random, controlled chaos. In the din, we'll regularly hear a shout of delight as someone makes a connection that can create luck."

Lara's luck circles were inspired by emergence theory—the idea that small things can interact and connect to create bigger payoffs. She transferred the academic theory to real life in her conferences, with the small circle leading to the bigger circle. After you state the one thing you need to get lucky in life, huge repercussions occur when others know about it and are inspired to help. As people move around, their paths cross, strangers become acquaintances, and somebody you never imagined has exactly what you need to get lucky.

Lara described one luck circle she ran where a young woman told her group of five that she wanted to get a job at a particular national foundation. Nobody in the group had an immediate way to help her. But as the small group expanded to the larger one, the foundation name got bandied about—and it didn't take very long for someone to remember a colleague who had once worked there and could make the right introduction. Wow! The young woman couldn't believe her luck. She just said the right words, and the luck popped up!

"Luck sounds mystical, but it starts from the very grounded place of knowing what you want," Lara told us. "Being declarative about your own desires and putting them into the world creates the conditions for luck. When you have clear ideas of what you want and see the world as something you can affect, you elicit lucky reactions. It's about openness and possibility and capturing chance."

Mathematicians would be quick to tell you that it was statistically reasonable that someone in the room was able to connect with the young woman's luck request. The more people you know, the more quickly your message will be spread and the more connections you can make.

Some of the most impressive work in exploring the power of networks has been done by a professor named Albert-László Barabási. He has so many professional titles that it seems like he could get lucky networking with himself—he's a professor of physics as well as of computer and information science at Northeastern University, runs that school's Center for Complex Network Research, and has appointments at Harvard Medical School and two major teaching hospitals. Born in Transylvania, Romania, he lectures so often around the world that it's a surprise he never ran into Mother Teresa on an airplane.

To explain how information (and luck) spreads, Dr. Barabási gives the example of a cocktail party with a hundred people who don't know one another. The host mentions to one of the guests (we'll call him John) that the red wine in the unmarked decanter is actually a rare and valuable vintage. The host figures that his wine is pretty safe—after all, how many people can John meet and share the information with during the course of the party?

The answer is: a lot more than you think. The cocktail party turns out to be like Lara's luck circles. What start out as small interactions can spiral into big payoffs. So at the start of the party, the guests will naturally break off into groups of two or three people to chat. The tidbit about the expensive wine is a good icebreaker, so John will surely share the news with his new acquaintances. Eventually everyone in the group will drift off to refresh a drink or grab an hors d'oeuvre or meet more people. If you figure that each of the three people in John's original group joins another group of three, the story of the vintage wine can now spread to nine more people. And eventually those nine will wander to other groups with their news.

According to Dr. Barabási, the mathematicians Paul Erdős and Alfréd Rényi studied the problem and concluded that it would take just thirty minutes "to form a single invisible social web that includes all the guests in the room." Just by going to that party and moving around, you can get lucky enough to taste the vintage wine.

But it also turns out that some parties will be luckier than others—as will some cities and towns and universities. Cornell sociology professor Victor Nee has been doing research to find out how people create luck for one another in a big-city environment, and why big cities tend to have so many creative and academic clusters. Doing research on knowledge-based economies, Nee noticed that after the financial meltdown of 2008, New York City rebounded with its usual strongholds in finance and advertising and arts, but it also developed what he called an "innovation cluster" that made it the second-largest technology economy in the country (behind only Silicon Valley and its epicenter at Stanford). He was curious to figure out what was behind both the resilience and the surge in innovation.

Barnaby and Nee often take walks together to toss around academic ideas, and one sunny morning I joined them for a stroll through Central Park. Nee had his English cocker spaniel at his side. The park was both beautifully peaceful and very busy—with joggers and bicyclists circling the reservoir and people holding casual meetings as they drank coffee outside the Loeb Boathouse. Nee's well-behaved spaniel (named Dustin) got attention from a variety of poodles and mutts and French bulldogs, and it was easy to see how New York could feel like a very small community as the various dog owners started chatting together.

Nee told us that as he did research into innovation in New York, he realized that "the spatial dynamic supports the serendipitous recombination of ideas." I asked for a translation, and Nee smiled. "It's a narrow, small island and easy to have face-to-face interactions. Look how simple it was for us to get together today. You just walk out of your apartment and you can encounter someone useful. The secret juice of New York City is that it's very easy for people to meet."

As a much-admired professor of sociology at Cornell and the director of the Center for the Study of Economy & Society, Nee goes well beyond making observations while dog-walking. He spent two years gathering millions of points of data on, as he put it, "every instant when people got together to talk about technology." He collected information on the 50,000 members of New York Tech Meetup, an organization that holds monthly meetings with speakers as well as social events and parties. He added in information on smaller specialized sessions that members organize and meetup groups in specific fields and much more.

He realized that people in the tech world attend meetings and parties big and small so they can be part of the swirl of ideas constantly percolating when creative people get together. "Those face-to-face meetings are important because most innovation is about taking existing ideas and recombining them," Nee said. "All the encounters increase the chance that someone will come up with a new combination." To people looking in from the outside, it feels like extraordinary luck when something original and exciting pops up. But those in the midst of the maelstrom of millions of meetings and exchanges know that it's a game of odds. The more interactions you have, the better your chances of hitting on the one combination of people and ideas that creates the explosive *pow* of innovation.

The frequent encounters also create what Nee calls "knowledge spillover." One person has an idea or insight that he can't use directly in his own work, so he shares it with someone else over a beer or at a meetup event. That person finds it to be just the link she needs in the company she's trying to start. "We expect people to be competitive and guard their ideas, but instead there's a great willingness to share without any expectation of getting help back," said Nee. "Making an investment in your reputation by sharing knowledge is very rational because others in the group see it and know you're a reliable person, so there may be indirect reciprocity." In other words, helping someone else gets everyone on your side—and makes them want to contribute to your lucky outcomes.

If you're outside the rarefied air of Stanford or the New York high-tech community (as most of us are), you can still use the principle of finding luck in other people. You may go to a moms' group, a book club, a yoga studio, or a Lions Club meeting to make some of those serendipitous connections. You can always read a book curled on the couch or do a side plank pose in your own bedroom, but you open yourself to lucky opportunities when you share the experience and have other people around you. Many of us like some time to sit alone and work or think or relax, and that can definitely be part of good days. But lucky sparks happen when people rub against each other.

I've always liked to think that being competent and talented is enough—but Barnaby convinced me that connections and personal networks often make the difference. What appears to the outside world as random luck often comes from networking behind the scenes. He pointed out that the movie *My Big Fat Greek Wedding* is regularly used as an example of a hit that came from nowhere. It's true that it was made on a shoestring (which now means $2 million), but writer and star Nia Vardalos also found a way to get the movie to Rita Wilson, who she knew was proudly Greek. Wilson agreed to help and brought it to her husband, Tom Hanks, who had his production company invest in the movie and work on its distribution. Luck, maybe—but the kind of luck that comes from connecting to other people.

So how do you actually start making connections? The easiest way to expand your luck network may be through social media. It doesn't take much effort to add a new friend on Facebook or up your number of Twitter posts. But this is only step one, and many studies suggest that online connections don't really replace face-to-face encounters. When social media guru Sree Sreenivasan used Facebook in his job search, it was just a way to invite people to meet with him in person via his daily walks. The vast majority of people looking for jobs use online sources, and there's no reason not to. But studies suggest that anywhere from 40 to 80 percent of people land jobs through direct contact with friends, colleagues, and connections. Having coffee with a former colleague may lead to more luck in the work world than another hour on LinkedIn.

The same pattern is true if you're looking to get lucky in love. Forty million or so Americans now use online dating sites, so these are a good way of expanding your potentially lucky links. But according to a 2016 Pew survey, even among people who have been with their partner for five years or less, fully 88 percent met through real-world connections. That may be changing—a recent survey from Match.com found that 39 percent of people now meet online. You can take these various survey numbers with a grain of salt (if not a whole shaker full), but you also have to remember that meeting is just the first step, and nobody gets married online. After you've swiped right on Tinder, you still have to do the face-to-face part: connect for a drink, get to know each other, decide if this is the person who will make you lucky in the future. You can't miss the overall conclusion that luck comes from connecting directly with other people.

Shortly after I graduated from college and moved to New York, I met a man named Henry Jarecki, who became a lifelong friend. He's

a couple of decades older than me and has made at least three fortunes on companies that he built and sold. Even if I don't see him
for months at a time, I always think of him as one of my closest
friends—and there are probably dozens of other people who keep
him on the top of their speed dial, too. However busy he is at work,
Henry always has time for the personal—connecting people, helping friends, making other people lucky.[3] People like Henry who are
always trying to make others lucky make themselves lucky, too.

Henry is an obsessive list maker, and he can produce an index of
all the lucky encounters he had over the years that helped create
some of his success. He also keeps a list he's written of all the
friends, colleagues, and associates who made a difference for him.
He is powerfully aware that nobody succeeds on their own.

"I marvel at how lucky I was to be surrounded by such smart,
talented people," he told me one day as we sat in his expansive
townhouse on Gramercy Park.

"But you made that luck!" I said. "You knew what you wanted,
and you made life interesting enough that everyone likes to be
around you."

Henry nodded, but he looked dubious, so I asked him what he
thought his number one secret was for making luck happen. He
didn't hesitate on that.

"I went to every party," he said with a grin.

Henry meant it both literally and metaphorically. He gets a lot of
invitations to parties and events and celebrations (and throws many,
too), and though he insists that he's mostly a cerebral kind of guy

---

3. Henry introduced me to Barnaby years ago, seating us next to each other at a black-
tie charity dinner that he sponsored. "I thought you'd find each other interesting,"
he said. So when I trace it back to the beginning, he was the lucky force behind
this book.

who would prefer being alone in his office with his papers than standing in a loud room with a drink in his hand, he always made himself go. The party he skipped might be the one at which he would have met the person who could change his life. He also realized that opportunities appear when you least expect them—and they were more likely to pop out at that party than in his office.

When he went to parties, Henry made a big impression on everyone he met. He doesn't hide the fact that he is a complete original. When he was young, he wore thick glasses and told great stories and wowed people as a charismatic intellectual. Now that he's older, he likes to entertain on one of the islands he owns in the British Virgin Islands, wearing a long caftan. He has a brilliant mind and a genius IQ, and as was true of Steve Jobs in his black turtlenecks or Mark Zuckerberg in his hoodies, Jarecki's style announces that he's going to head in his own directions in both his business life and his personal one. If you like that message, you can come along. If you have a more traditional or conservative approach, you might want to talk to someone else at the party.

People like Henry with strong personalities and their own style stand out at parties and are more likely to be remembered—others think of them when an opportunity arises. But you can make luck with other styles, too.

When I discussed Henry's go-to-every-party approach later with Barnaby, he turned to one of his nature analogies again and said that it reminded him of fishing. Cast five lines into the water, and you're more likely to reel something in than if you use just two lines.

And since you can't have too much of a good metaphor, Barnaby pointed out that commercial fishermen rely on a variety of techniques depending on what they're trying to catch. The big factory ships toss out huge nets to catch everything in the area. They have to decide how big the holes in the netting will be—because with very small fish you also pull in a lot of sea junk and garbage. When they're after specific kinds of higher-quality fish, they'll take the time to use separate hooks and bait each one with care. And for the biggest and most valuable fish—like the bluefin tuna, where a single fish can sell for hundreds of thousands of dollars—fishing companies use helicopters to scout from the air and find the fish to target.

The bigger point here is pretty clear. You have to know what you want before you start fishing for luck—and one technique doesn't work for everyone or every goal. Throw a big net, and there's a good chance you'll haul in something you want, but you have to be willing to put up with a lot of junk, too. Cast just a couple of lines, and the odds are lower but more focused.

I thought of my friend Marnie, who is gregarious and outgoing and so full of energy that she could talk to a rock and make it her friend. Lucky things seem to happen to her all the time—but (as we're now discovering) it's not random. Since she talks to everyone, she's like the fisherman who casts five lines and always pulls something in. When she was going to Austin, Texas, recently to visit her older son, I asked where she would be staying, and she laughed and rolled her eyes. "One of those crazy lucky things that happen to me," she began. On her last trip to Austin, she had gone to a funky local coffee shop and (of course) started chatting to the woman next to her in line. By the time their artisanally brewed coffees arrived, they were laughing and having so much fun that they sat down together to keep talking. When they finally left, the woman explained that she traveled a lot, so Marnie was welcome to stay in her condo in Austin anytime she visited her son.

"So that's where I'm staying!" Marnie said delightedly. "Can you imagine how lucky that is?"

Yes, lucky—but I could also imagine how many other people could go to that same coffee shop and not end up with a new friend who offered to be their local innkeeper. Marnie's good luck occurred for the same reason that Sree's did—both of them discovered the advantages of having many lines out to catch unexpected luck. (It's also noteworthy that it wasn't a close friend who offered the condo but a . . . weaker tie.)

The big-net approach doesn't work for everyone or every goal, and that's okay, too. Being thoughtful and focused in your interactions (a couple of carefully baited lines) can sometimes lead to even more luck than a brasher and more scattershot approach. If that tends to be your style, you can still be lucky. Back in 2003, writer Jonathan Rauch wrote an article for *The Atlantic* called "Caring for Your Introvert", which was one of the magazine's most popular pieces online for many years. He clearly hit a chord among people tired of being told that they needed to talk and socialize more to be successful. Rauch pointed out that introverts aren't necessarily shy—they're just calmer, more reflective, and usually more independent minded. Extroverts are energized by other people, while introverts tend to wilt after being social for too long and need to be alone to recharge.

Author Susan Cain expanded on that idea in her 2012 bestseller, *Quiet*, pointing out that our current culture of personality has made it seem that everybody needs to be an extrovert to function well. But introverts form loyal alliances through one-on-one interactions, and they're the ones getting luckier and luckier these days. In a follow-up interview a few years after his famous article, Rauch noted that geeks—the classic introverts—have been romanticized by Silicon

Valley, so "the digital economy is giving introverts a new place in the sun."

But none of this is an excuse to hide away and turn on the TV. Introverts can be as sociable as anyone else. If you want to make luck, you have to connect to people—in one style or another—and that means making yourself go to the party or start the conversation. Sometimes you have to make yourself do something that's not completely natural to make luck. Your own temperament may determine whether you talk to everyone at the party or sit quietly with just a couple of others. But with the right focus and attitude, you can make the connections that will help you capture luck.

Since I enjoyed testing out the theories Barnaby and I were creating, I decided to see if I could get lucky by making an effort to connect with someone I didn't previously know. I happened to be traveling a lot giving speeches, and typically on flights, I'd put on my Bose headphones and talk only to the flight attendant to order my Diet Coke. But returning from Montreal one afternoon, I left off the headphones, and as we taxied down the runway, I glanced over at the man sitting next to me. He had a stack of magazines like *Variety* and *Hollywood Reporter*—which suggested we might be in similar fields. That was interesting. Maybe I should cast a (well-curated) line and try to make luck.

I smiled at my seatmate but had no idea how to open the conversation. So I said something clever like "You have a lot of magazines there."

He nodded and then gestured to the cover of one of the magazines. He had a much better way to start.

"Do you think it's real?" he asked.

"Is what real?" I asked, confused.

"That." He moved the magazine closer to me and pointed. "Kim Kardashian's butt. I don't think it's real, do you?"

Kim Kardashian's butt did *not* seem like a road to luck, but heck, you have to see where things lead.

"I'm not sure I really care about the Kardashians," I admitted.

"I'm in the entertainment business. I have to care about everything," he said with a friendly smile.

I mentioned that I'd been a TV producer, so we started talking and playing the who-do-you-know game, and before long I felt like Marnie—making a new friend. His name was David Steinberg, and it turned out he was (among other things) the personal manager for huge stars including Bette Midler and Billy Crystal and the much-missed Robin Williams. When I told him that I was now investigating luck, he gave a big smile.

"Making luck happen is what I've done my whole career," he said.

Working with Billy and Bette and Robin, he'd seen how even the biggest talents needed to see possibilities and grab opportunities (or sometimes craft their own). He had so many stories that the ninety-minute flight wasn't nearly enough. When we landed, we agreed to have lunch together sometime in New York.

I got off the plane feeling the same exhilaration I had on my lucky Friday the thirteenth. Making luck happen wasn't just a theory—I could actually do it. Maybe not every time and certainly not every day, but just being aware of the principles (*luck is other people*) changed your focus and let you pay attention to the right things. In this case, I'd cast a line and met someone interesting. He wasn't lending me a condo in Austin, but not every connection needs an immediate payoff.

Over lunch at the Redeye Grill a couple of weeks later, I realized that David had something even better (for me) than a condo—great stories about people making luck for other people. He said that when he started out in his own career, he didn't realize how he was making his own luck. But reflection (and many years) made it all clearer.

"Can I include your stories in my book?" I asked.

"Sure, if anyone wants to hear about a guy from Milwaukee," he said with a laugh.

David grew up in Wisconsin, put himself through college selling aluminum siding, and quickly realized that this wasn't the job he wanted for his whole life. He moved to Los Angeles and got a job in the mailroom of an ad agency. "But I didn't like that, either," he said. "I wanted to be one of the guys sitting in an office getting my mail delivered to me."

So he started calling people to get a lead, and it turned out that he had a cousin who was married to a guy who knew another guy in Hollywood who . . .

I smiled to myself. I didn't really need to get the connections right. It was just more proof of how weak ties make luck.

The various connections led to a publicist doing a favor and giving David a job at his agency—which was where David met Sammy Davis Jr. They immediately bonded. David was half Sammy's age, but they both liked to go to every party. At the time, Sammy was part of a celebrated circle of celebrities—and there was no bigger star.

"He wanted to have as much fun as I did," David said. "I had a credit card with a $250 limit, but I was traveling around the world with him and going to dinner parties with Frank Sinatra and Lucille Ball. I met everybody." Those connections led to possibilities—and eventually he started his own PR company out of the back of

Sammy's office. "I just kept running. Whenever there was an opportunity, I put myself in that place," he told me.

David instinctively realized that if you want other people to make you lucky, you need to make them feel lucky, too. Life doesn't track one way. Early in his career when he was (as he joked) "apparently successful but realistically broke," David was going to dinner at the Hotel Bel-Air one night with six Hollywood friends. He saw it as his chance to be generous, so he gave his credit card to the maître d' ahead of time—not realizing that one of the guests, the actor Peter Sellers, had preordered for the whole table.

"All of a sudden there were mounds of caviar coming out and rack of lamb, and I thought, 'I am now one credit card statement away from disaster,'" he said. But he let the card go through, amazed that it wasn't denied. He knew it was important to give as well as take.

Later, when he became a manager, he produced various shows for Robin Williams and Billy Crystal, took notes on their live performances, and helped them develop some of their material. "My job was just to make them look good," he said. A manager's motivations can be tinged by self-interest—"we're human, not robots"—but since he was known for integrity and putting his clients first, his career kept getting bigger. By making others lucky, he increased his own luck, too.

"I flunked out of college twice, and I was a discipline problem growing up, but I had good instincts and understood comedy," he said. "I never took myself too seriously or told anyone why I'm so important. But I was interested in other people and liked to get new experiences—and that all made me lucky."

Other people can make you lucky when you give to them without worrying about what will come back. You pay for dinner at the Bel-Air, you help a big star become even bigger, you offer to work for free just to be around interesting people (he did that early in his career, too). David had met me on a plane, but he spent three hours at lunch sharing great stories and insights without expecting a return. And when the check came and I reached for it, he grabbed it and rolled his eyes. "Really?" he asked.

Making someone else feel lucky without knowing how (or if) you'll get it back can be a risk. But it's a risk worth taking. Not every person you meet is going to help you make luck, but you need only a couple. (And you can still have fun and interesting times with the rest.) David was the Hollywood example of what Professor Nee had described as investing in your reputation by sharing knowledge. As so often happens to people who do that, what came back for him was buckets of luck.

Dr. Barabási, who had shared his cocktail-party theory, pointed out in one of his books that "once upon a time people were born into communities and had to find their individuality. Today people are born individuals and have to find their communities." Being part of a community opens you to a network of possibilities. Being part of *many* communities expands your weak ties and invisible webs and dramatically increases the chance of lucky events coming your way.

I left the lunch thinking of all the different ways that luck comes from other people. And I also realized that to make that luck happen, you need to take action within your social circles, however you define them, and do so in a way that feels genuine to you. You might pick up the phone and call an acquaintance you haven't spoken to in a year. At a coffee shop or a local park or on an airplane, look up and take in the people around you. Maybe there is someone sipping their latte or walking their dog who can help you plant the seeds for luck. If you think about what you need to get lucky and let as many people as possible know about it, you can essentially form your own luck circle—and watch it pay off.

The luck we bring each other can be mutual and expansive. You have to know how to take the opportunities and share them and give them back. Because whoever you are—from New York's chief digital officer to Bette Midler's manager—you need other people to help you get lucky.

CHAPTER SIX

Zig When Others Zag

Take your own path. . . . Be willing to think different. . . .
Cultivate unpredictability.

The more I got to know Barnaby, the more I realized that he was . . . unconventional. Growing up in Alaska as the oldest of five children, he was mostly self-taught and spent a lot of time in the outdoors. (You can learn a lot watching salmon swim upstream.) The first time he stepped into a real classroom was when he arrived at college.

He wondered for a while what he had missed—and even volunteered at two local-area high schools his freshman year at Harvard to find out. "I realized that I was lucky to have been able to follow my own interests and learn how to solve problems for myself," he told me one morning. "When everyone else was on the main road with a standard curriculum, I was on a side street and getting my own view."

Barnaby was convinced that swerving off the main road was sometimes the best way to make yourself lucky. Most people stick with what he called the "main institutional flow," but that can keep you from seeing different and original approaches.

"Lucky people are often the outliers who find a path that others missed," he said. "Social and institutional structures set the norms, but if you are willing to take some risks and step around those, you sometimes find better ways to create and capture value." The people who look for possibilities outside the accepted flow often create the greatest luck for themselves—and others.

The previous day, Barnaby had visited his friend Dr. James Watson at the Cold Spring Harbor Laboratory. Though close to ninety, Dr. Watson remains vigorous and outspoken. He wanted to be a professional ornithologist when he was young (a passion he shares with Barnaby), but he took up the emerging field of genetics when he was a student in graduate school. He had strong opinions and a curious mind and was definitely not a go-with-the-flow guy. The willingness to think in completely new directions helped Dr. Watson back in 1953 when he discovered (along with Francis Crick) the structure of DNA. It was one of the greatest scientific breakthroughs of the century and led to his winning a Nobel Prize.

"A lot of luck in life is seeing what others don't see," he told Barnaby. "You rarely make great breakthroughs by staying only on a standard path."

In any field, there are social pressures to follow others and work on what is currently popular, but over lunch, Dr. Watson had exhorted Barnaby not to worry about being conventional.

"One must think for oneself!" he said. "Being novel does not always come naturally, but to be special and know what you can do, you must try new things."

Dr. Watson could discuss science and the double helix all day (and night), but as his wonderfully titled memoir *Avoid Boring People* suggests, he doesn't want to bore anyone. The title has a second meaning that's just as important—the renowned biologist doesn't like to be around anyone, or anything, boring or expected.

"Too many people go in obvious directions, and they don't recognize new possibilities," he told Barnaby. "People are afraid. They don't take the new paths because they worry what others think of them. They are weak." For Dr. Watson, the excitement of life came from always pushing forward in new directions, even if it was sometimes in opposition to what most around him believed.

If you're willing to be like Dr. Watson and avoid the mundane and obvious, you can make luck outside the laboratory, too. Back when I was a television producer, I worked with a network executive named Mike Darnell, who was one of the most daring people I'd ever met. Smart, innovative, and creative, he had more cutting-edge ideas in a day than most people have in a year. And he didn't care how off-the-wall or unusual they were, or how much his bosses bristled when he proposed them. In a business where everybody imitates each other, Darnell made a career of being a complete original.

I couldn't wait to talk to him again, and I was thrilled to discover that after many years at Fox, he was now running the television division at Warner Bros.

"You're the main person I miss from my TV days!" I told him.

"I miss you, too—we had so much fun!" he said with the joyous excitement that was always his hallmark.

I loved hearing about Darnell's new position, because he didn't look like a guy who would be top dog at a network. Just over five feet tall, he had kept the long curly hair and elfin smile that brought him success as a child actor. He liked to wear jeans and cowboy boots (though he'd stopped wearing the matching hat). Back when we worked together, you could tell it was a really important day if he was wearing a button-down shirt instead of a flannel one. I probably shouldn't have favorites among TV executives, but he was always my favorite.

In the late 1990s, well before reality television became its own genre, Darnell did specials at the Fox network like *When Animals Attack!* and *Breaking the Magician's Code* that caused controversy but also got big ratings.

"All those crazy specials—nobody else thought of doing those shows when I started. I was looking for a lane I could take where I didn't have to compete with everyone," Darnell told me now. "Really, that's how I started. Looking for a different lane that would be my own."

Darnell swerved into the reality television lane and, at the time, found himself virtually the only one there. He was slightly offended that the rest of the TV community looked down on his shows, but he had a tough skin. He liked getting ratings and attention and just shrugged when one competing network exec snottily announced that he'd rather fail with quality than succeed with garbage.

"He definitely found a way to fail," Darnell said with a laugh, "but I wanted to succeed." He was given a title as head of alternative programming, and really, that's what he was—an alternative direction for the network.

Other executives were never quite sure what to make of Darnell, who clearly followed the beat of his own drum. He was regularly late for meetings and sometimes drove an hour or two in the middle of the day in order to go home and have lunch with his wife, Carolyn. If the others warily accepted his quirkiness, it was because he seemed to have a recipe for success that nobody else could quite copy—and the main ingredient in his formula was to go in a direction different from that of everybody else.

"Sometimes it's finding a path that nobody else takes that catapults you to success," Darnell said. "I almost got fired a few times, but everyone in this industry gets fired. I'd rather go out screaming and yelling and making a big deal than just trying to get along."

At about the time that Darnell was swerving into a new lane with his TV specials, Apple launched an advertising campaign that featured iconic figures from Thomas Edison to Gandhi to Amelia Earhart and urged people to "Think Different." As one of the commercials put it: "Here's to the crazy ones. The misfits. . . ."

Apple and Mike Darnell and James Watson all understood that being one of the crazy ones can bring you the smashing success that seems, from the outside, to be the epitome of luck. You can be perfectly happy following a standard route. But if you want to make luck and change your own corner of the world, it helps to go in a different direction.

As we continued to talk, Darnell reminded me that when music mogul Simon Fuller came to Hollywood to pitch a show, none of the other networks' executives would take a meeting with him. Darnell eagerly met with him—and, excited by Fuller's idea, bought his show as a summer replacement. Darnell had seen similar shows that aired in the United Kingdom and instinctively knew that he wanted this one—called *American Idol*.[1] Yup, Darnell was the guy who brought America *American Idol*. Unless you've taken a side trip to Mars in the last decade, you know the rest. The show became a cultural icon and one of the most successful programs in television history.

Taking a bold stand for what you want can bring in huge luck returns, but it takes a certain amount of courage. Darnell, though, laughs at the word. He insists that he's not one of those rare wild and crazy guys whom you can admire but not emulate. "In real life, I don't like roller coasters or scary rides and I take no risks. I don't

---

1. Elisabeth Murdoch is often credited with convincing her dad, Rupert Murdoch, who founded the Fox empire, to bring *Idol* to the United States. But Darnell had already signed up the show by the time she got involved. Her support just gave it a slightly bigger launch budget.

even like change. I'm married to the same wife, and I stayed at Fox forever," he said. But taking a risk at work is different. "In business, I've always been bold. There, I'll do anything to be different."

If you want to go into the lane where nobody else is driving, you have to be prepared to be attacked. The challenge is to keep believing in yourself and pushing forward. New ideas always sound like nutty ideas at first. And let's be clear: Not every original idea is worth fighting for, so trying to be different also requires a certain amount of honest reflection. If nobody is buying the wasabi-and-peppermint rice pudding that you've just created, there could be a reason for that.

But sometimes it just takes patience. For a while, nobody wanted Darnell's flavor of the day, but then everyone did. The daring direction he took quickly became mainstream, and with *American Idol* number one in the ratings—often by large margins—the network execs who had once berated him soon tried to copy him. He went from being the alternative guy at Fox to being the king of television at Warner Bros., overseeing some of the studio's biggest programs.

Darnell believes that going in a different direction from most people is an especially good idea when you don't start with the traditional credentials. If you're a classically handsome six-foot-tall rugby player who graduated from Harvard and was president of the Hasty Pudding Club, you can get attention by being the same. Your fellow Harvard alums (who are now showrunners at the networks) will be happy to invite you in for an interview. But with his unusual size and style, Darnell knew that he wasn't the obvious guy to get lucky in the intense, image-driven world of television executives. So he decided that to make his own luck, he needed to forge a different path. He had to zig when others zagged.

In setting out on a jagged path, Darnell unwittingly undertook a strategy that researchers call "systematic unpredictability." Charles Darwin would have seen the value of Darnell's approach, at least theoretically, since it turns out that evolution may favor people and species that take unusual paths. British biologists P. M. Driver and D. A. Humphries spent three decades studying animal behavior and figured out that doing the unexpected is one of the best survival skills around. In one of their early studies, they simply tracked rabbits as they raced across a field and noticed how they made quick and nimble changes of direction. This behavior is called "jinking," and the biologists originally thought that it was done specifically to dodge a predator. But then they realized that the twists and turns are different every time and take place even when the furry little rabbit isn't being pursued.

Taking an unexpected path even when there's nobody on your tail gives you a leg (or paw) up when there *is* a predator around. Basically, it works so well that it has become an innate behavior in many species. The biologists call this "single erratic display," and they've observed it in rabbits and squirrels and songbirds and snipes and mullet and eels and waders and many, many others. They described one bird called the black-tailed godwit that will display "a quick ascending flight . . . alternating with steep dives inclusive of leaf-scattering and quick zig-zag flight low over the ground, often with sudden changes of flying direction." Whew. Now that's *definitely* being different. If you're unpredictable, you're less likely to get caught and more likely to survive—and there's nothing luckier than staying alive. So natural selection seems to have favored the animals, including us, who learned how to zigzag through life.

A biologist would probably note that Darnell's systematic unpredictability explained his luck (and survival) even early in his career.

When he first started out, he landed a lowly job at a local news station and tried various stunts to get himself noticed. His antics eventually caught the eye of hotshot executive Barry Diller, who was running the newly launched Fox network.

"Diller said to me, 'You're shameless, but you're doing a good job,'" Darnell said now with a big laugh.

With that encouragement, Darnell spent a couple of months planning his next "erratic display"—or lucky move. After discussing possibilities every night with his wife, he finally took an old Panasonic tape recorder and recorded the theme from *Mission: Impossible*. Then he voiced a message saying how much he wanted to work at the network and ended it with: "Either Mike's career or this tape will self-destruct in five seconds." He showed up at an event that he knew Diller would attend and convinced the parking valet to give Diller the recorder. He put a big red arrow next to the play button so that Diller would know what to do.

"I was scared to death about what would happen," Darnell told me. "My entire career was on the line. I left the tape on a Thursday. Friday I didn't hear anything. I panicked all weekend that I'd blown my career. Then Monday morning, Barry Diller called and said, 'What do you want to do at the network?' And I had no idea! I had spent months planning this, but I didn't have an answer to the simplest question. Here's the lesson—be prepared for the moment. When luck is going to hit, you've got to be ready for it."

When Darnell finally got to the network, he expected that his bosses would all be geniuses. But they weren't. And that may be one of the surprises of any job. You figure there are so many people who know a lot more than you do that you just follow along. You're afraid to take a new direction because there must be someone with more experience who knows the right way to go. Eventually you discover that the people who think they have the answers aren't always right. You make your luck by figuring out what works best for you and going for it. The person who has the temerity to challenge the accepted wisdom and zig when everyone else zags could end up soaring.

Mathematician Steven Strogatz has such powerhouse credentials that he could have decided to follow the straight line throughout his career (going from point A to point B, as it were). He has degrees from Princeton, Cambridge, and Harvard and is now a chaired professor at Cornell. But he's also charming and amusing (not just for a math guy) and believes that you can create luck with the unexpected. One of the sections on his website is called "Fun." He has written popular math columns for *The New York Times* and has the best-named mathematics book ever: *The Joy of X*.

Strogatz's zigs come with a touch of genius attached. Some of his most admired (and brilliant) breakthroughs happened because he was open to unconventional thoughts. "If you want to get lucky or do something original and creative, you have to be willing to entertain odd ideas," he said when Barnaby and I spoke to him.

Some years ago, he was working on the question of how biological rhythms get in sync—and specifically how crickets synchronize their chirps. His then PhD student Duncan Watts began talking with him about the six degrees of separation theory. You probably know the research—or at least the concept—suggesting any two people in the world can be connected through a small number of links. Back in 1967, the psychologist Stanley Milgram famously found that it took just five intermediaries to get a package from a random person in Omaha, Nebraska, to a stockbroker in Boston. Since then, other researchers have tried similar experiments online that allow bigger samples (and save on postage). They've gotten roughly the same results.

The idea that we're all connected seeped into popular culture in a play by John Guare called, reasonably enough, *Six Degrees of Separation*, which then became a movie starring Will Smith and is frequently revived on Broadway and in theaters around the country. Watts wondered if that connectedness concept being batted around in social sciences could somehow be related to Strogatz's work and anything that has links—from the human nervous system to national power grids.

"It was a wacky idea at the time and a risky idea, and there were all kinds of reasons for me to avoid working on it," Strogatz said. "But I was curious and liked playing around with the concept. It ended up being the biggest thing either of us will ever do in our career." The mathematical paper on small-world networks, which they published in the journal *Nature*, is famous in the field and cited more often than any other by researchers around the world.

Strogatz says that when he was working on the small-world networks project, most of the established scientists and mathematicians he spoke with were dismissive. But he liked the idea of going down a path that others ignored. "Sometimes the best areas to pursue are the most unfashionable," he told us. There's less competition and a better chance of making your mark. At times a path is *so* unfashionable that it gets written off as a complete dead end—and everyone advises that you'd be nuts to head down it. Everyone except Strogatz. He thinks revisiting dead ends can be a productive strategy in many fields, including business and academics. "Think about the problem again, or have a young person think about it, because they won't be stuck in the traditional way of thinking that got you to the dead end in the first place," he said. Maybe all that's needed to open it up again is a small tweak, a slight change, or a new twist.

Often everybody knows that some particular direction can't work—until it works. Then everyone is equally certain on the other side. For example, no mainstream publisher would go for a book with graphic sex and S&M until Erika Mitchell, calling herself E. L. James, self-published a book called *Fifty Shades of Grey*. People loved it—and after it was picked up by a traditional publishing house, it sold more than 125 million copies and was one of the fastest-selling books of all time. Sequels and movies (and even more profits) followed—and suddenly sexy books seemed like a great idea. For James, going down a dead end turned out to be an expressway to success.

Mathematical theorists who study game theory, such as the late John Maynard Smith and Martin Nowak, have reached the similar conclusion that the best move under highly competitive conditions is often the unpredictable one. If you want to get lucky when you're playing poker, you don't want to tip your hand so that the others at the table can predict what you'll do. Football coaches who've taken a lesson or two from game theory try to stay unpredictable enough that the opposing team doesn't always know how to line up against them. So when they're close to the goal on a fourth down, they may occasionally have the quarterback throw the ball rather than trying to rush for the end zone. The randomness matters, or the opposing team will always know exactly how to respond.

In the 2015 Super Bowl, there were just seconds left to go when the Seattle Seahawks had the ball on the one-yard line. Coach Pete

Carroll called for a pass play instead of the expected rush—and the pass was intercepted. What had looked like potential victory became a miserable 28–24 defeat. Being unpredictable may work statistically, but (as with anything) it's not going to work for every play. Some mathematicians tried to argue that Carroll did just what he should have, but the more fan-focused *Washington Post* called it "the worst play call in Super Bowl history." If you move away from what's safe, you can sometimes suffer, too.

When Mike Darnell concocted his *Mission: Impossible* tape, he realized that unconventional actions can blow up into huge luck—or just blow up. Even though he was panicked, he went all in with his big risk and didn't have a backup plan. Strogatz took a more balanced approach. While pursuing what he calls "paradigm-busting science" in his project with Watts, he continued gathering good data from his more conventional research with the crickets. He thinks that knowing they had another option allowed them to be bold.

Going down an unusual path doesn't mean being reckless. In fact, you're most likely to get lucky if you stay realistic. "If you're trying something wild that's high risk but also high payoff, you don't want to bang your head on the wall for too long," Strogatz said. "Take the flier, and if it's a dud, get out quickly." When he and Watts were doing their unexpected project, they kept it top secret and met every week to assess their progress. If it wasn't going right, they were back to crickets.

Sometimes the best way to get lucky is to take the most unexpected path of all—and just let yourself have fun. Strogatz is convinced that lucky discoveries happen if you're willing to be playful. He is as obsessive and hardworking as anybody else in high levels of academia, but he doesn't overlook the value of having a good time. "When a problem seems like fun, you'll stick with it and work on it incessantly—you'll think about it when you're in the shower or driving the car. And that increases the chance of hitting on lucky good results," he said. Playful people also try things that nobody else would dare. The sense that they're just having fun gives them the excuse to try far-out ideas—which leaves them open to new possibilities and (what seems like) good luck.

But remember what we said about new ideas being met with ridicule? It happens over and over, in every field. So if you're going to be playful or unexpected or zig when others zag, you also have to be able to shut out criticism and have some faith in yourself. When Dick Fosbury was growing up in Oregon in the 1960s, he liked sports, but he wasn't very good at any of them. He didn't make the school football and basketball teams, so he decided to try the high jump. Unfortunately, he wasn't too impressive at that, either. Though he was six-foot-four, he could barely clear five feet four inches. In those days, high jumpers got over the bar with either a scissors kick (one leg and then the other) or a straddle. He tried both styles of jumping, but neither made him a winner. Then at one meet, he decided to improvise something completely different. If he couldn't win in the normal fashion, maybe he'd have luck going over the bar—well, backward. He did his takeoff and rotated in the air—and soared over the bar. In a sport where success is counted in quarter-inch increments, he went an amazing six inches higher than his previous best.

Over the next couple of years, he continued honing his style and jumping higher and higher. His technique got wide attention and even a clever moniker associated with it—the Fosbury Flop. But however successful he was, the standard-bearers of the sport considered Fosbury (and his flop) a sideshow amusement. The so-called experts warned that he'd never achieve anything with his backward style. Sports journalists went out of their way to find sneering metaphors to describe his technique, one describing him as looking like a guy falling off the back of a truck and another invoking the image of a fish flopping on the bottom of a boat. But Fosbury ignored them and continued to believe in his distinctive jumping style. He surprised everyone by qualifying for the 1968 Olympics in Mexico City.

As a kid from Oregon, Fosbury didn't want to miss anything about the experience of being in Mexico. The night before the opening ceremony, he drove to the Aztec pyramids at Teotihuacán with two friends and stayed there all night. In the following days, while his teammates went out to practice, Fosbury often stayed behind or tried just a few jumps. Some thought he was slacking, but he knew himself and realized that more practices wouldn't help. He needed the rush of competition to do his best. Then came the actual high jump competition, and the naysayers were caught up short. Over two days in Olympic stadium, Fosbury didn't miss a single jump. He won the gold medal with a new Olympic record of 7.35 feet (2.24 meters)—flopping his way to glory.

But even the gold medal didn't convince everyone. People who follow more standard approaches don't trust those who zig when everyone else zags. Instead of seeing that there's luck to be had by going in a new direction, they feel threatened. Fosbury's backward jump meant that after he went over the bar, he hit the mat neck first. The (tradition-bound) Olympic team coach warned that if kids tried to imitate Fosbury, it would "wipe out an entire generation of high jumpers, because they will all have broken necks." The kids did copy him and (happily) all necks stayed intact. Soon the Fosbury Flop was the only style any high jumper used. Every single Olympic medal in the high jump since 1972 has gone to a Flopper.

To be lucky in any area of life, from love to the high jump, you often have to be the outlier, willing to be the exception and find the pathway that others have missed. If you're trying your best and things just don't seem to be working out, maybe it's time to zig a bit. Like James Watson, Mike Darnell, Steve Strogatz, and Dick Fosbury, if you have the courage to think different, it often looks like you've gotten very lucky. But really you've just zigged when all the others zagged.

CHAPTER SEVEN

The Power of Persistence and Passion

Create a lucky personality with persistence and passion. . . .
Get on a lucky path. . . . Develop the power of optimism.

On the train ride back from Princeton one week, Barnaby happened to be looking out the window as we passed Edison, New Jersey. The connection to the great inventor Thomas Edison—the guy who said that genius is 1 percent inspiration and 99 percent perspiration—got Barnaby thinking.

"If you want to make luck, you have to be persistent," Barnaby said. "Many of life's failures are people who did not realize how close they were to success when they gave up."

"That's lovely," I said, reaching for the notebook I always carried. "Let me write it down."

"It's a quote from Thomas Edison," Barnaby said with a smile. "He also said that the most certain way to succeed is always to try just one more time."

Edison invented the lightbulb, the phonograph, the movie camera, and a thousand other things—or make that 1,093, the number of US patents he holds. But he didn't hit on any of them by random chance. He once explained that he never failed, but he had found at least 10,000 things that didn't work.

Barnaby has a soft spot for Edison because he shares the great inventor's intensity. He is convinced that if he wants something fervently enough, he will get it. He's not spoiled—he's just persistent. And his focus and intensity have made him seem very lucky. For example, when he was just seventeen, he decided he wanted to study with the great evolutionary biologist Ernst Mayr at Harvard—and he was going to make it happen no matter what.[1] He flew in from Alaska and showed up at Mayr's office. His passion was so convincing that Mayr invited him to stay—and Barnaby may be the only person who ever studied at Harvard without SATs, grade transcripts, or teacher evaluations.[2]

"You get lucky when you have focus and won't quit," Barnaby told me.

The comment that "the harder I work, the luckier I get" has been attributed to so many people that it's hard to know who actually said it. Probably all of them—from Thomas Jefferson to Samuel Goldwyn to Oprah—would agree with it. But after our conversation, Barnaby spent the next week thinking about how hard work translates to luck. Were the hardest-working people really the luckiest?

The connection turns out to be subtler than it seems. The persistence and focus that lead to luck come in many forms—and don't necessarily equate to hours put in. Far more important may be the attitude and intensity you bring.

"Knowing what you want and where you're aiming is really the key," Barnaby told me when we met the following Wednesday, this time sitting at the dining room table in my apartment. (I'd come to think of it as an auxiliary Luck Lab.)

---

1. Mayr understood people with passion and persistence, since he had those qualities himself. In the name of research, he had braved cannibalistic tribes in the thick rain forests of Papua New Guinea in the 1920s.

2. Barnaby points out that he actually got into Harvard the old-fashioned way—by direct interview. The current system of standardized tests and complicated applications is under a hundred years old.

Barnaby had spent the morning with his new friend Deepak Chopra, the spiritualist and New Age guru. As a scientist, Barnaby had initially been a little wary of meeting him because Chopra's ideas on alternative medicine have been attacked by many mainstream scientists. But as he got to know Chopra over several months, Barnaby was won over by Chopra's openness toward a bigger picture of reality and his insights into how we can exert control over our own lives. Through his inspirational talks, Chopra shares the idea that we can make things happen for ourselves by our own thoughts and attitudes.

I had learned that telling other people in your networks and community what you want could cause lucky connections and breaks to happen, but I had a hard time believing the cultural gurus who suggested that if you simply whisper your desires to the universe, then the universe will (mysteriously) respond. But Barnaby said that Chopra had a deeper approach that was worth considering.

"He suggests that you start each day with a routine of calm focus where you ask yourself, 'Who am I?' and 'What do I want?'" Barnaby told me. "That way you get your actions in harmony with your goals."

In a much more down-to-earth way, I could see that if you're truly driven to get something—whether a job, a lover, or a good deal on a new Prius—you'll try hard and perhaps never give up. The grit and fortitude and steely resolve that come with being passionate make positive things happen. Putting your desire out to the universe just means that you know what you want. Once you've declared it to yourself, you're more likely to aim your energy and emotion in the right direction. It looks like magic, but it starts from knowing what will make you feel lucky.

When I started investigating, I discovered that these ideas aren't off-the-wall or New Agey at all. You don't get more respected and mainstream than Nobel Prize winner Daniel Kahneman, and some of his research suggested that simply *wanting* can change your luck for *getting*. So, for example, in analyzing one study, he found that people who said when they were eighteen years old that being very well-off financially was important to them ended up wealthier twenty years later than others.

"Goals make a large difference," Kahneman asserted, noting that in the years after they stated their financial aspirations, "many of the people who wanted a high income had achieved it."

Kahneman reached his conclusion by looking at a study that followed 12,000 people over twenty years, beginning when they were just starting at elite universities. The initial questionnaire had students use a four-point scale to rank how much they cared about money. On the follow-up twenty years later, Kahneman looked at one group and discovered that for every extra point they had given on the money-importance scale, they were making an additional $14,000 in income—the equivalent of more than $22,100 today.

It's a pretty striking result. Announcing as a teenager that you're a four rather than a three on the want-to-be-rich scale results in a luck bonus that's enough to buy a new Honda every year. Most of us wouldn't mind that kind of lucky input to our own bank accounts. And we can all make that kind of luck. If you've told yourself at age eighteen (or any other age) that having money is a top goal, you're going to set yourself on a course (consciously or unconsciously) to make that happen. You'll put in serious effort, get to know the right people, and land an entry-level job when you graduate that allows you to rent your own apartment. Your parents' friends (whose children are all back living at home) will wonder how you got so lucky.

You can tell them that in order to find a pot of gold, you need to identify it. Only then can you can follow the right rainbow.

The study Kahneman analyzed didn't ask the eighteen-year-olds how important it was to them to become parents, work in the fashion world, star in a TV show, or volunteer in Ghana. But if it had, I'd be happy to bet that those who ranked any one of those options as a four-out-of-four in desirability would be more likely to achieve it than those not as driven. Once you've acknowledged to yourself what you consider a lucky life, you start putting into place all the pieces to get there.

Barnaby told me that he had recently met with Leonard Mlodinow, the Caltech physicist whom I admired, to talk about some mathematical theories. Barnaby wondered if I'd like to chat with him, too.

"Of course I would!" I said.

In addition to his academic work, Mlodinow has authored books with Stephen Hawking and written for popular sci-fi shows like *Star Trek: The Next Generation*. In his own books, he has pointed out that randomness plays a bigger role in some successes than we like to admit. A lot of things we find miraculous ("I was walking down the street and ran into an old college friend!") are examples of simple statistical chance. But I was interested in whether a guy who studied randomness thought we could affect our own luck.

Yup, he did. When we gave him a call at his home in California one morning, he was charming and thoughtful—and he quickly agreed that random chance is only one element in the success equation. He thought that luck usually lands with certainly personality types.

"I just watched the old John Wayne movie *True Grit*," he said as we began our conversation. "Have you heard of it? It reminded me that successful people are usually the ones who don't give up. If you're thinking about luck as a rope with many strands, persistence is one of the big ones."

As Mlodinow described it, talent and ability are important, but the willingness to forge ahead can balance them out. "You have to keep trying and accepting failure, because the more at bats you have, the more likely you are to get a hit, no matter what your skill," he said.

He gave the example of two people of different abilities—one who succeeds 99 percent of the time and one who succeeds only 1 percent of the time. Sometimes the less talented person can seem to be incredibly lucky at landing a great job or acting part or loving spouse. But there's a good chance that he's changed his odds by not giving up and so having more at bats. "If you try a hundred times, you might very well succeed, because then statistics are on your side," Mlodinow said. "It's how you turn a 1 percent person into a 99 percent person." In other words, the less obviously talented person who tries a hundred times can have the same success as the superstar who tries only once.

As the child of Holocaust survivors, Mlodinow understands at his core that we can't control everything and are sometimes caught in swirls of history much bigger than ourselves. He also recognizes the power of randomness in daily life and admits that he likes to trace back the instances that made a difference—and how they occurred. We can all do that. If you left your office a moment earlier, you might have been hit by the drunk driver rather than watching the accident happen to the guy in front of you. Or if you hadn't sat a little longer to have an extra cup of coffee, you wouldn't have met the person who became your best friend. Physicists are very good at seeing life as Brownian motion writ large—humans being the equivalents of the little particles suspended in air, being tossed about randomly by the fast-moving atoms around us.

Scientists have been fascinated by this kind of motion since the Roman poet and philosopher Lucretius wrote about it in 60 BCE. He described looking at the dust particles in a sunbeam streaking into a building and realizing that "their dancing is an actual indication of underlying movements of matter that are hidden from our sight." Albert Einstein and others later brought some mathematical precision to the mystery, making the causes of the dancing less hidden. In real life, we may be tossed in Brownian motion, but that's not the end of the story. As Mlodinow put it, "What really matters in your life is how you react to the opportunities and challenges that randomness brings your way."

With all those random particles knocking into one another, the more times you head into the field, the more opportunities you'll find. One of the best ways to up your luck is to keep taking chances. And that's where Mlodinow's formulation that successful people are the ones who don't give up brings science and real life together.

Once something has become hugely successful, it's hard to imagine how there could have been any other outcome. You look at what happened and take it as proof that it *had* to happen. But it didn't. Writer John Grisham has sold more than 275 million books worldwide, but his first legal thriller was turned down by twenty-eight publishers before one small house finally said yes. Beloved Dr. Seuss (Theodor Geisel) had a similar number of rejections. He planned to burn the manuscript of *And to Think That I Saw It on Mulberry Street* when a chance meeting with a college classmate convinced him to give it one more try. He has sold over 600 million books, and even these many years after his death, he remains the number one bestselling children's author in America. And J. K. Rowling had twelve rejections of her first Harry Potter book before a London publisher gave her a meager advance of £1500 and did an initial print run of an even more anemic 1,000 copies. Now that the Harry Potter books have sold 450 million copies and been made into movies that earned some $6 billion, it's easy to imagine that the world was simply begging for Harry. But what would have happened if Rowling (or her agent) had decided that a dozen rejections was enough?

It's not just authors and actors who face endless rejections (theirs are just easier to count). Just about everybody has to decide consciously or not how many times they're willing to put themselves on the line. Pushing forward with passion is how you get lucky, but it's also how you get disappointed. Teenagers assiduously court an attitude of being cool as a way of proving that they don't really care what happens. If you're too cool for school, you don't have to worry about getting As. If you're too cool for the prom, you don't have to care about getting invited. What works to protect a teenage ego backfires for anyone seeking more profound success in life. You get lucky when you admit what you want and go after it.

But there's a flip side to consider. Maybe your novel was turned down twenty-eight times because it just wasn't very good. Luck, as we've said, occurs at the intersection of chance, talent, and hard work, and while talent involves traits like recognizing opportunities and having the right networks, it also includes . . . talent. How do you know when the likelihood of persistence leading to luck has (at best) diminishing returns?

Sometimes you get lucky by quitting at the right time. Mathematicians and economists have analyzed the question of optimal stopping, using such elaborate equations that when I looked at them online, I didn't even recognize some of the symbols. I showed the equations to Barnaby, who offered a more down-to-earth view.

"A simple method is just to look at how close you've come to your goal," he said. "If you're trying to be an actor and get a lot of callbacks but no parts, then keep going. You're close, and the persistence may bring luck. But if you always get polite rejections in the first round, it may be time to look for other opportunities."

On my next trip to Los Angeles, I drove over to the very cool offices of movie producer Doug Wick.[3] A red, industrial staircase outside led to a lobby with a wooden-planked reception desk. Two handsome guys in their early twenties, both with perfect three-day stubble, welcomed me and said that Doug was running a little late (de rigueur in Hollywood). While waiting for him, I went into a bathroom that was the size of a small apartment and had a gorgeous kimono encased in plexiglass filling one wall. Doug later told me it had been a gift from Steven Spielberg, his coproducer on the movie *Memoirs of a Geisha*.

When he finally arrived, Doug was gracious and warm and took me to his spacious, light-filled office. Movie posters in the hallways chronicled his successful career, from the 1988 hit *Working Girl* to the recent sci-fi favorite *Divergent*. He had wanted to be a producer for as long as he could remember and told me that while in college, he had been a teaching assistant (TA) in a film course. One of the students in the class was related to the great film director Alan Pakula.

---

3. Though alums of the same college, Doug and I had never met, so I asked a classmate I barely knew to connect us. It turns out weak ties and networking really do work!

"She introduced me to Alan, who gave me a job—and that began my career. So I guess I was incredibly lucky," Doug said. Then with a smile he added, "Though it's also fair to say that I was a very good TA."

Doug's passion for producing helped him land a deal with a studio. He came up with the idea for *Working Girl* and pursued it for two years—but nobody was interested. His deal was about to run out, and "I could feel the building people checking out my space for the next occupant," he said. But having heard that a "no" in Hollywood is just a postponed "yes," he kept scrambling and sweating—and finally got the movie script to famed director Mike Nichols. Nichols liked it enough to go ahead. The movie, with stars Melanie Griffith and Harrison Ford, was nominated for an Academy Award for Best Picture.[4]

"You can't let yourself be beaten down or start reacting to life with fear," Doug told me. "You have to persist with optimism. But it's got to be an informed optimism or you're just a delusional busboy."

To Doug, the secret to looking lucky is to love the work you do and never let your attention waver. Over the years he has worked with stellar actors, including Brad Pitt, Leonardo DiCaprio, Nicole Kidman, Russell Crowe, Sigourney Weaver, Will Ferrell . . . the list goes on and on. He gave Angelina Jolie her breakthrough role in *Girl, Interrupted* (she won an Oscar and a Golden Globe) when she was still early in her career. Thinking about Cassie, the young would-be actress I had met on my last trip to LA, I asked Doug what

---

4. That was just the start. Doug's movies have had twenty-two Oscar nominations and seven wins, which means a lot of time spent in tuxedos.

might have happened if he had cast a different actress. Would she have been the one to end up Angelina-famous?

He shook his head. "There was only ever Angelina to play that role because few people have her power and wit and presence on-screen," he said. "But that magic is only the first step to a brilliant career. You have to keep caring and focusing."

Doug learned about what really makes luck the first time he met Jack Nicholson. "I went to his house figuring I was the smart young guy and would easily manage the old fogey. But as we talked, I realized he was three chess moves ahead of everyone else. And I had that idiot moment where I thought—'Of course!'" Nicholson might grin wickedly on camera or play the tipsy lothario, but "to prevail and stay on top in a tough business, you have to be perceptive and attentive to every detail."

Recently, some movie studios have turned to data-driven algorithms (and the quants who love them) to try to figure out how to make box-office magic. The analysis might suggest that beloved actor A tied with hot-handed director B equals a Netflix miracle. One company uses what it calls "neural networks" to analyze scripts with more than a hundred different components to determine if the resulting movie will be a box-office success. Back in 2004, a guy named Ryan Kavanaugh started Relativity Media on what he called a "Monte Carlo model"—a risk-assessment algorithm (borrowed from Wall Street) that looked at past performance and churned through tens of thousands of combinations of actors, director, budget, release date, genre, and on and on, to decide what would make a profitable film.

It sounded like a great idea—a way to bring some stability to a business where, as screenwriter William Goldman said, "nobody knows anything." But the math and regression analysis didn't know all that much, either. Relativity had some dramatic ups and downs—and filed for bankruptcy in 2015.

Doug took a different path—relying on his own conscious study. At one point he went back over the last one hundred years of movies (practically the entire history of the genre) and looked at the top twenty hits of each year. Seeing how different themes cycled back led him to decide to do *Gladiator* with Russell Crowe. But when he first pitched it to Sony, "an executive there lectured me that swords and sandals was dead," he said. He was in good company for being rejected. Two studios turned down the original *Star Wars* before 20th Century Fox made billions of dollars with it. Steven Spielberg's *E.T.* was snubbed by a studio that chose to make something called *Starman* instead. Ever heard of it? Me neither.

Doug bought the rights to what became the four-movie Divergent series when the first book was an unpublished manuscript by an unknown author.

"That was kind of gutsy," I said.

"The moment I read it, I realized it hit every element on my checklist of what makes a great movie. It was a genre story with a compelling heroine, and the world it created made an inviting destination for the audience. Only an algorithm could have missed it," Doug said with a laugh.

As Doug and I discussed all the uncertainties in the movie business, he seemed surprisingly calm. Though he had explanations for the movies he'd made that didn't work out, it wasn't the dollars or the fame that kept him going. "People call Hollywood a stone tit—you can keep suckling and not get a drop. I like that metaphor because it makes me think, 'If I'm doing this, what am I getting?' And I remind myself that the nectar is the pleasure of good work and good collaboration. Love what you are doing, and the luck is there."

When I saw Barnaby again, I told him about my trip and the questions I still had about Hollywood. Doug Wick was a great guy and clearly a talented producer—but like many successful people, he wondered what role random chance had played in his triumphant career. "Any movie involves a few crazy years of getting an idea, developing a script, casting, and finding the right director," he had told me. "My percentage in making the right choices keeps getting higher, but it's still only a percentage." I couldn't decide if he was being modest or accurate when he pointed out that getting a break-out performance from a young star—as happened with Russell Crowe in *Gladiator*—is never fully under your control.

As usual, Barnaby took out a piece of paper, and this time he drew a bell curve showing what success looks like in the movie business.

"Most movies do moderately well—that's the big bell in the middle—and a few are at either end, doing very badly or extremely well," Barnaby said. "Doug is right—you can't really change that curve. If you make one hundred movies—any one hundred movies—you'll end up with roughly the same distribution."

"But what about those algorithms being tried?" I asked. "Aren't you more likely to be lucky if, say, you have Matt Damon in your movie?"

I've interviewed Matt Damon a couple of times, and I think he's thoughtful, smart, and pretty darned terrific. He's also one of the most admired actors of his generation, hailed for hits like *The Martian*, *The Bourne Identity* (and its sequels), and *Good Will Hunting*. But as we talked, Barnaby reminded me of a few others. How about *Stuck on You*, *EuroTrip*, and *Hereafter*?

"You can't say a movie will be a success just because he's in it," Barnaby said.

"I'd put Matt Damon in any movie," I said, remaining loyal.

"And you'd be right!" he said. Because he had an interesting theory to propose.

On the same sheet of paper, Barnaby made another bell curve to the right of the first one. He explained that you can't necessarily change the existence of the bell curve in movies (or most things in life). But you *can* make luck by influencing where the whole bell curve sits.

"Matt Damon movies are also going to fall into a bell curve—but that big cluster in the middle may be more to the positive side than movies without Matt Damon, and the big hits on the tail will be even farther out," he explained. You can't guarantee success, but using the right elements, you can at least move the entire curve over so you have a better chance of being at the positive end where you want to be.

And that's just what Doug Wick had done. With his persistence and passion, he had been able to move the bell curve over and look very lucky. Legend says that luck in the movie business gets made at the corner of Hollywood and Vine—but real luck in Hollywood occurs at a very different corner (where tour buses can't go)—the intersection of talent, hard work, and random chance. Doug knew that he could control the first two, and that let him shrug off the randomness that he couldn't do anything about.[5]

---

5. Doug's partner in his production company is Lucy Fisher, who was a top executive at both Sony and Warner Bros. She also happens to be his wife. Maybe the passion that leads to luck takes many forms.

It's common to look at those who have one triumph after another and mutter that "some people have all the luck." And it's true. Once you have one success, you're more likely to have another one. The casting agent knows your name, your book gets put in the front of the store, or the executive in charge of hiring knows that he can justify bringing you on. Research done recently at the Santa Fe Institute by economist W. Brian Arthur has led to what's known as a theory of increasing returns, which has quickly become a paradigm-changing explanation for breakaway success in high-tech companies. He has shown that a product that is popular has a greater chance to become even more popular. Arthur made his name analyzing market share, and his theory of positive feedbacks is true with colas or computers or Harry Potter. Once you get on the lucky path, more good events follow.

A lot of people work hard and don't get what they want. If you want to be one of the people who have all the luck, you need to nurture both persistence and passion. Those are the great luck-making personality traits, and you don't have to be born with them. Urging young people to follow their passions is a regular theme of commencement addresses, but the message leaves a lot of new graduates despondent. They don't yet have a passion, so they wait for the epiphany that will give them one fully formed. But that's just not the way it happens. In her book *Grit*, psychologist Angela Duckworth points out that passion for your work "is a little bit of *discovery*, followed by a lot of *development*, and then a lifetime of *deepening*."

Those commencement speakers would be better off advising that you explore for a while until you find what you care about. Then nurture your interest and decide that you will stick with your approach. At that point, your persistence has the power to bring cascades of luck tumbling in your direction.

Thinking about the power of persistence reminded me of an artist named Mark Ulriksen I'd met a year earlier at the Tucson Festival of Books. We'd both been invited by one of the sponsors, the *Arizona Daily Star*, and I was impressed to discover that he had done more than fifty covers for *The New Yorker* magazine over the years.

"That's an incredible number!" I said when he mentioned it.

"Not nearly as incredible as the number that got turned down," he said with a little laugh.

Mark told me that cover artists regularly made and submitted dozens of sketches, and only a small percentage ever got selected. Getting four covers in a year was considered a big success. He'd had years with just one. More than once he had worked all night to get in three or four ideas for a topical cover and then simply heard nothing.

"I'd get pissed for a few days and decide I was going to quit, but then I'd get over it and tell myself to grow up," he said. "I know some great illustrators who have stopped submitting because it's just too painful. But all that means is they *never* get a cover!"

Mark told me that the odds were even more brutal for cartoonists, who needed serious persistence to get lucky. The magazine's cartoon editor, Bob Mankoff, was the guy who said yes or no every week.

So I got in touch with Mankoff, and he generously invited me to visit him in his office in the Freedom Tower in Manhattan. I took the subway down and walked around the memorial for a while before taking the elevator to his high-floor office. Mankoff had the good grace to look exactly the way a cartoonist should—as slim as a rail, with a slightly scruffy beard covering his face and flowing silver hair that curled long past his ears. He would be easy to draw.

"Hi, come in, sit down," he said, gesturing to a round conference table piled high with cartoon sketches.

He was obviously busy but also happy to take the time to talk about luck. I told him my theory of luck being at the intersection of chance, talent, and hard work. He nodded, pointing out that his good luck started when he grew up in a family where curiosity, humor, and intellect were all part of the mix. "The home environment is the primordial soup from which personality emerges," he said. His mother was an early believer in finding a passion and pursuing it to create a lucky life. "She used to say, 'You can be whatever you want as long as you're happy. You can be a garbageman as long as you're the best one.' I told her, 'I'm sloppy, so it will be hard to be number one at that.'"

Garbageman was out—but it took him a while to know what he wanted to do. After college, he pursued a PhD in psychology and then wanted to be a stand-up comic. When he decided to veer toward cartooning, he submitted something like five hundred cartoons to *The New Yorker*—all of them rejected.

"You must have thicker skin than I do," I said. "I don't know that I could persist that long."

"Persistence needs to be focused," Mankoff said thoughtfully. "People get distracted by the personal slight and angry at the person or institution that rejected them. They'll explain why that person is a moron and doesn't recognize great talent. They're not benefiting from their failure. If you're rejected, it's probably for a reason."

Mankoff kept trying to understand the reasons and develop his

119

style. The persistence paid off and (what luck!) he eventually sold a cartoon to the magazine. Then he sold more and more. For twenty years he continued submitting batches that would be (at least) 90 percent rejected, since "only about one in ten cartoons ever works." Persistence eventually starts to look like luck. One of his own cartoons became wildly popular and among the most reprinted in the magazine's history. It shows an executive on the phone saying politely, "No, Thursday's out. How about never—is never good for you?"

As the cartoon editor since 1997, Mankoff doesn't say never, but he's very good at no. He has about fifty regular contributors, and he advises each of them to submit (as he did) about ten ideas at a time. He gets similarly sized stacks each week from his extensive bench of younger cartoonists as well as unsolicited ideas from all over the world. What's the chance of even the best cartoonists getting the lucky call? There's space in the magazine each week for fifteen or so cartoons. You do the math.

As Mankoff was describing these odds to me, he got a phone call from David Remnick, the magazine's editor in chief, who wanted to review Bob's choices for that week's issue.

Mankoff hung up and looked at me apologetically. "I'm sorry, I was supposed to meet David later, but he has time now. Can you stay here for a few minutes?"

"Sure," I said.

Mankoff scooped up the sketches he had chosen and left behind on the table dozens and dozens (and dozens) of cartoons he hadn't selected.

"I won't peek," I promised.

"Peek away," Mankoff said, walking out.

Who could resist? Many were by famous cartoonists whose distinctive styles were immediately recognizable. Some were funny enough to send to a friend. Others were clever enough to evoke a giggle. A few were beautifully drawn and must have taken a long time to create. As Mankoff had pointed out, it would be very easy for those who were rejected to get angry at him or complain about his bad taste.

Mankoff came back quickly—Remnick liked his choices—and he tossed the rejects from the table into a wire basket. An assistant came in and whisked them away. Some of the best cartoonists in America were about to find out that this wasn't their lucky week. It occurred to me that when you know the very *best* case is that 90 percent of what you do will be rejected, you need dogged determination to keep going. Only those with the passion and persistence to submit one more batch would make luck for themselves another week.

But when he sat down again, Mankoff had more on his mind than cartoons. In his view, anybody who wanted success had to understand failure. You want to get lucky? Then sit down and put in the effort. But it had struck him that the persistence we were talking about had much bigger ramifications.

"The real issue isn't that I became the cartoon editor, but that I'm still alive and here at all," he said.

When he was in his mid-forties, he went through a period of abject depression. He told me that he didn't talk much about it, but after his second wife left him, "I went into a mental institution, spent three months there with my mind scrambled, and wanted to kill myself. There was nothing. Just nothing. But eventually I was able to reconstitute myself and become successful. Some little pilot light of life was still stirring," he said.

Talking about that time of despair, Mankoff pointed out that persistence can do a lot more than give luck in a career—it can be the very source of life. "Everybody's rejected in their work, okay.

What's the big deal? Your cartoons are rejected, you'll do more or you'll do something else. But maybe the real inspiration is to know that you can be as far down as I was and still find within yourself the luck in life."

Mankoff is now happily remarried and has a grown daughter. His advice to her is "always give it a shot. The thing that holds us back is the fear of failure or finding out that we're mediocre. People stop growing when they find people are better than them. But motivation and perseverance count for a lot. So many people are doing nothing but watching television."

To Mankoff, the goal is to turn off the television and have faith in yourself and the opportunities you can create. "When I talk to young people, I tell them that the odds of succeeding in a creative field are small—but they're zero if they don't try. So your chance is between zero and small. To get lucky, you need a positive delusion of your chances of success."

When I left Mankoff's office, I thought about that pilot light of life that we need to keep burning. Luck doesn't come in a straight line (however well drawn), and it's in the toughest times, when you think you'll never be lucky again, that you need to find the tenacity and courage to persist. Sometimes it gets you a published cartoon, and sometimes it gets you out of a mental hospital. In both instances, you've made yourself luckier than before.[6]

I told Barnaby about my conversation with Bob Mankoff and mentioned his insight that it helps to have a "positive delusion."

6. Mankoff retired from *The New Yorker* shortly after we spoke and is now the cartoon editor at *Esquire*. He will continue being both funny and insightful wherever he is.

"I think that's another way of saying that optimism matters," I said.

Barnaby nodded and quickly agreed that a positive attitude—whether delusional or not—was a key to making luck. It seemed like we had now defined at least one triumvirate of traits included in the talent bucket that led to luck—persistence, passion, and optimism.

"If optimism is part of luck, we have to talk to Marty," Barnaby said.

Our friend Martin Seligman, a chaired professor of psychology at the University of Pennsylvania, is the go-to person for any discussions about optimism and positive attitude. He more or less created the entire field of positive psychology, and the power of his work and the impressive students he has taught and sent into the world (including Angela Duckworth) have turned the focus of much research in psychology from curing the negative to inspiring the positive. How can we make ourselves happier, improve our well-being . . . and increase our luck?

When we called Marty—Barnaby and I have both known him for a long time—he immediately agreed that a positive outlook could be a key to creating luck. And because he has a complicated mind, he took an interesting turn.

"Your question about luck made me think of the science fiction novel *Ringworld*," he said.

He explained that in the story, a character named Teela is brought along on a space expedition as the person who would bring the mission luck. She was descended from six generations of lucky ancestors and would therefore be lucky herself. In real life, there's no evidence (yet) of a genetic predisposition to good luck, but Dr. Seligman didn't think it was so far-fetched. You could at least mold a lucky personality type.

"If I were looking for a lucky person to take along on my space travel, the number one ingredient that I'd select for would be optimism," Dr. Seligman said. "Optimistic people have the cognitive disposition to take advantage of good events and not get bogged down hugely by bad ones."

As with passion and perseverance, optimism can be learned—and it doesn't take six generations. Dr. Seligman considers himself among the naturally pessimistic—"gloom-and-doom scenarios are constantly running through my head"—and that doesn't sit well on the man who is often dubbed the father of positive psychology. So he is constantly seeking a brighter outlook.

"Optimism is eminently changeable," he told us. "You get people like me to recognize the self-defeating, pessimistic things they say to themselves. Then you get them to argue against their catastrophic flaws, as if it were a person who was a rival for their job or wife."

As an example, he darkly pointed out that he was over seventy, the best of his career was over, and it was all downhill from here. And then he quickly argued the other side—he had just gotten a research paper accepted by *The New England Journal of Medicine*, he had attended a very exciting conference, and he had a new book coming out.

Optimism connects to luck in part because it encourages you to keep trying. Early in his career, Dr. Seligman did groundbreaking experiments on learned helplessness, showing that when animals are put in negative situations that they can't control, they eventually stop trying to escape. People too have a tendency to lie down and whine when they think they are victims of bad luck. What appears like good luck is often the result of a willingness to believe in a positive future.

"If you don't believe you can create a lucky future for yourself, you don't capitalize on the good things that come across your path," Dr. Seligman told us. "Believing that you have some control over what happens fuels trying. If there's a potentially good event for me, am I going to seize the opportunity and follow up, or am I going to be passive?"

At an academic celebration in his honor many years ago, Dr. Seligman met Sir John Templeton, the financier and philanthropist who had started a foundation to support big thinking and new ideas. He told Dr. Seligman he would like to support his vision and asked what he could do.

"I sent him a grant request for $20 million," Dr. Seligman told us with a laugh. "I learned later that nobody had ever asked Sir John for that much money. He turned it down, but I think it was very important that I acted on it."

His optimistic approach didn't bring an immediate payday, but it led to a relationship that lasted for decades and included many large grants from the John Templeton Foundation to support his work. Barnaby had a top role at the foundation for many years, and he confided later that—ironically—all the grants Marty received probably added up to that twenty million after all.

"To the extent that you can imagine the future in a positive way, you capitalize on it," Dr. Seligman told us. "So optimism plus imagination lets you try for the rich scenarios ahead."

A few days later, I walked over to the Paramount Hotel in Times Square at eight A.M. to meet the just-announced nominees for the Tony Awards. Early morning is not usually prime time in Times Square, but the hotel was a hub of activity as the nominees drifted in. Some of them (like Hollywood stars Michelle Williams and Jeff

Daniels) were old hands at awards shows, but many looked slightly dazed—reflecting both the early hour (for a late-night crowd) and the surprise of the recognition.

Great theater requires a lot of elements—brilliant script, pulsating score, stunning set, charismatic star—to mesh in some magical kismet. Nobody is ever quite sure how it happens, and (just as in sports) everything occurs in real time in front of an audience. However well you have trained and prepared, there's always the chance of an unexpected twist that leads to sudden triumph or disaster. Luck always seems to be hovering in the wings.

But nobody gets lucky in theater without caring enough to put themselves on the line. If passion, persistence, and optimism were key traits for creating luck, I expected to see them on full display here. And I was right. As I spoke to one nominee after another, I realized that the passion in the room was hot enough to ignite a rocket ship. Many had decided early on that they would do *anything* to be a part of the theater world. Some had left comfy childhood homes to venture to New York and live in a garret in Hell's Kitchen. Many told me how they got turned down repeatedly but wouldn't give up. All knew what they wanted. With persistence and passion, they made their own luck.

One bright-eyed actor bounded into the room with a cheerful smile and an energy that you could feel at fifty feet. Nominated for his role as the humorously thin-skinned King George in the blockbuster musical *Hamilton*, actor Jonathan Groff plopped down in a chair across from me and immediately described himself as the luckiest guy around.

"The first time I saw *Hamilton*, I loved it so much that I burst into tears," he said. "Lin looked at me and asked, 'Are you going to be okay?'" Lin-Manuel Miranda, *Hamilton*'s much-heralded creator, had just offered him the role of King George. Groff could hardly believe his luck.

Groff's luck hadn't fallen from the sky—it evolved from burning desire. Growing up as the son of a Mennonite and a Methodist in conservative Lancaster, Pennsylvania, he wasn't exactly raised to think of acting as a high calling. But he sang in local productions and knew that he loved the stage. Like many would-be stars, he said good-bye to his hometown after high school and set off on his dream. Coming to New York, he took acting classes and got a job as a waiter at a restaurant called the Chelsea Grill. It was a good choice—since it happened to be a hangout for theater types.

"A guy at my table one night said, 'You must be an actor—would you like to see the ends of shows and collect money in buckets afterward?'" Groff recalled. The offer wasn't as strange as it may sound since the guy ran the nonprofit Broadway Cares, which raises money for the sick and needy in the theater community. For a few weeks every year, actors stay onstage after their curtain calls and make a pitch to support the cause. As the audience streams out, volunteers in the lobby hold out collection buckets.

Groff was thrilled at the chance to be a bucket boy. He juggled his schedule of acting classes and waiting tables to show up for (volunteer) bucket duty almost every night. "So I was hanging around theaters and getting to know people just at the time that *Spring Awakening* was coming," said Groff of the show that was to become a huge hit. "They were looking to cast kids in their teens and early twenties, and there I was."

Yes, there he was. He got the lead role and scored his first Tony nomination (this was his second) when he had barely reached drinking age.

In Groff's energetic telling, the leap from bucket boy to breakout star was random luck. Hang around the theaters, meet some people, and boom! You're a star. But Groff had been putting the pieces in place since he was in fourth grade. He had been so passionate about singing when he was in elementary school that "I recorded the Tony Awards on VHS tape and brought it to school to play for everyone in math class. I couldn't believe people could sing like that. It made me so joyful!"

His passion would have been as obvious to a guy ordering a steak sandwich at the Chelsea Grill as it was to the casting agent for *Spring Awakening*. Getting lucky often requires sticking with something long after others would quit. If you love what you do and deeply believe in it, you're less likely to get discouraged. Holding a bucket (even for a good cause) could feel tedious or even demeaning to a lot of people, but if you see it as part of a bigger framework, you'll do it with energy, passion, and perseverance. And that's what might make you lucky.

Groff had spent way too long talking with me, and since the publicist was getting anxious, I wished him luck and sent him to other reporters who were waiting. I watched as he hugged a few people and grabbed a bottle of water—and it occurred to me that if luck happens at the intersection of chance, talent, and hard work, he had them all. He was a great example of all the principles Barnaby and I had been discovering. He put himself in a place where good things could happen (which wasn't Lancaster) and looked for every possibility. He knew what he wanted, so when opportunities came, he grabbed them. He had the skills to shine on Broadway—terrific voice and acting chops, winning personality, and adorably curly hair (not required, but nice). Add to that the hard work he was willing to put in to achieve his goals, and it's not a surprise that he was a return invitee at the Tony breakfast. He might have liked to focus on the random chance of being a bucket boy—but really that was the least important element in the whole story.

Talking to Jonathan Groff and Bob Mankoff and Leonard Mlodinow and Marty Seligman had convinced me that any of us can create a lucky personality. Passion, persistence, and optimism don't guarantee luck—but it's pretty hard to be consistently lucky without them. They are essentials to what Mankoff poetically called the "pilot light of life." They light the fire that needs to keep burning brightly for luck to emerge.

CHAPTER EIGHT

How Many Eggs in Your Basket?
(And How Many Baskets?)

Take many opportunities. . . . Don't try to be a cowboy. . . .
Enjoy the moment but have a backup plan. . . . Failure can
be a badge of honor. . . . It's okay to line up serial baskets.

One morning Barnaby rushed in to our usual Wednesday meeting a few minutes late and full of apologies. Having run a few blocks, he dabbed at his forehead with a white (well-pressed) handkerchief and sat down to catch his breath.

"Sorry, it's been a busy morning."

I glanced at my watch. It was just a few minutes past nine. So far this morning I'd eaten a yogurt, washed my hair, and walked over to our meeting.

Barnaby had been somewhat more productive. He'd had an early breakfast with a billionaire who wanted his advice, discussed philanthropy with a colleague in Berlin, and done yoga with an entrepreneur from Silicon Valley who was in New York for the day.

"You do a lot," I said mildly, thinking that maybe I could have taken the time to put some berries in the yogurt.

"Well, the Berlin discussion was just a phone call," he said, clarifying.

I laughed. "I'm glad to know that even you can't fly back and forth to Germany before nine A.M."

A lot of people I know are busy (it seems the requirement of the age), but Barnaby's activities cover a wider range than most. He'll discuss karma with Deepak Chopra in the morning and innovative financial strategies with hedge fund genius Paul Tudor Jones in the afternoon.

"You get lucky by diversifying," Barnaby said. "You never know which opportunity will pay off, so you need to keep a lot going."

My dad used to refer to that as having a lot of balls in the air. For some people it's a great idea. Juggling a lot of balls is exciting—but if you lose concentration, all those balls can come crashing down.

When Barnaby left his position as a top executive at the John Templeton Foundation, he had opportunities from many other philanthropies that wanted him to come on board. He turned them down, wanting to explore new areas. It was going to be more of a challenge—but exactly the kind of challenge he had been missing and wanted more of in his life.

My career has been like that, too. I've been a magazine editor and a television producer and I've written books. Sometimes I wondered if I would have been more successful sticking with just one. But I loved the variety, and having many options meant I always had a next step and an exciting possibility ahead. I never thought of it as diversifying—I just liked new adventures.

But Barnaby saw having those many baskets—magazines, television, and books—as a smart strategy.

"You never know exactly what's going to work, and if one thing goes away, you're already attuned to other possibilities," he said. "If you want to capture luck, you have to be able to shift your focus fast if you need to."

Barnaby pointed out that to be lucky, you want to diversify your life—in the same way that experts recommend you diversify your financial investments. Even if you're the kind of (irrational) person who thinks you can beat the market in picking stocks, you're not going to plunk all your money in just one stock. Or at least you generally shouldn't. Just ask the people who invested in the companies that became the famous flameouts of the dot-com boom, like Webvan and Pets.com. Sure, they looked good early on, but if one of those baskets held all your eggs, you didn't feel very lucky afterward when they got scrambled.

A reasonable investment plan would have you put some money in bonds and some in stocks (and maybe a little bit in commodities), and if one portion goes down, another portion probably balances it out. The nice, safe, diversified strategy is also the one that can make you feel lucky when you're able to retire to Palm Springs and sip a mai tai cocktail while lounging on your deck.

But what about the big lucky hit that everybody wants? One guy I know boasts often about having bought Microsoft when it first went public in 1986. The two thousand dollars he invested then is worth about three-quarters of a million dollars today. Nice. So how did he get so lucky? I gave him a quick call to ask.

"I had done a lot of research into Microsoft, and I had a feeling that Bill Gates—"

"Come on, be honest," I said, interrupting. "How many other stocks did you buy that same year that I never hear about?"

There was a long pause. "Okay, I guess that's true. You got me," he said with a little laugh.

In other words, he didn't get lucky by picking the *right* stock—he picked *a lot* of stocks. He just never discusses the dozens of others he bought at about the same time that didn't go anywhere. People do that regularly. Maybe your brother-in-law happens to mention every Thanksgiving how much he's made on the Apple stock that he bought way back when and has split more times than he can count. Next time he brings it up, ask him what else was in that original mix. Perhaps some shares of Pets.com he doesn't mention? If you don't want to ruin the whole dinner, you can point out that making his luck by diversifying was actually a smart strategy. It's the same reason you have a pecan pie and a pumpkin pie and an apple pie on the table. However much you try to predict, you can never really know which will be the best. (Yes, this also creates an excuse to take a slice of each.)

The venture capitalists who put money into companies in the early stages generally figure that they'll get a return on one in ten of them. If nine bomb but one turns into a Microsoft or Facebook or Alibaba, everybody looks brilliant. Following that model, diversifying means you're not betting the farm (or the retirement fund) on a gut feeling or a tip from that same brother-in-law. Rather, you're spreading the risk and setting yourself up for at least one or two lucky returns.

Nassim Nicholas Taleb, the mathematician and author of *Fooled by Randomness* and *The Black Swan*, has spent a lot of time thinking about how to set strategies that can make you lucky in (what he considers) a random world. What he calls "black swan events" are those that seem to come out of nowhere and can't be predicted— like world wars and stock market crashes and terrorist attacks. Taleb gives the example of a Las Vegas casino that had planned for every contingency on its gambling floor but was almost destroyed by completely unprecedented events—a star performer was mauled by a tiger, an employee hid important records, and an owner's daughter was kidnapped. Events like these, rare but with an extreme impact, cause disaster for most people who count on the status quo—but can create huge windfalls for others.

Taleb's view is that if you want to get lucky from black swans, you should invest in the extremes. Think of it as the barbell school of life, in which you stay away from the middle and load up on things at either end that are extremely safe and extremely risky. So, for example, you might squirrel away 90 percent of your savings in something like well-protected Treasury bonds and then put the remaining amount—the amount you're willing to lose—in extremely high-risk possibilities like Bitcoin or oil wells in Alaska. If you like the idea of the big chance, it's a good plan. But most of us would rather be a little more cautious. Betting on black swans is one theoretical way to create luck—but if you're not careful about how much you're willing to risk, you can end up broke (or crazed with anxiety) long before the black swan appears.

So in both finances and life, you can either diversify with a normal, middle-of-the-road approach or go to the extremes that Taleb suggests. But there's not a mathematician or analyst around who would recommend anything *other* than diversifying in most circumstances.

Great. So we're all in agreement. From every rational perspective, having many eggs in your basket (or many different baskets) sets you up to be lucky. You have more opportunities for success. If you break one egg, you still have several others, smooth and shiny and ready to go.

But come on, now, admit it. That cautious approach (even with the Taleb twist) doesn't inspire much excitement. We live by the American legend that you go big or you go home. We've all watched *Who Wants to Be a Millionaire?* (and endless other similar game shows), where the more you risk, the luckier you can get. If you really believe in something, you put everything you have into it.

"Like the Fred Smith story," Barnaby said, when I brought up the problem. "Gamble everything you've got and get so lucky that you create a huge company."

Exactly. A few years after Fred Smith graduated from Yale, he had the crazy idea for an overnight delivery service. He raised many millions for the company, which he started in 1971, but over the next couple of years, fuel prices started going up and the company's finances went down. On the verge of bankruptcy and millions in debt, he made a last-gasp pitch for financing to the board of General Dynamics—and got turned down.

Smith had $5,000 left in the bank. Give up? Nope. He flew to Las Vegas and played blackjack all weekend with the last of the company's money. He made $27,000. On Monday morning, the senior vice-president of operations was stunned to see the money in the bank. Terrific! It was enough to pay fuel costs for the week. He asked Smith where the money had come from—and heard about the big gamble.

"You mean you took our last $5,000? How could you do that?" asked the senior vice-president, stunned.

Smith pointed out that it really didn't matter. The $5,000 wouldn't have been enough to keep them aloft for the week, so it made sense to risk it. He'd had the courage to put all his eggs in the blackjack basket and win.

Now *that's* a story! Bet everything you've got—and create a company called Federal Express! Shortly after the gambling weekend, Smith raised more money—to the tune of eleven million dollars— and was able to keep going. A few years later, the company was profitable, and it became so successful that Smith is personally worth close to five billion dollars. And you have no doubt gotten a FedEx package delivered to your door sometime recently.

At the risk of ruining a good story, I think this kind of mythologizing does everybody a disservice. The lesson is supposed to be that if you truly believe in yourself and what you're doing, you should put all your eggs in one basket and go for broke. (Nobody mentions that you might truly *go* broke.)

But the truth is that Fred Smith didn't make himself lucky with that one weekend of gambling. He had been building the foundations for his company for years. As an undergraduate, he wrote a paper for an economics class about automation and transportation and how you could deliver stuff by small planes. He later joked that he didn't remember his grade but guessed it was probably his "usual C."[1] After he graduated from Yale, he spent three years in the Marines, flying in planes (though he wasn't a pilot) and learning military logistics. All that helped when he started what was then Federal Express.

By the time of the Las Vegas story, Smith's innovative Federal Express was already flying eight planes and gaining a lot of attention. The $27,000 might have felt nice that Monday—but what really mattered was the $11 million he pulled in shortly afterward. The notion of gambling it all in Vegas makes an excellent fable, but it clearly wasn't the only option he had for saving his company.

Once I started thinking about it, I realized how often we fall prey to the all-in-one-basket mythologizing. My closet is full of Kate Spade pocketbooks and shoes and dresses (and my kitchen has more of her adorable plates and serving pieces than I should admit), and I've always liked the story of how she quit her job as a magazine editor to start the company. Friends and family thought she was

---

1. He was in Skull and Bones along with George W. Bush, who also boasted of his low grades. Did anyone successful ever get better than a C at Yale?

crazy—how could she give up that glamorous job at *Mademoiselle*?[2] Back then, she was Kate Brosnahan, and she teamed with her boyfriend Andy Spade to risk it all on making pocketbooks.

Kate has talked about how close the company came to closing. But she stuck with it. Not mentioned as often is that Andy (whom she soon married) worked in the company—but also had several high-level jobs in advertising. By my count, that makes for at least two eggs in their basket, the company and Andy's career.

The extra egg makes the Kate Spade origins story a little less sexy—but it also helps explain how she got so lucky. You need time to make a big splash in a crowded fashion pool. Having that sideline support helped her keep paddling.

Adam Grant, a wunderkind professor at the Wharton School at the University of Pennsylvania, used to believe in the eggs-in-one-basket mythology for entrepreneurs. He is known for having an open door for advising students, and among those seeking his wisdom a few years ago were four guys getting their MBA who had an idea to sell eyeglasses online. He was happy to talk with them, but when they asked him to invest, he wanted to be sure that they were fully devoted to their idea. So he asked if they had taken internships the previous summer. Well, yes, they had. And were applying for jobs after graduation? Again, yes. Just in case. A backup plan, because you never know what will happen with a start-up.

"So I obviously declined to invest," Professor Grant said. Successful entrepreneurs wouldn't hedge their bets—they would sleep on

---

2. *Mademoiselle*, which Condé Nast shuttered in 2001, was a fashion magazine that also published a stellar list of writers. The magazine ran a famous college competition every year, and the winners came to New York to be guest editors for a month. Sylvia Plath wrote about her experience in *The Bell Jar*. Other winners over the years included Joan Didion, Ali MacGraw, Ann Beattie, Curtis Sittenfeld—and me.

the floor and eat pizza! Believe in their idea to the ends of the earth! Put all their eggs in the start-up basket!

The company launched in 2010 as Warby Parker—and became an almost instant success. It's now valued at more than $1 billion. Professor Grant jokes that after his bad decision, his wife now handles the family investments.

"I thought to be an entrepreneur you have to be a risk taker and you have to be all in. And what I didn't realize at the time was, first of all, successful entrepreneurs are much more likely to play it safe and have backup plans than failed entrepreneurs. And second, all of the time they spent working on other things was giving them the freedom to do something really original," Grant said.

Like Kate Spade, the Wharton four had some backing that allowed them to take their time and make good decisions. (They tested two thousand names before they settled on Warby Parker.) However hard they worked on the company, they were also going to classes and thinking about other options—which probably gave them a more expansive view of their own company. As Dave Gilboa, one of the company's co-CEOs, somewhat awkwardly explained a while ago, "Warby Parker wasn't the basket that I wanted to put all my eggs into."

I happen to have heard the Warby Parker founders give talks a few times recently, and as they tell and retell their story, something curious has started to happen. Those extra eggs in baskets they kept around don't get mentioned anymore. Smart guys, they know what the start-up legend is supposed to be, so they focus on how hard they worked and how little they slept, how they zeroed in on unpacking boxes and responding to consumers to the exclusion of schoolwork and paying attention in class. It's all true and very inspiring, but I'm glad Adam Grant is willing to remind us of the other side. You need to focus and take some risks to get lucky—but you don't have to be crazy and exclude everything else.

Finding the right balance of eggs in baskets to make yourself lucky isn't always obvious. Back when I was the editor in chief of a big national magazine, I had lunch with a glamorous friend who had the same position at another magazine. This wasn't her first experience as an editor in chief, and a few years earlier, she had been unceremoniously fired from the top spot at a hugely popular women's magazine. In the merry-go-round of media, that happens regularly, and it certainly wouldn't be a black mark against her. But she had loved that particular job, and losing it stung badly. Now that she was running another magazine, she was wary—and determined to keep herself hedged.

"Your problem is that you're too involved with your current job," she told me as we nibbled on our Greek salads with extra feta cheese. "I've learned that you have to spend less time thinking about your current job and more time thinking about where you'll be next."

Having a backup option wasn't just her proverbial Plan B—it seemed to be Plans A through Z. Constantly setting herself up for future opportunities, she saw her current job mostly as a stepping-stone. She was networking, appearing on television, and even getting a master's degree in an unrelated field that just happened to interest her. If magazines completely collapsed, and that seemed very possible, she had an entirely different way to go.

Preparing for her job to end, she had all her eggs well separated into different baskets. She kept two phones and two computers—one each for the office and home—and had all her work contacts on both. "I don't have a single personal item in my office except a box in one desk drawer with my makeup and a hairbrush and a few other things," she told me. "The day this job ends, I turn in my work phone and computer and I walk out with my box and never look back."

I understood her instinct, but listening to her made me squeamish, too. If diversifying your life too dramatically meant never investing yourself fully in where you were, you were missing out on some present-moment fun. My friend's job did end eventually, as did mine, and we've both moved on to other projects that make us happy. But thinking about our positions, it occurred to me that part of luck was enjoying where you were at the moment. If your backup plan felt more important than real life, something was wrong.

Barnaby knew a young guy named Alex Abelin who had left Google a couple of years earlier and launched an interesting company called LiquidTalent. It was essentially a mobile app to connect web developers and designers with the people who might hire them.

"Let's follow his progress for a while and maybe learn some lessons about luck," Barnaby suggested.

We arranged to talk with Alex on a Wednesday a few weeks away. When the day came, the conversation didn't go exactly the way we had expected. After some cheerful hellos and assurances that he was eager to talk about making luck, Alex hesitated only briefly when Barnaby asked how he was doing.

"It's interesting that we're talking today, because I sunsetted the company on Monday," he said

Sunsetted? I had an image of Alex and his team taking an idyllic boat ride into a glowing sunset. I looked at Barnaby for clarification.

"He shut it down," Barnaby whispered in surprise.

Oh. So the boat had indeed sailed, but it wasn't idyllic at all.

Alex explained that the company had simply run out of

financing. He still believed in the concept, but it just wasn't sustainable anymore, so it was time to let go.

"It was a tough decision, but I believe in the adage that when one door closes, a window opens," he said, sounding unexpectedly upbeat.

Alex didn't need to search for that window, since it was already part of his blueprint. After he left Google, he was excited to start his own company, but he also wanted to be rational. So when he was beginning LiquidTalent, he also became an advisor to a start-up launched by a colleague called LiquidWiFi. "You can't have all your eggs in one basket," Alex said as Barnaby and I exchanged a sideways smirk. "I always knew that if one didn't work, I had an opportunity with the other."

The second egg wasn't solely a backup in case the first one broke—it enhanced both of them. Alex was quick to point out that he had thrown himself wholeheartedly into being CEO and that "both companies were made more robust by our connections with each other." The interactions between the two meant he had a bigger network and more talent to draw on. But now Alex was additionally pleased about the double role because he had someplace to go the next morning.

We all agreed that failure was no longer an embarrassment—it was more a badge of honor. It meant you had experience that would help as you moved on. Barnaby knew of companies in Silicon Valley where failure was so lionized that they threw regular "congratulations—you screwed up!" parties. To incentivize risk-taking, they celebrated failure. You didn't hang your head after something didn't work—you swaggered on, proud to have tried. Two days in, Alex wasn't swaggering yet, but he had a good perspective.

As Alex saw it, the company failure hadn't come from anything big but from "the little moments that add up." If one or two more people had said yes to financing, he'd still be going strong. Or maybe it was the split with his girlfriend that distracted him and affected his attitude. "Business is about people, so emotion always plays a role," he said. Over the company's three years, they'd had big media attention and ran events that brought thousands of people together. If you looked at success as a moment in time, they'd had plenty of it.

After we said good-bye to Alex, Barnaby and I hung out to talk a little more. Barnaby was still surprised by the sunsetting. From what he'd seen early on, Alex had done everything right. He'd brought in top talent and planned his moves carefully. "Maybe that changed his chance of success from one in a hundred to one in two, but it still wasn't guaranteed," Barnaby said thoughtfully. "That's why you need the fallback plan—so you can land on your feet no matter what."

And the wisdom of Alex's backup plan became very apparent when we followed up with him sometime later. He had immediately moved full-time to the second company—and shortly after that, it was purchased by Verizon for a hefty sum. Alex sounded delighted. They now had plenty of money to go ahead with a plan to put internet kiosks in cities and parks and even at the Super Bowl.

"It sounds like we set this up!" I said to Barnaby. "His first plan failed, but then his backup paid off royally. Proof of your eggs-in-baskets theory."

"We didn't set it up, but he did. He doubled his chance of making luck, and it worked," Barnaby said.

"He surprised us all along—but it turned out to be a good story. And it even has the advantage of being true," I said with a laugh.

At his Princeton Luck Lab, Barnaby had been looking at various scenarios for risk-taking and diversification. He found that for eons, biology has shown the value of diversification, and more recently, successful financial institutions and investors had demonstrated the same. So the question—how many eggs and how many baskets were optimal? He didn't have a single answer, because a lot depended on your talents, aspirations, and appetite for risk. But he'd come up with a few general principles.

"It usually makes sense to diversify across two or three options," he said. The simplest plan was two similar options—a primary and a fallback, as Alex had done. But you could also throw in a third option that was completely different, in case the first two failed for the same reason.

When Alex first left Google, he thought he wanted to travel and have new adventures. "Google is a huge biosphere, but it's still a biosphere with walls and ceilings, and I wanted to see the world and do a lot of things," he told us.

So he essentially had that third, very different option. If both of his companies closed, he could pack up and take six months to explore New Zealand and Fiji and Bora Bora (or wherever he wanted). Options aren't always about having one job or another. They're about seeing that life offers many different opportunities, and luck comes from taking the different paths that will make you happy.

Having two options, with a possible outlier third option, seemed like a generally good route to getting lucky. But surely there were exceptions. I started my career as a sportswriter and regularly heard coaches thunder about the need to give 110 percent. If you were coming up to bat in the World Series with the score tied at the bottom of the ninth inning, you weren't going to think about a backup plan. You focused everything you possibly could on that single at bat.

Now Barnaby nodded. "I can think of only two exceptions where it makes sense to put all your eggs in one basket," he said. The first was where the payoff was so high or the opportunity so narrow that you needed to throw caution to the wind. That would include the ninth inning of the World Series or, as Barnaby suggested, when you're trying to win an Olympic medal or the love of a special person.

"The second exception is when that single basket is all that matters for survival," he said.

That seemed reasonable. If you want to get lucky making alternate plans for tomorrow, you have to make sure that there will *be* a tomorrow.

After I said good-bye to Barnaby, I walked home thinking about those tomorrows. It occurred to me that when we're in the midst of one adventure, we don't realize how many more are to come. Maybe we can make ourselves lucky by plopping those eggs into our baskets one after another, rather than all at once.

A few days later, I got a call from my college friend Jim Bennett. We hadn't seen each other in a long time, but we would always be bonded by wrestling. No, not *that* kind of wrestling—we were just good friends. But one of my first assignments for the college newspaper was covering the varsity wrestling team, and Jim was one of the stars. It was a fun beat because the wrestlers were smart and determined and incredibly driven (with great biceps, too). It got even better when Jim won the National Collegiate Athletic Association wrestling championship—which was an impressively big deal.[3] He was as close to a campus hero as a wrestler can get.

---

3. Jim won the NCAA Division I individual championship in the 142-pound weight class. Weight divisions have since changed.

On the phone, Jim told me that the NCAA wrestling champion-ships were being held this year at Madison Square Garden and he had purchased a suite for the three-day event. Did I want to come by? Some members of the old college team would be there, as well as some of Jim's current colleagues.

So on a Thursday evening, I made my way over to Madison Square Garden and found Jim's spacious suite, which had plenty of seats facing the arena, a large comfy area for chatting, and a big center table filled with enough beer and wine and snacks to make it a good night. Jim looked fit and happy and not too far above the weight class in which he once competed. After college, he had worked for financial firms and then started his own company, Ben-nett Management. Given the suite, which was usually leased to big corporations, my best guess was that he had achieved the financial equivalent of an NCAA championship.

Jim was busy being a gracious host to his many guests, so I started talking with a guy who had been a top executive at Jim's company. He told me that Jim invested in distressed assets and at one point had two billion dollars under management. It was a tough, competitive business, and several other similar companies that had started at the same time had since folded.

"So what do you think made the difference?" I asked. "How did you guys stay lucky?"

"What made us lucky is all this," he said, gesturing toward the arena floor where the college wrestlers were on the mats competing. "Jim was a wrestler—an NCAA champion—and he never gives up. He spent years developing dogged persistence and tenacity. He's the same in business as he was on the mat—patient and purpose-ful, and he waits for the right opening. Then he has incredible stamina and doesn't mind hurting a little bit. Wrestlers always have something that hurts. But Jim figures out every move and has stay-ing power."

"Nice hagiography," I said with a smile.

"What's that?"

"A description of a saint."

He laughed. "Jim doesn't pay me anymore, so I don't have to say it. But it's all true."

Sitting down a few minutes later with a beer (for him) and a Diet Coke (for me), I told Jim what his colleague had said. Jim gave a little smile. "Wrestling does train you to be persistent, and maybe that helps in business," he said. He knows some other wrestlers who had gone on to big success on Wall Street, and the step-by-step approach he took to wrestling had surely helped when he was evaluating com-panies. "Maybe I was willing to be more methodical and spend more time studying details than most people," he said. At least a third of Jim's competitors went out of business in the 2008 recession, but he didn't panic and got through just fine. "You keep working and looking for opportunities and trying to make your luck," he said.

It struck me that Jim was a serial eggs-in-basket guy. He threw himself fully into whatever he was doing—but always had that next egg hatching. He had focused intently and worked endlessly to be-come an NCAA champion—but he was still at an Ivy League school and studied hard. He did well enough to get into Harvard Business School and set up his next round of luck. Now he brought incredible intensity to his business, but he also took ten weeks of vacation a year, spending time with his delightfully ebullient wife and their young children.

"When you work seventy or eighty hours a week, you can burn out. I want to keep going," he said.

Wrestling was still a big part of his life. In fact, he had just been named the team leader for the USA women's team at the 2020 Olympics. But always modest, he didn't want to take too much credit for his long-ago national championship. Understanding my concept that luck was based on talent, hard work, and random chance, he suggested that he'd needed all three.

"Everyone who gets to the top level has talent and works hard," he said, "but when you get to those last matches, something can just go your way or not."

After a while, Jim got up to return to his hosting duties, and I sidled over to the ringside seats to watch the college wrestlers on the mats below. Jim was probably right that some chance would be involved, as it always is in sports—a bad call, an unexpected injury. But as a general rule, the best wrestlers would win their medals through a combination of talent, hard work, and determination.

The winners would be very proud. They deserved to be. They had trained in the gym for hours, run on the streets for miles, and probably eaten celery for days in order to make weight. They'd given all they had to the sport. But I hoped that they also understood that life was long and college wrestling would end—and that (like Jim at the same age) they had another egg hatching in their basket, preparing them for the next stage of life.

After I gave Jim a hug good-bye, I left Madison Square Garden thinking how life is both shorter and longer than you realize. Shorter for all the obvious reasons (*Was college that long ago?*) and longer because you have more cycles and opportunities and chances than you realize when you're starting out. If you want to be lucky, you have to both throw yourself fully into the moment and also be prepared for the future. That takes a couple of eggs and a couple of baskets—and just might be the formula for a lucky life.

CHAPTER NINE

The Lucky Break That Really Counts

The big break might start out small. . . . Lay the founda-
tion for luck. . . . Why Alexander Fleming's chance discov-
ery wasn't chance. . . . The lucky breaks that can change
the world.

As we took a walk together one day through Central Park, Barnaby brought up the subject of lucky breaks—and I began thinking about a lovely young woman who works in the grocery store near my house in rural Connecticut. Always eager to help, she has a gentle style, a warm smile, and an air of competence that her IGA apron can't hide. Plus, she's quite beautiful, with the slightly exotic looks of the first assistant I hired when I was a TV producer.

But there she was in rural Connecticut, packing groceries. I imagined that she came from a family without a lot of advantages. And how would she ever get a chance to be lucky?

"I wish I could be her fairy godmother and bring her to New York and get her a job in television," I said. "Could you imagine what she'd do with a break like that?"

"It might be amazing, or it might lead to disaster," Barnaby said. "Not everybody knows how to handle a lucky break when it comes along."

Really? A lucky break that doesn't make you . . . lucky?

In the best of all worlds, a lucky break is the monumental event that changes everything. Your boss quits and hands you his job, your start-up sells for a billion dollars, or your YouTube video goes viral and makes you famous. Actress Shirley MacLaine was just out of high school and an understudy for the Broadway production of *The Pajama Game* when the starring actress broke her ankle—and MacLaine landed center stage. A very literal lucky break! (Though only for one of them.)

Those earth-shattering events do happen, but Barnaby was right. Like MacLaine's, your lucky break could lead to a career marked by six Academy Award nominations—or it could lead to absolutely nothing. Because if you're not prepared, you're going to blow the chance you've been given.

The real secret is knowing what to do *after* the big opportunity comes—because a lucky break is not the same as a lucky outcome. In our slot machine of chance, talent, and hard work, a lucky break is the big cherry of chance. But you still need those other two cherries lined up. We've all heard the stories of athletes with multimillion-dollar contracts who get arrested and thrown out of their sport, or lottery winners who end up penniless and angry. A lucky break turns out to be like any other opportunity. You can recognize that it's in front of you and make it part of a lucky life. Or you can mishandle it so it leads to nothing—or disaster.

You'll be able to make the most of a lucky break only if you've laid the proper foundation for it. MacLaine didn't just waltz (or tap-dance) onto the Broadway stage—she had been preparing to be a dancer since she was three years old. Acting was also in the family genes. (Her brother is actor Warren Beatty.) When she had the chance to be onstage, she was fully prepared. Similarly, if you buy a lottery ticket with an actual idea of what you'll do with any winnings, you'll be in a better position to handle the windfall than if you've just fantasized that big bucks will change your life. The chances of winning are so small that preparing ahead probably isn't worth it in this case. But you get the point.

Many times a lucky break isn't a huge rupture in the earth but just the tiniest little crack. A small advantage can grow into something big and bigger. If you're waiting for the big break, you'll miss the truth that most luck builds and builds on itself. The challenge is to realize how a tiny lucky break can become an enormous one.

As an example, Barnaby suggested that he would like to give me a lucky break in the form of a penny that doubled every day. He would give me the value at the end of a week. How was that for generous?

I looked up at him (he's tall) and turned up my nose. Wouldn't you? It doesn't take a lot of math skills to figure out the magic penny will be worth only 64 cents at the end of the week.[1]

"Okay, I can do better than that," Barnaby said. Could he lure me with the penny if it kept doubling until the end of the month? Was that good enough for a lucky break?

Now I sighed.

"Really, Barnaby, you're supposed to be offering a lucky break, and instead you're playing with pennies!"

He could feel my pain. So now he gave me a choice. At the end of the month, I could have the value of that doubling penny—or $1 million. Which would I like?

A million bucks! There must be a catch, but I still couldn't resist. I told Barnaby I'd take the million.

Barnaby looked a little smug.

---

1. This is apparently a popular problem in high school math classes—but I had never heard it before. To start out, the 1 cent today becomes 2 cents tomorrow, 4 cents the next day, then 8, 16, 32, 64.

"Wrong choice!" he said. "The doubling penny will be worth more than a million dollars at the end of the month."

"It can't be!"

"Trust me on this."

I didn't trust him because it just didn't make sense. How could a penny be the right choice? He sat down on a bench and quickly wrote out the numbers to prove it. (You can find the full rundown in the notes at the end of the book.)

A million bucks was fine with me, and I hadn't done badly in taking it. But the real opportunity came with the doubling penny, which I (and probably you) passed right by. Hard as it is to believe, that penny would be worth $10.7 million at the end of the month.[2] So I could have been ten times luckier if I had realized the power of cumulative advantage.[3]

As he said, small bits of luck can turn into big ones.

Instead of waiting for the magical million that will change every-thing, you would be better to start thinking about—and collecting—the pennies that will build and make you a real (or proverbial) fortune. Luck builds on luck. The biggest lucky break of all could start out as nothing more than a copper coin. Lucky people set themselves up for the big break by taking those dancing lessons or getting the penny or simply being open to possibilities in different ways than others.

---

2. If you get the offer for the doubling penny in February, ask to wait until March. There's a big difference in value after twenty-eight days versus thirty-one. (That's the power of doubling.)

3. Barnaby quickly clarified that all this was theoretical. He wished he could give me that doubling penny!

We're all suckers for stories about the big life-changing (or world-changing) moments of luck. Everybody has probably heard by now that penicillin, Post-it notes, and Velcro were discovered by accident. Supposed lucky breaks like those take on almost mythic proportions. But you have to be careful about giving too much credence to the serendipitous lucky break that led to the discovery or invention. Because that undermines the truer story of the determined efforts (before and after) that really create luck.

So let's start with the story that penicillin was discovered by sheer chance when Alexander Fleming found mold growing in one of his petri dishes. As the story goes, he went away for a month-long family vacation in September 1928 and left several petri dishes with *Staphylococcus* bacteria on the windowsill of his lab. When he got back, one of the dishes was contaminated with mold. And lo and behold, the bacteria surrounding the mold had been destroyed.

He didn't shout, "Eureka!" or go running naked through the streets (as Archimedes reportedly once did),[4] but he did realize that the mold might have inhibited the bacterial growth. And there you have it—one lucky break and millions of people have been saved from diseases like strep throat and scarlet fever, as well as wound infections.

"When I woke up just after dawn on September 28, 1928, I certainly didn't plan to revolutionize all medicine by discovering the world's first antibiotic, or bacteria killer. But I suppose that was exactly what I did," Fleming said later.

The revolution wasn't quite as casual as all that. During World

---

4. Archimedes was trying to figure out how to assess the purity of gold. He settled himself into a tub and realized that the water displacement equaled the volume of his body (or the part submerged). He jumped out of the tub, shouted, "Eureka!" and ran home naked. The story was first told two centuries after it supposedly occurred—casting some doubt on its veracity. But we refuse to stop believing in that tale.

War I, Fleming had been in the Royal Army Medical Corps doing research into wound infections and antiseptics. After the war, he returned to his lab at St. Mary's Hospital at the University of London, and by 1921, he had made his first big discovery, finding an enzyme that fights bacteria.

That research reportedly began when Fleming had a cold and dropped some mucus into one of his bacteria cultures. Are you starting to see a pattern here? The dropped mucus and the plopped mold were serendipitous, but they were common events. It wasn't their occurrence that was so lucky and magical, but what Fleming made of them.

At the time of his family vacation, Fleming had been working on questions about bacteria and the human immune system for more than a decade. As is often the case in science, he had many small breakthroughs and lots of incremental steps. Many of the things he tried didn't lead anywhere. When one does pay off, it's not random luck—it's the result of months and years of focused energy, and plenty of experiments that didn't pan out.

You get lucky only when you know what you're looking for. Someone else coming into Fleming's lab after that vacation might have tossed away the contaminated petri dish without a second thought. One man's scientific breakthrough is another man's yucky, moldy mess.

And despite the lucky break, Fleming didn't revolutionize medicine on September 28. The real challenge came afterward, as it so often does. He added two researchers to his team, but he wasn't successful in isolating and purifying the "mold juice." Not long after, two scientists at the University of Oxford, Howard Florey and Ernst Chain, led a team that finally created the first usable doses of penicillin. They ultimately shared a Nobel Prize with Fleming.

Florey and Chain never got much media attention because all they offered was the moral that intelligence and hard work pay off. Fleming's story had magic and mystery—the distracted scientist, the messy lab, the mold plopping into a dish placed on a windowsill. Luck . . . serendipity . . . and the world is changed! But the lucky break was only one step in the chain. Much had to occur ahead of time for it to mean anything, and even more had to happen afterward for it to pay off.

The lucky breaks we remember are the ones that pay off. If Fleming's colleagues hadn't ultimately made penicillin, we wouldn't be telling the story of the moldy petri dish. Lots of understudies step into the starring role, but since they don't become Shirley MacLaine (or her equivalent), we don't have any reason to remember them. The lessons of the past are helpful only if we can use them to recognize the lucky break when it happens to *us*.

Josh Groban is now one of the biggest pop stars in the country, but when he was eighteen years old, his future wasn't that obvious. I was (happily) invited to a small dinner with him recently and was struck by how smart, thoughtful, and serious he seemed. Really, shouldn't a pop star be a little more vacuous? He told me that shortly after he started as a freshman in the prestigious theater program at Carnegie Mellon, he was offered a recording contract from Warner Bros. Records. He remembered sitting on the bed in his college dorm, wondering what to do. Was this the lucky break that would shoot him to stardom? Or if he blew off school, would he end up coming back a semester later, tail between his legs?

"I expected I'd be a failure and come back. But if I didn't do it, I imagined how much I'd resent being in dance classes the next semester," he said.

Recording contracts don't come out of the blue. For Groban, luck led to luck when he stood in for the famed Italian tenor Andrea Bocelli at a rehearsal for the 1999 Grammy Awards. Singing a duet with Céline Dion, he immediately impressed Grammy host Rosie O'Donnell, who had a TV talk show at the time. She invited Groban to come on the next week and sing, and the appearance led hotshot producer David E. Kelley to write a role for Groban on the then hugely popular TV show *Ally McBeal*.

So was the lucky break filling in for Bocelli, appearing with O'Donnell, impressing Kelley, or getting the recording contract? Like our doubling penny, it all compounded. But then Groban had to take all these breaks and make them into something beyond one-time opportunities.

He took the risk to leave school and performed with big stars all over the country. His eponymous debut album in 2001 quickly went from gold to double platinum. A few years and several records later, he had four multiplatinum records and was the bestselling artist in the country.

Even as a big star, Josh continued to make his own luck. Though he hadn't done musical theater since he was a teenager ("I was sailor number four in *Anything Goes*," he joked), our dinner was to celebrate the announcement of his Broadway debut in an offbeat show called *Natasha, Pierre & the Great Comet of 1812*.

"I wanted to do something new that scared me," Josh said. He was learning to play the accordion for the part and expected to wear a heavily padded suit to look more like the stout and dissolute Pierre.

The show had been conceived by a cool downtown writer named Dave Malloy and directed by the equally cool Rachel Chavkin. Both had high cred as unconventional artists who didn't care about popular audiences. Knowing that Rachel and Dave traveled in a crowd of experimental artists, Josh admitted that he was half-dreading and half-amused at the thought of the downtown crowd coming to see him—one of America's biggest pop stars—on Broadway.

"I want all Dave's and Rachel's friends to leave the show thinking, 'I really liked Josh, and I'm ashamed of myself,'" he said with a laugh.

When the show opened, it was pretty clear that everybody (even the cool friends) really liked Josh. The reviewer for *The New York Times* called him "absolutely wonderful" and said he went to see the show twice in two days. Groban got a Tony nomination.

Benefiting from a lucky break is easier when you have the talent and drive of Josh Groban. But whatever your situation, you need to recognize that an opportunity could be in front of you—and take the risk to get up from your college dorm bed and pursue it.

A lucky break becomes meaningful only if it falls on fertile ground. Barnaby and I both have many talents (we hope you agree), but singing is not among them. If I had the chance to perform at a Grammy rehearsal, the result would not be Groban-like pop stardom but rather many people wearing earplugs.

For a lucky break to have an impact, you need to be ready for it, like Alexander Fleming, and able to make use of it, like Josh Groban. Giving someone a lucky break that pays off isn't as easy as it might sound. Back in 1981, the philanthropist Eugene Lang was speaking to a group of sixth-graders at the school in East Harlem that he had attended fifty years earlier. As he looked out at the sixty-one children from low-income families, the idea struck him of offering them a collective lucky break. He made an impromptu offer: He would pay the college tuition of every one who graduated from high school.

The kindly fairy godfather sprinkling lucky dust on a school of children made headlines around the country. In interviews, Lang pointed out that it wasn't just the money that made the difference but the ability of the children to dream. Somebody cared about them. He quickly realized that the big break he was offering—free tuition—wouldn't do anything if the kids didn't have the grit or interest or vision to stay in school. So he put people in place who could tutor and help support the kids and their struggling parents.

And the result? The ground wasn't as fertile as it needed to be. One boy robbed a grocery store and went to prison, and several girls got pregnant. Others dropped out of school. But about half of the original sixty-one students took advantage of the lucky break and went on to college—some to schools as prestigious as Swarthmore and Barnard. That doesn't sound like a lot—until you hear that before Lang's offer, the principal had estimated that only one kid from the class would ever make it to college.

Lang's program spread, and his "I Have a Dream" Foundation inspired programs all over the country. Other philanthropists followed Lang's lead, adopting inner-city classes and offering college tuition to kids who make it through high school. The appeal is obvious. Those who have been successful in their own lives can often look back and recognize the people along the way who helped and supported them—parents or a teacher or the first guy who gave them a job. They feel fortunate. The idea of giving a lucky break to kids who wouldn't otherwise have one is compelling.

These luck interventions have gotten more formalized since Lang's spontaneous offer, but the results are often similar. Graduation rates do go up, and some kids who would never have had a chance to shine take advantage of their lucky break. But not everyone. When one generous donor tried to give the lucky break to 112 students in a blighted community in West Philadelphia, he ended up with more felons than college graduates. Only one student had a smooth passage through college. He is now an aeronautical engineer.

Two wealthy men, Abe Pollin and Melvin Cohen, got on the lucky-break bandwagon when they set up a Dreamers program at one of the poorest schools in Prince George's County, Maryland, in 1988. Pollin was well-known at the time as the owner of several big sports teams, including the Washington Capitals in the National Hockey League and the Washington Bullets of the National Basketball Association. He regularly wore a big smile and a big gold NBA championship ring.

The two men did everything right. They put a mentor in place to help the kids and parents and promised to pay full in-state tuition at the University of Maryland for everyone. They brought the kids to the Capital Centre to watch the Bullets games and got to know them all. The effort got a lot of media attention, and as the kids appeared on the local news, they understood how lucky they were. Just for being in the right fifth-grade class, they had opportunities for the future. The ultimate lucky break.

But once again, despite a huge effort and big bucks, the results were equivocal. As *The Washington Post* reported in a follow-up of the fifty-nine students more than twenty years later, one student became a doctor and another a cellist. But the successes were mixed in with disasters: "One would kill herself. One would kill his father. One would become a politician. One would become a cop. One would become a drug dealer."

The mixed results suggest that the upshot of a lucky break can range from heartwarming to heartbreaking. The kids in East Harlem and West Philadelphia and Prince George's County had many obstacles making it tough for them to take advantage of the opportunity. Sharon Darling, who founded the National Center for Families

Learning back in 1989, advised Lang at one point on how to get families involved. Part of the problem, as she saw it, was that the college tuition didn't feel like a lucky break to everyone.

"The parents didn't go to college themselves, and they expected their kids to get a job after high school and earn some money. They certainly didn't want them to move away," she told me. If you're a teenager, it's hard to take advantage of a lucky break if your parents are seeing it as an obstacle. And it's even harder to see advantages that will accrue in the long term if you're suffering in the short term.

Many of us don't have those same overwhelming barriers—but we put others in our way. We don't see the opportunity or simply don't realize that it could be life changing. We're so used to our usual patterns that we're reluctant to take a risk and veer in a new direction.

So, for example, if someone offered you the chance to travel six thousand miles away for a new job, would you consider it a ridiculous idea—or a lucky break? A man I recently met named Gustavo Rymberg faced that question some years ago when he was in his late twenties and living in Buenos Aires. He and his lovely wife, Marisa, had both grown up in Argentina and had no thought of leaving. But then representatives of the Jewish community from the city of Winnipeg in Manitoba, Canada, arrived with an offer. Wanting to bring new young energy to their community, they were encouraging Jewish families from South America to immigrate by offering help with jobs, housing, and schooling. Winnipeg, they promised, would be a supportive and warm community.

Warm in spirit, anyway. Temperatures can drop to minus forty degrees on Winnipeg's windswept prairie, and the average temperature in January is about two degrees. Snowdrifts outnumber people, and they're usually taller, too. By any estimation, Winnipeg is in the middle of nowhere. The closest big city is Minneapolis, more than four hundred miles south. (And when you have to go *south* to get to Minneapolis, you know you're in cold climes.)

But Gustavo was intrigued. He had grown up at the time of the military junta in Argentina, when thousands of people were "disappeared." Democracy had been restored, but the economy was shaky, the peso continued to be devalued, and there was a bombing at the embassy of Israel. Gustavo wasn't convinced that Buenos Aires was the best place to raise a Jewish family.

"Our daughters were four years old and ten months at the time, so maybe it was crazy," he told me over a hearty Canadian breakfast of eggs and home fries. "I tried to think about possibilities not just at the moment but into the future." He envisioned what the opportunities would be for his children in both places, and within a month he and Marisa packed up their house, their two children, and their high expectations. They got on a plane, ready to take advantage of the lucky break that had been offered in Winnipeg.

"But believe me, it didn't feel like a lucky break at first," he said with a laugh (and a charming accent). "There was a seventy-degree drop in temperature from when we left Buenos Aires to when we arrived in Winnipeg. That first winter, all of us were sick."

But the community was as welcoming as promised, and Gustavo and Marisa quickly found jobs and a sense of belonging. "We were the first family to arrive under the immigration program, so we were practically local celebrities," he said. "Everybody wanted us to be happy."

They *were* happy. In that supportive community, their opportunities expanded and their luck seemed to multiply. One job led to another, and they stayed for nine years, eventually moving to Toronto (where the winters are slightly better). Gustavo says that moving to Winnipeg didn't necessarily look like a lucky break to his friends. Trade long sunny days at the beach for short dark ones on the prairie? No thank you.

"They couldn't understand what I was thinking," he said. But now those same friends from Buenos Aires come to visit often, "and they see we have this nice house and nice life and I have this good job—and they say, 'Oh, you're so lucky.' They don't know how hard that first year was, or how many nights we lay in bed crying because we missed our families. So I say, 'Lucky? No. It's what you choose to make happen for yourself. It's what you do now because of where it can lead in the future.'"

In retrospect, the lucky break may look like sun-kissed (or snow-kissed) serendipity. You happened to be one of the kids in the class that a rich guy decided to support. Or you were in the right place when a Jewish community was looking to expand. But in order for that chance event to pay off, additional elements from our luck equation of talent and hard work must come into play. You have to recognize that there is an opportunity—and then run with it.

Gustavo and Marisa got to watch their daughters grow up in a nurturing environment and attend good colleges. Maybe it was difficult to move with babies, but new research suggests that was exactly the right time to give them the lucky break. Raj Chetty, now a professor of economics at Stanford, should know something about early starts—he got his PhD from Harvard at age twenty-three and was one of the school's youngest tenured professors. He has found that the greatest gains for upward mobility and other advancements come for children who move to better environments when they're very young.

Chetty recently looked at the data from a 1990s Clinton administration project called Moving to Opportunity, which helped some families move from the poorest housing projects to more economically mixed areas. Researchers who first followed the results were disappointed. They had expected that the people who moved would get better jobs and family outcomes—but that didn't seem to happen. Chetty decided to look at the results from a different perspective. Many of the families had small children when they moved. Did the lucky break change *their* lives? Some twenty years later, Chetty discovered that the results were actually quite remarkable for the kids who moved when they were under five.

"You see extremely clearly that they are doing dramatically better today as adults," he said. The lucky move meant that their incomes were significantly higher. They were more likely to go to college and less likely to be single parents than children who stayed in the projects or who moved later in their lives.

Using lucky breaks to create social change can work—but with caveats. As with the housing moves, the lucky break has to be given at the right time in a child's life. And as with the college-tuition programs, it won't work for everyone. The people who receive the lucky break still have to recognize that they've been handed an opportunity and act on it.

Getting a lucky break is always the start of the story, not the end of it. The twenty or so men and women who receive the "genius awards" every year from the MacArthur Foundation aren't required to act on their lucky break, since each one gets $625,000 over five years with no strings attached. The winners have already proven that they have talent and a willingness to work hard—two strands of the luck equation. But when given the final strand of chance (in the form of the unexpected fellowship), they recognize the lucky opportunity and want to take advantage of it, even if nobody is checking up on them. When I called Cecilia Conrad, the MacArthur Foundation managing director who oversees the awards (officially called a MacArthur Fellowship), she immediately concurred.

"The no-strings aspect seems to convey its own kind of responsibility," she said with a laugh.

The genius grant can feel like luck at its most magical. It's all handled through a confidential nominating and evaluation process so nobody knows they're being considered. And even if you have a suspicion that you're in the running, you can't sit around waiting for the news because there's no fixed date for the announcement. So when the winners get the call from Conrad announcing their award, they're usually flustered and flummoxed. It feels like a bolt from the blue. The ultimate lucky break.

Once they're over the initial excitement, the fellows use their lucky break to run in many directions. Conrad said that for many, "It gives renewed push and commitment to their path. Others see it as a safety net to take new risks. Some see it as a chance to become more public scholars or intellectuals."

The fellowships are meant to celebrate creativity in every field imaginable. Yes, poets and playwrights win, but MacArthur has also recognized blacksmithing and bowmaking (for stringed instruments— not arrows). Anne Basting, who got her fellowship in 2016, uses theater and storytelling to improve the lives of people with dementia.

"When people at cocktail parties ask what I do, I never knew what to say, and my husband would step in with something pithy," Basting told me when we spoke by phone one morning. "I always tried to legitimize my work, but I don't have to do that anymore. It's a relief and a savings of energy."

Basting heard the news about her genius award—the luckiest break she could imagine—one day when she was driving in her car and the phone rang. She didn't recognize the number but picked up anyway. Conrad, who has a very cheerful voice, introduced herself and asked Basting if she was in a place to have a private conversation. Hearing that she was in the car, Conrad suggested she pull over.

"But I told her that I was in a construction zone with no place to pull over, so we'd have to chat for a mile until the next exit," Basting said with a laugh.

Didn't she realize then what was coming?

"You never want to open yourself to disappointment. So I thought maybe she wanted me to give a reference for someone else." Ultimately, it was wise that she finally pulled over—since when she heard the news, she burst into tears.

Basting was the first person from the University of Wisconsin at Milwaukee ever to win a genius award, and only a handful of the winners (close to 1,000 since the awards began in 1981) have ever hailed from that state at all. The foundation created a map showing where all the MacArthur Fellows were born and where they lived when they won the award—and (aside from the international winners),[5] New York and California come out on top in both counts. When you adjust for population, the prominence of winners *born* in those states isn't surprising, but much more dramatic is where people *ended up*. Well over half were living in New York, California, and Massachusetts when they got the lucky fellowship.

If you want to increase your luck in any creative field, from arts to science to humanities to teaching, you may need to buy a plane

---

5. The very largest number of winners were born in countries other than the United States, though all lived here at the time of the award. What that says about the value of immigration to American progress is another topic altogether.

ticket. "There's an element of putting yourself in places where luck might find you," Conrad said. "The complementarities for people in the same place make more opportunities for luck to happen. Big cities draw more creative and original types, and there are also clusters around top educational institutions."

Lucky breaks (and $625,000) don't just fall from the sky, and Conrad thinks you pave the way for your own good fortune. It starts with "basic competency, skills, and hard work—and being passionate about possibilities," she said. Then comes a willingness to pursue your passions without an obvious end in sight. "The payoff may be far off and outside the norm. You have to take risks and be willing to fail—which is a form of resilience."

Anne Basting is a perfect example of all that. She got lucky by caring only about the deep impact her work would have. "I don't follow the same benchmarks for success that other people do," she admitted. "My satisfaction for the work is what keeps me persevering. I count the importance of my work by how it makes me feel. And I know that when others see it, they feel the power of it, too." A willingness to find your own niche and dance on the creative edges, no matter what the result, brings its own good luck. You become the only judge of what matters, and with or without a fellowship, the work feels like a lucky break.

Speaking with Cecilia Conrad and Anne Basting, I realized that there's another sort of follow-through at play here—a lucky break can have a huge multiplier effect. When you change one person's life, you can have a domino effect on others. Anne Basting works with people with dementia ("please don't call them patients," she said), and her lucky break with the genius award means she can spread the wealth and the opportunities to more of the elderly who need it.

The MacArthur Foundation is now trying to support that domino effect by getting into the lucky-break business in the biggest way possible—offering a hundred-million-dollar grant to a single project. A hundred million dollars. That's big bucks no matter how you look at it. Conrad told me that the foundation's 100&Change competition gave a payout ten or a hundred times bigger than the biggest grants that foundations typically give. And it came with almost no guidelines. The idea wasn't just to figure out the solution to a problem—but to decide what problem needed to be solved.

"I always said I have the coolest job when I was working just with the Fellows. Now I have the double coolest job because I'm doing this, too," said Conrad.

Conrad had expected a lot of proposals, but she and her colleagues were taken aback when more than 1,900 proposals came in. But there was a lesson for the rest of us in that, too. A majority of the proposals were dropped for not meeting basic requirements, and only 800 were passed on to the judges. If you want a lucky break on a massive scale, you have to be prepared. You have to put in the time and effort and not expect miracles.

The eight proposals selected as semifinalists ranged from a plan to cure river blindness in Nigeria to a new concept from *Sesame Street* to educate displaced children in countries like Syria. The real lucky break from all this wasn't just to the winner of the contest—it was to the millions of people who would be the beneficiaries of the project.

So can giving a lucky break change lives on a grand scale, creating a domino effect in the best possible way?

"We hope so," said Conrad. "And it's inspiring, isn't it?"

———————

Yes, I was inspired. But I still couldn't help thinking about the young woman packing groceries in Connecticut. She could try to set herself up for a lucky break by working hard, taking some risks, and being willing to try an original path. And if she did get a break—of any kind—she needed to be willing to recognize it and have the courage to move forward.

The next time I went to the grocery store, I thought I would talk to her and find out a little more about who she was and what her future might hold. But she wasn't there. When I didn't see her the next time, either, I asked the store manager if she had left.

"She sure did. She got a college scholarship—not a huge one, but enough for her to get started," he said with a bit of paternal pride.

I smiled and walked away. It struck me that the college scholarship was like the lucky penny—the perfect start for luck. If the young woman from the grocery store saw the possibilities and kept multiplying the opportunities, she could turn the small break into a huge windfall. I thought of the great Russian writer Boris Pasternak, who said that "when a great moment knocks on the door of your life, it is often no louder than the beating of your heart, and it is very easy to miss it."

You have to know when your lucky break has knocked—in any size or form. You don't want to miss it, and you need to be ready to make it grow.

PART THREE

TARGETED LUCK

Look on every exit as being an entrance
somewhere else.

—Tom Stoppard,
Rosencrantz and Guildenstern Are Dead

If opportunity doesn't knock, build a door.

—Milton Berle

CHAPTER TEN

How to Get a Job at Goldman Sachs (Or Anywhere You Want)

Don't follow the usual routes. . . . Listen to your hairdresser. . . .
Have the courage to recognize an opportunity. . . . Drop out
of Harvard . . . if you want to.

Barnaby regularly insisted that our principles of luck had to be "robust"—a word that always made me think of a chubby, red-cheeked toddler. But in science lingo, it means the rules can hold up in most circumstances. The term is adapted from computer programmers who use it to ensure that their coding will work even if there are errors during input—and you probably don't want to get too deeply into this lingo, because then you find out about fuzz testing, which involves putting in random data and seeing if it crashes the whole program.

We were pretty sure that our program for making luck wasn't fuzzy at all, and the principles—from being attentive to zigging when others zagged—were definitely robust. They could get you through anything.

But now that we had figured out the big theories, I wondered how they would work in everyday situations. Making yourself lucky in a theoretical sense is nice—but it's a lot better if you can get lucky in the areas that really count, like love, work, and family.

We decided to start with work. What was the best way to get to that intersection of chance, talent, and hard work that would make you lucky in your career?

Barnaby told me a funny story about the go-getters who apply to be first-year analysts at Goldman Sachs. Most are at the top of their game and the top of their class (at an Ivy League school, preferably), and with so many high-level people competing, any little edge can make a difference. So they write carefully crafted cover letters, deliberate about whether their résumé should be in Helvetica or Arial font, and look for the bon mot that will make them stand out.

One year, the Goldman Sachs managing director who was overseeing recruiting piled all the résumés of potential analysts on his desk, then divided them into two smaller stacks. He deliberated for a moment—and then tossed one of the stacks into the wastebasket.

When his colleagues looked at him in surprise, he gave a little shrug. "You have to be lucky in this business," he said. Then pointing to the résumés still on his desk, he added, "We might as well pick from the lucky ones."

I laughed. It was a great story—and a pleasure to think of the most elite guys around being subject to the laws of randomness. I asked Barnaby if this tale was really true or just Wall Street legend.

"I haven't been able to pin down the source," he admitted. "But nobody I've ever met in business doubts that it's true."

If you have ever applied for a job or spent time trying to build a career, you know that randomness seems to determine outcomes more than seems fair. Your future and fate may depend on whether the human resources person has a headache the morning she meets you or whether the executive who interviews you played squash at the same college you did. A whimsical executive tossing out résumés just to make a point seems like it's all part of the game.

The story got us thinking. If you're trying to make your own luck (as we've been describing all along), how can you possibly make sure that your résumé ends up in the pile that stays on the desk? Once we'd posed the question to ourselves, we spent some time batting it around. Had we finally hit on an example where the randomness, which you can't control, was the operating force in luck, well beyond the other elements that you can control, like talent and hard work?

"Unless you have magical powers, you can't move your résumé to the pile that stays on the desk," I said worriedly.

"Right," Barnaby agreed. But he looked perturbed for only a moment or so before immediately brightening up. "So you don't want to be in one of those piles at all!"

Aha! The managing director at Goldman Sachs was right that you're going to need luck to get a job—but remember that the luck we've been describing comes at the intersection of chance, talent, and hard work. The whimsical decision to toss away half the résumés is a perfect example of random chance. If you're in the wrong pile, there's nothing you can do. And while you can't remove random chance from life (unless you do have those magical powers), you have to be prepared to work around it. You can't always anticipate the unexpected, but you can focus on elements that *are* in your control, and thus make chance less . . . chancy.

So let's say you're applying for that job at Goldman Sachs. The trick is to make sure that your résumé ends up in a *third* stack—a small selection that the managing director has already pulled and knows he'll look at and consider.

Now, it may seem like we're working backward here—because when you're applying, you can't possibly know that the managing director is going to do something so random. But whether you're in the year of the lucky-versus-unlucky résumé piles or not, it's a good bet that a basic résumé, even one set in Helvetica and accompanied by a brilliant cover letter, won't be enough to get you hired. Standard techniques rarely work in a hypercompetitive environment. You need something that will make you stand out from the beginning so that your résumé isn't in either of the stacks on his deck.

One approach is to imagine the person who would definitely be lucky in this situation. You can, for example, figure that if some top-level executive had a child applying for the Goldman Sachs job, he'd call the CEO directly and make sure that his prodigy's résumé was at least seen. Instead of stomping around and complaining about how unfair it all is, you can figure out how that example applies to you. Assuming your family ties lean more toward plumbers and accountants and sales reps than investment bankers, what's the best next step?

Clearly you need to find somebody else who can pick up the phone and make that call for you. And that's not as hard as it sounds. Don't worry about what your mom and dad can (or can't) do for you. Remember that sociologists have shown that luck doesn't always, or even usually, come from the people closest to you. You need to rely on the strength of weak ties.

Barnaby had come across an executive coach named Don Asher who has written a dozen books on how to get a job, so we tracked him down to get his advice on the topic. He said that you're most likely to find the person who can make that call if you "cross the boundaries of the bubble where you normally live. You miss a lot of luck if you interact only with your own friends."

Asher told us about one client who was in retail sales and wanted to break into the fashion business. He told her to ask everyone she encountered if they knew anyone in the field. "She was in the gym with her personal trainer, Helga, and told her the situation—and it turned out that one of Helga's clients was the vice-president of finance for a major designer," said Asher. Connection made.

We called two other career coaches, and it turned out that the Helga story wasn't an anomaly. People such as hairdressers and personal trainers—whose professions naturally let them cross boundaries—are unexpectedly good sources for luck. Know specifically what you're asking for, and you can trigger a lucky connection while you're taking a hip-hop dance class or getting a layered bob with blond highlights.

One of the strongest of the weak ties often turns out to be college alumni connections. It's hard to say exactly why the fact that you attended Notre Dame rather than Penn State should make someone want to talk with you—but it works. Psychologists have shown over and over that people form tribal allegiances over often insignificant ties. Give half a group red T-shirts and the other half blue ones, and all of a sudden people are fiercely loyal to their color-mates. They'll be more likely to lend them money and cooperate with them in games.

Our neurologically wired instinct for group identification has led to tragic events throughout history, from religious wars to genocides to immigration bans. Turning that instinct on its head and using group identification for positive purposes seems like the very least we can do to start balancing the scale. So if you're applying for that job at Goldman Sachs (or elsewhere), check out LinkedIn or your college alumni directory and find someone at a high level at the company who attended your college.

Or you can try something even more creative. I happened to meet a young guy named Tyler who told me that he spent much of his senior year in college trying to find a job through the usual channels. He applied to companies that did on-campus recruiting and put his résumé into the school's career directory.

"Nothing lucky broke my way," he said. "I was at a small Division III school, and the firms I was interested in didn't even come here."

Tyler thinks of school in terms of NCAA divisions because he happens to be a talented lacrosse player. Toward the end of his final season, he went to his coach and asked if he could get a list of lacrosse alumni and their current contacts. The coach had it easily available since he often invited alums to celebrate at post-game parties (and maybe make a donation).

Tyler noticed one guy on the list who had worn the same number he did—and had even played the same midfield position—twenty years earlier. He now ran an insurance business in Atlanta.

"I sent him a picture of myself in uniform with the number clearly visible and told him that I'd be very interested in his company," Tyler said. "I wrote: 'As you know, midfielders are the backbone of any team.'" A couple of days later he got a call from the alum.

"I checked with the coach, and he said you've got speed, stamina, and hustle," the alum said.

"And determination," Tyler added.

"Lots of determination, obviously," the alum said with a laugh.

After two trips to Atlanta (and a winning lacrosse season), Tyler had a job.

"I think my parents were embarrassed that I got the job through lacrosse connections—like they'd spent all this money for college and the only thing that paid off was my stick-handling. But I figure whatever makes you lucky is okay."

In this case, I have to agree with Tyler rather than his parents. He knew the kind of job he wanted, and when luck didn't naturally come his way, he made the luck for himself. The fact that Tyler and the alum played the same position and wore the same number was definitely a bit of random chance. But Tyler then had to capture the luck by being skillful enough to recognize the opportunity and find a creative way to pursue it. Chance, talent, and effort—and bingo, you seem lucky.

I wondered if I could be exaggerating the need for connections to keep you from the tossed-résumé pile until I talked to Jack, a thirty-one-year-old executive at a quickly expanding e-commerce site. Smart and hardworking, Jack is exactly the kind of inspired and thoughtful manager most people would like as a boss. He's figured out that supporting the people on his team works out for everyone.

Jack needed to hire some twenty people when he started out, and the human resources group flooded him with hundreds of elegant résumés (and properly written cover letters) from applicants who boasted of impressive colleges and business schools and wide-ranging experience. How do you make the distinctions?

"Most of the people I hired had made some effort to reach out to me directly, or they tracked down someone in the company who could put in a good word," Jack said. He wanted people who were self-starting and could take charge—and making the effort to connect with him was one way to prove their skill. Networking or weak ties gave them an edge. "I hadn't really planned it that way, but when someone shows they're eager and goes that extra step, you notice them."

The new online company was acquired by a bigger firm—and Jack and everyone he hired seemed very lucky when their stock options were paid out at a generous number. But they had gotten lucky by reason of making good connections to start with.

Some people look at networking of that sort as being slightly disreputable, as if they're stealing an advantage they don't really deserve. And sometimes it can make you feel a little queasy. When the HBO show *Girls* was first announced, I remember being a little taken aback by the cast. Creator Lena Dunham had selected three women to costar with her, and two of them—Allison Williams and Zosia Mamet—had famous parents and the third, Jemima Kirke, was Dunham's high school friend.[1] All were talented, but I kept thinking about all the equally talented young actresses who didn't have their edge. I pictured rows of young actresses standing in line for their audition, not knowing the odds were stacked against them. It didn't seem fair.

But then a funny thing happened. Over six seasons on the air, Williams and Mamet and Kirke so defined their characters that it was impossible to think of anybody else in their roles. Mamet continued honing her skills, and I went to see her in an off-Broadway play in which she was stunningly good. And that's when I realized—connections can give you a foot in the door, but just like any other lucky break, what really matters is what you do with them.[2]

Still, the networks and weak ties that make luck for some people effectively block the path for others. In terms of social mobility and possibilities for everyone, we need to think about ways to distribute opportunities equitably in work and finance and entertainment. And some people are doing exactly that. My friend Julian Johnson

---

1. Allison's dad, Brian Williams, was then the anchor of the NBC evening news, and Zosia's father, David Mamet, was a renowned playwright. Dunham, then just twenty-three, had to realize—consciously or not—that in launching a new show, it couldn't hurt to have a famous playwright and a powerful broadcaster on your side. Her high school friend Jemima Kirke also had an impressive pedigree—her father had played drums with two big rock groups.
2. An even more curious thing . . . Williams's father was deposed from his position at NBC by a scandal, and Mamet's dad wrote a couple of terrible plays. The daughters became more successful than the dads.

is the executive vice-president of Sponsors for Educational Opportunity (SEO), a nonprofit that offers career programs for students from underserved communities. If you want that job at Goldman Sachs but come from a poor town in southern Alabama, Julian might be your guy. Over the years, he and his colleagues have helped thousands of minority students land jobs in finance and law and investment banking.

"We help create networks for people who don't have them," Julian told me. Minority students at small schools, for example, might not have any obvious route to Wall Street since investment banks usually offer jobs to students from only a few select colleges. But SEO makes the network much wider. You provide the hard work and determination—and they'll make sure you get the opportunities to connect with the right people.[3] When Julian and I spoke, SEO had students from 105 different colleges about to start in summer internships. That's a large number of schools. SEO was opening lucky doors for a lot of people—and they expected that 80 percent of the interns would get full-time offers.

Julian pointed out that to make luck in your career, you need to do more than study and work hard. That might have paid off in grades K–12, but in the real world, it's no longer enough. Instead of keeping your head down and expecting the work to speak for itself, you need to find mentors and advisors and sponsors who will help you advance. Julian told me that the SEO teams stay with the students after they get the internships to help them understand how to ascend within the company—"because your network becomes your net worth."

---

3. SEO provides training, too. College students get thirty hours of coaching just to prepare for their first interview with an investment bank

Personal channels open unexpected paths, and wherever you start in life, you owe it to yourself to develop and take advantage of them. You have to give yourself a fair shot. Whether it's your dad or a hairdresser or a varsity teammate (some years removed) or an organization like SEO, opening your networks changes your luck.

My friend David Edell has been thinking about luck in careers for a long time now—at least in part because he knows that he's the guy who sometimes delivers it. As the head of DRG, an executive search firm that deals mostly with nonprofit organizations, he has placed more than a thousand top executives in their jobs. To find them, he has approached tens of thousands of people who weren't expecting to hear from him at all.

David and his wife, Marsha, happen to live across the street from me in Manhattan, so one rainy evening I crossed the street and joined him for a drink in his pretty apartment. As an executive recruiter, David told me that he knew how surprising it could be to some people when they heard from him.

"I'm the random phone call—the guy who calls and says, 'Hi, I have this good opportunity and thought you might be interested,'" David said with a smile. "You have just come back from lunch and weren't thinking about changing jobs, and now I present an opportunity that you had no clue even existed. So the question is—what do you do when that drops into your lap?"

From long experience, David has found that people typically fall into one of three categories. He described the first group as people who "throw up a hundred defenses right away as to why it won't work." Sometimes the problem is real life getting in the way of opportunity (if your teenager is a junior in high school, you may not want to move), and sometimes they're just uncomfortable with change.

People in the second group are also slightly wary and show it by "digging in and asking a lot of questions—who they'll report to, why the last guy got fired, what their responsibilities would be. They want all the information before deciding whether to even have the conversation." Then there's the third group—"the people who listen and say, 'Great. I wasn't expecting your call, but I'm in.'"

David finds the initial response to be a good measure of how the person will do going forward. The naysayers in the first group usually won't work out even if they change their mind and decide to pursue the opportunity. Those in the second group who ask a lot of questions may be thoughtful and analytic—and David appreciates that. But he's also careful to see if they're the kind of people who will continue to throw obstacles in the way and find reasons not to go ahead. Those in the third group are most likely to be successful at recognizing new and lucky opportunities—but he wants to be sure that they're not reckless.

"Luck comes to the people who have the courage to recognize an opportunity when it arises and are open to thinking about how to operationalize it," he said.

David had his own experience with an unexpected opportunity very early in his career when he was working as a fund raiser for a very large nonprofit organization. "And then the craziest thing—I got a call from Citizen watch company asking if I'd teach their salesmen how to sell watches. I was thirty years old and didn't know a thing about watches." One of the top executives had seen him in action as a fund raiser, knew he was persuasive and good on his feet, and recommended him. "So I went to the Acapulco Princess in Mexico for five days with my wife and did sales training for a $75 million watch company. Courageous? Okay, yes. Lucky that it came my way and I didn't screw it up? Definitely. It was always a reminder for me going forward that when you have opportunities, you take them."

David continued leading those sales trainings for several years and began to see opportunities for himself outside fund-raising. Taking an expansive view of his own career, he made the leap to start his own executive search firm. From his own experience, he encourages people to have a general sense of what's on their radar but not to be *too* focused on exactly what they want.

"Creating luck doesn't mean taking every opportunity. But it does mean that you have to be open to exploring whether yes or no is the right answer," he said. He doesn't mind pursuing a possibility with someone—and ultimately getting a well-reasoned no. He's very respectful when people present him with the specifics of why they're turning down one opportunity and can explain what it would take instead for their next step.

"The other side of that is adopting a willy-nilly strategy so the next call you get is the next job you take," he said. "That leaves you depending on randomness rather than generating any real luck."

A call from David (or someone like him) can seem like the ultimate out-of-the-blue bolt of good luck—but to David, it's not random at all. Someone has told David that a particular person is worth meeting.

"When I'm doing a search, I rely on people to tell me about the talented people they've encountered. I'll hear: 'Oh, you should meet Joe because he's doing interesting stuff.' Or 'I heard him speak at a conference and he was really good.' The things you do create the opportunities."

You can advance your professional profile—and get noticed—by speaking at conferences or being part of committees or writing interesting papers or blogs. David doesn't think of it as networking as much as enhancing your profile and letting the world know about the good work you're doing. But shouldn't good work speak for itself?

"Sometimes it does," David said with a smile. "I might hear that somebody has been doing interesting work, so I'll call them. But then they have to speak about the work, right? They have to want the opportunity and take the next step."

Barnaby and I chatted about the jobs we'd each had over the years—and we were surprised to realize that between us, we had hardly ever applied for a job. We didn't have to worry about the tossed-résumés problem because we'd never really submitted résumés. We'd always taken an alternate way around.

My career had followed a one-thing-leads-to-another pattern. Many times an executive I worked with in one job asked me to come with her to another—and I did. It wasn't carefully planned, but sometimes the best way to make a career (and a happy life) is to recognize opportunities when they come and grab them. When I first got a job as a TV producer, I didn't even own a TV.

Barnaby always created his own lucky directions and took even less traditional routes. His parents were both risk takers who retired early from executive posts and moved to Alaska with their five children. When he was about seven or eight, Barnaby lived with his family in the middle of the woods with no clocks or calendars, no electricity or running water. He spent a lot of time relying on himself and watching out for bears. He couldn't rely on standard paths because there weren't any. He had to find his own solutions.

Barnaby told me that his first real job before college was with Disney—and he certainly didn't find it online. Back then, he thought it would be exciting to study the behavior of unusual birds. So he went to visit the curator of Discovery Island (a precursor of Disney's Animal Kingdom theme park) and asked if he could study the varieties in their collection.

"No such job existed," Barnaby said, "but I was sufficiently excited about the idea that the director made up a position for me on the spot."

Barnaby's first research was on a large bird called the brush turkey, which comes from the deep rain forests of northeastern Australia and spends its time scraping dead leaves into a giant compost mound. The leaf compost generates heat and can then be used as a nest. Clever, right? Studying compost may not sound like *your* dream job, but Barnaby was so passionate about his work that he became a popular character at the wildlife park. He even became the subject of a coloring book the park used. Keeping his luck going, Barnaby announced that he was curious about the behavior of vultures. He wanted to follow those residing at the park—and why not? Disney arranged for him to use a private airplane that was specially fitted with radio-tracking devices.

I'd like to say you can't make this stuff up—only you *can* make it up. That's the whole point about creating your own luck. As a little side note, Barnaby told me that Walt Disney himself understood about making your luck—he failed many times in business but never gave up. Early on, Walt applied for a position as a postal clerk and was rejected as too young. He came back, dressed better and having penciled in a shadow of facial hair. He got the job. Another time, Walt was fired from a job because someone said he "lacked imagination and had no good ideas." If you want to get lucky, you persist. You create your own magic kingdom.

Personalized jobs come when somebody trusts you and is willing to take a flier on an original idea. Some years ago, I got a job that had never existed before, creating television shows for a popular magazine brand. I spent five happy years in the role. One of the shows I produced was a multiyear TV awards special that attracted some of the biggest names in television at the time. In one of my favorite personal pictures from the first year of the show, my husband and I are walking down the red carpet. He's handsome in black tie, and I've been decked out by a publicist in a borrowed designer dress that shimmers in the lights and a million dollars' worth of diamonds on loan from a store on Rodeo Drive. Talk about luck!

"A perfect way to get lucky is to follow a passion and make up your own position," Barnaby said.

My older son, Zach, got the concept of making your own luck when he was still in school and attended a campus talk by the president of an online-payments company. Zach went up to the executive afterward, said how much he admired the company, and asked if they could get together. The president agreed to a meeting—but just to give advice and information. He didn't have any openings for a student with Zach's background.

Zach came to the meeting well prepared—always a way to make yourself lucky—but he also listened carefully. As the president described how they were trying to reach customers, Zach offered an idea on how collecting and analyzing a certain kind of data might be helpful. The president nodded thoughtfully. He hadn't thought about that approach before—and he asked if Zach might be able to do it.

"Yes, I'd be excited to take it on," Zach said.

"Can you start this afternoon?" the president asked.

"Happy to," Zach said.

You don't have to worry about your résumé being tossed away if you're sitting with your would-be boss and solving a problem for him. Having something very specific to offer changes an answer from "can't use you" to "can you start this afternoon?" Working at this very cool company looked to Zach's friends like the ultimate in good luck. But it was luck that he had made.

Proud of my kid? You bet.

Wanting to avoid the vagaries of randomness, more and more people are trying to make luck by going in their own direction. Sometimes the best way to end up in the third stack is to be in a spot where those first two stacks don't even exist. Or as a very successful friend of ours put it, "People always talk about thinking outside the box. I never even knew the box existed."

In an increasingly entrepreneurial world, the barriers to entry in most fields keep getting lower (you can now create a company with a laptop instead of a factory). So abandoning standard career paths and making your own trail isn't crazy—it could be one way of entering the good luck club.

Barnaby suggested I meet a young woman named Rebecca Kantar who was a master of going her own way and creating luck. In her mid-twenties, she was already a serial entrepreneur. So one afternoon we headed over to the offices of the Gerson Lehrman Group (GLG), where she sometimes works. It was one of those super-chic spaces where you immediately feel that everyone around must be cooler than you. The front area featured red and orange chairs in a flex space, an upside-down fish tank, and hanging lights in the shape of brass globes. Behind the cool spaces were rows and rows of people on computers.

Smiling, Kantar came out to greet us. Slim and graceful with long blond hair and a beguiling style, she could have easily passed for a high school cheerleader. But she's not and never was. When we sat down at a corner table, Kantar quickly admitted that she's always been an original, going in her own direction. She surprised everyone a few years ago when she decided to drop out of Harvard after her sophomore year. She considered it a good way to get lucky.

"The average income for Harvard dropouts is higher than for Harvard graduates," she said briskly.

Barnaby suggested that maybe the average was being skewed by the outsize fortune of Harvard dropout (and Facebook founder) Mark Zuckerberg.

"Yes, Zuckerberg and Bill Gates and Matt Damon were all Harvard dropouts who raise the average," Kantar said. She liked to see herself in their mode. She too wanted to be an original who took big risks and looked very lucky when they paid off. When she was at Harvard, she hadn't felt inspired by her classes and didn't see where her degree would lead.

"My parents were panicked, but I tried to talk them through and ask what they were worried about," she said. "My mom pointed out that I wouldn't be able to get a traditional job in investment banking or consulting without a college degree—but I said I didn't want one. She also worried about what would happen if I eventually wanted to go into politics. I said that my generation would like to see someone who had done something interesting rather than just what's expected."

Kantar had gone in her own directions from an early age. Growing up in suburban Newton, Massachusetts, she took Chinese, got obsessed with origami, and played the trumpet. For her bat mitzvah, she took her friends snow tubing ("I hated dance parties"), and later in middle school, she started asking her (baffled) parents for a donkey.

"I thought it would be nice to have one in the backyard. No particular reason. I liked donkeys," Kantar said with a smile.

Trying to avoid a bigger argument, her parents explained that their suburban home wasn't zoned for farm animals. Kantar was too young to drive, so she walked over to city hall one afternoon and filed a petition for rezoning. She got it. (But she still didn't get the donkey.)

The donkey story pretty much summed up Kantar's attitude. Go after things that are different. In high school, she didn't want to take the standard classes and asked to devise her own curriculum. The school said no. So she wrote to the deans of the Ivy League schools where she had applied and said she wanted to quit her AP classes and do an independent study project for the rest of the year. What did they think of that? Most of them responded that it would be just fine. Rebecca spent the rest of senior year outside the classroom. "It was the best academic experience I had," she said.

While she was still at Harvard, Rebecca developed a company called BrightCo, which connected young entrepreneurs with corporations and investors who could use their insights. The idea was that the younger group knew about innovations that might upend the traditional models.

"Coca-Cola might not know that some twenty-year-olds were developing a sprayable caffeine that could completely disrupt their business," Kantar explained. "So we put them together."

The company was still small when Kantar dropped out, and she knew it would never be Facebook. But eventually GLG made an offer to buy it. GLG has become hugely successful by connecting experts with the businesspeople and investors who want their information. They were really buying Rebecca's brain—and gave her the title of entrepreneur in residence.

Kantar is now developing a company to change how testing is done for both colleges and employment. She is convinced that the standard tests currently being used—whether IQ tests or SATs or personality analyses—don't find the original thinking that is most important for success.

"People who are pointy-headed or jagged in some way are the ones who create big lucky change," she said. "You have to let them go their own way. We need sheep in the world, but when you find the black eccentric sheep, let them be blacker."

Kantar recognizes that going along a standard path puts a floor on bad outcomes. "If you go to Harvard, the worst that can happen is you become a cog at an investment bank," she said. "But dropping out creates a huge possibility tree for better or worse."

When we left, Barnaby told me that a few months earlier, he was at an elite conference of innovators that Kantar told him she wanted to attend. He made inquiries with the organizers on her behalf, and when she didn't get one of the coveted invitations, she still found a way get inside. I was impressed. Even though Kantar looked like a cheerleader, she apparently had the ferocity and intensity of a Navy SEAL. When she had a mission, she didn't let anything get in her way.

When someone is an original, you never know what will happen. Kantar could end up being the next Steve Jobs—or she could end up with no jobs at all. Trying to crash the party, you sometimes just crash instead.

Being willing to take unusual risks is one more way you can get lucky in a job. Sometimes it pays off big, and sometimes it doesn't. Yet failing isn't always a bad thing. Barnaby told me about a conversation he had with Naveen Jain, the entrepreneur who founded a company called InfoSpace in the late 1990s. It was briefly one of the largest internet companies in the country—making Jain worth some $8 billion. Then came the dot-com crash and a series of lawsuits, and suddenly his stake was more in the $200 million range.

"Failing is part of becoming good," Jain told Barnaby when they talked recently. "In basketball, the best player on the best day will only score about 50 percent, and the other 50 percent aren't considered failures but part of the success. Fail well."

Interested in space exploration, Jain cofounded a company in 2010 called Moon Express, trying to be the first to land a robotic spacecraft on the moon and send back images. He has secured a launch contract with NASA.[4]

"Life depends on your outlook," Jain said. "For any new venture, you think, 'What can happen?' and 'What could be possible?' This prepares you for both good luck and bad luck, which are going to be coming in the future."

Jain was convinced that going in your own direction requires some risks—but once these are analyzed, they may not be as dramatic as they seem. In his view, for example, having a private company try to get to the moon wasn't crazy at all.

"For space travel, government tries to eliminate 99.99 percent of risks because failure is not a political option. The last 1 percent of the risk abatement adds 99 percent of the cost," he said. A private company can make the unmanned rocket "good enough"—then buy private insurance to cover the cost if something goes wrong. Jain sees that as a metaphor for how to lead other pursuits.

---

4. At this writing, he was one of five teams still competing for the Google Lunar XPRIZE. The winner needs to land a robotic vehicle on the moon, travel at least 500 meters, and send back high-definition images. There's about $30 million in prizes at stake.

"Forgo making it absolutely as safe as possible," he said. "Nothing is ever 100 percent safe anyway."

You have to know yourself and your own willingness to take risks. Barnaby and Rebecca Kantar are probably the types who would climb on Jain's spaceship and see where it took them. I'm not sure I would. I'm willing to get lucky through making the right connections, working hard, and taking opportunities, but I'm not a big risk taker. Some people will probably get a lot luckier with a willingness to try a completely unknown approach.

Trying to get lucky by going your own way doesn't work every time, but when it does, you end up with one of those stories showing the value of being original. So, for example, Barnaby didn't drop out of college like Kantar did, but he did switch universities several times, moving from Harvard to Cornell to a year of research at Oxford. (He actually planned it all, wanting to work with the world-renowned ornithology professors at each.) Later, he wanted to win a Rhodes scholarship to return to Oxford and needed to be endorsed by his school. Cornell initially said they couldn't support him because he didn't have enough credits on their campus. Barnaby went higher and higher in the administration, finally banging on the president's door. He figures that he contacted close to fifty people in various capacities to get support for his application.

"It wasn't the standard approach, but in this case, being original made me stand out," Barnaby told me. "I met a lot of people, and some of them even became new friends."

Whether you want to get to the moon or win a Rhodes scholarship or land a job at Goldman Sachs, you get lucky when you make your own path. Sure, some randomness can come into play. But you'll expect that ahead of time and do everything to work around it. You'll put yourself in the third résumé stack—instead of one of the others that might be tossed away. You'll speak to the right people, find your own direction, and be willing to stand out. It won't work every time—and you might get a chance to learn from your failures—but when it does, you'll look very, very lucky.

CHAPTER ELEVEN

Get Lucky in Love

Don't expect a supermodel to make you lucky. . . . Invest in the relationship. . . . Look for love in new places. . . . Pick the right grazing ground.

My husband and I recently marked a big anniversary with a dreamy trip to South Africa. We stayed one night at a glorious hotel called Le Quartier Français and indulged in a nine-course dinner (yes, *nine* courses) in a famed restaurant called the Tasting Room. Over crazy good food, we held hands, stared moonily at each other, and talked about our amazing good luck. We still made each other laugh, shared the same sense of adventure (all those lions and rhinos in Africa!), and had been great partners in raising our two terrific sons.

It was probably enough to make anybody overhearing us want to throw up.

But it wasn't until much later that I thought about *how* we had gotten so lucky. Was it random chance that I had stumbled on the perfect guy all those years ago? Out of seven billion people in the world, had I somehow found (at age twenty-four) the one person destined to be my soul mate?

I wish I could be that romantic. Sure, Ron was handsome and fit, and as a doctor, he had a kind, caring style that I admired. But, as I suspected after all the research I'd been doing, our luck in love had less to do with the magic of meeting the right person than with the effort we had put in afterward. Nicholas Sparks would never sell a book if he wrote about the nitty-gritty that makes a good marriage—turning the other cheek when one person is snitty and turning to the other side of the bed when the other person is snoring. But ultimately, those are the twists and turns that make others think it was all just good luck.

Most of us are realistic about what it means to be lucky in love. In the national survey Barnaby and I conducted, only 7 percent said that you needed to find the perfect person. The very largest number—a full 80 percent—said that the secret to being lucky in love was to pay attention to the other person's needs as much as to your own.

Back home over a more normal one-course dinner (grilled chicken and vegetables), I asked Ron what he thought had made us lucky in love.

"Probably Netflix," he said.

"Netflix?" I asked, puzzled.

"Right. We can never find anything to watch because you're trying to pick something I'll like, and I want to pick what you'll like. It cuts down on how many movies we see. But it's why we feel very lucky with each other."

I liked that explanation. When you let the other person's desires ride as high in importance as what you want (and your partner does the same), you both feel loved and lucky and supported. Ron's definition of lucky in love matched our survey. But there are some bold names who would contribute a different view.

On his first solo album in 1985, Mick Jagger roared out a song called "Lucky in Love." For the racy rock star with the wandering hips, the song was a fairly obvious way to boast about sexual conquest. He might be unlucky as a gambler with cards, horses, roulette, and craps, but he could crow that with women, it was easy. "Yes, I've got the winning touch," he bellowed.

Jagger is one of those guys who (in the teenage parlance) get lucky on a regular basis. Model Jerry Hall hung around to have four children with him, even though she knew he was unfaithful from the beginning. He has fathered a host of children with half a dozen different mothers and has managed to keep the sex-symbol moniker well into his seventies. He's clearly lucky at sex. And if he says he's lucky at love, we believe him.

But Jagger's definition of luck isn't shared by as many people as you may think. Soon after our trip to South Africa, I was on a book-tour stop in Iowa and met a woman named Phoebe who told me that she had been married to her high school sweetheart, Al, for more than forty years. The two of them had never been with anyone but each other. (Or so she said. I didn't press.)

"Nobody could be luckier than me," Phoebe said, reaching over to take his hand.

Her adored husband was slightly balding, with a belly that spilled over the top of his khaki shorts. They didn't have any children, but they had a mostly blind (and beloved) German shepherd and a little cabin on a lake two hours away that they retreated to on warm weekends.

"The love nest?" I asked, teasing.

"No, just a cabin that's falling apart," she said with a little smile.

An accountant, Al had lost his job a couple of years earlier and was working from home as a consultant.

"He doesn't get a lot of work, but I still have my job as a nurse, and we manage just fine," she said.

Adding up all the elements—the lost job, the schlumpy appearance, and the falling-apart cabin—it occurred to me that at least superficially, some people might think Phoebe wasn't so lucky in love after all. But Phoebe was dedicated to Al and had a way of looking for the good in him. Focusing on the positive and giving lots of love and support made them both feel lucky.

Phoebe had clearly found a formula that esteemed psychologist Barry Schwartz would immediately understand.

"A lucky relationship is created, not discovered," Dr. Schwartz said when Barnaby and I called him one morning.

A longtime professor at Swarthmore, Dr. Schwartz became nationally known for his surprising research on the paradox of choice. (He popularized it with a book of that name and many TED talks.) He showed that while we think having many choices will make us happier, it actually leaves us less satisfied. When you have too many options, you're always thinking about the alternatives that you passed up.

Dr. Schwartz joked about how happy he used to be years ago when his local store offered only one kind of jeans. Then along came choices like slim fit, easy fit, relaxed fit, button fly, stone-washed, acid-washed . . . and on and on. Now when he leaves the store, the jeans fit much better, but he feels much worse. Adding options increases expectations, which, he said, "produces less satisfaction with results, even when they're good results."

What's true for jeans is equally true for spouses. "If you're looking to find the best, you're never going to put in the time and effort to make what you *have* the best," he told us. "It's the Tinder effect. Why invest the time and commitment necessary to make a relationship grow when another option is just a swipe away?"

Married for more than fifty years, Dr. Schwartz has been investing in his own marriage for a long time. "We've known each other a lot longer than that—she was my best friend in eighth grade. So she doesn't like it when I talk about finding a spouse who is 'good enough,'" he said with a laugh. "But really, that's what you want."

Phoebe might similarly object to the idea that her husband is "good enough." But it's pretty clear that whatever his traits, she got lucky in love by investing effort and taking positive actions, including holding hands, sharing smiles, and visiting that cabin. Like Dr. Schwartz and his wife, Phoebe and Al met when they were young (in high school, in their case), and they have stayed close to their hometown.

"Living in a small town, you have fewer options, so you're more likely to be of the mind-set to find someone and see what you can make of it," said Dr. Schwartz. "You don't have as many distractions."

Nobody likes the idea of "settling" for a spouse, but Dr. Schwartz points out that we're usually lousy at knowing how to evaluate potential mates, anyway. After all these years, he knows that his wife is kind, empathetic, and intelligent and has a fierce moral core—plus she's the great first reader for everything he writes. But he didn't focus on any of that when they met. "I was attracted to her because she was the first girl I ever met who loved baseball—more specifically, the New York Yankees. Liking the damn Yankees—what kind of basis is that for a relationship?"

Obviously, it was a good one. Or good enough. If you get your lucky-in-love ideas from Hollywood romantic comedies, you would probably focus the script on the beginning of the story: Barry and Myrna meet as kids and become best friends, he works hard to make her his girlfriend, and eventually they get married. Music plays. Fade to black. End of story.

But the luck of their marriage wasn't made the day they met or the day of the wedding ceremony. That was really the beginning of the story, not the end. The real relationship developed in the following years as they trusted each other and turned to each other for support and love.

"You always hear people say, 'Oh, they're so lucky they found each other.' But no. Really, they found each other and turned it into something others wanted. That luck happens much more often than kismet," said Dr. Schwartz.

The fantasy version can make for the unluckiest relationships around—because when you focus only on the days leading up to the wedding, you forget to think about what happens afterward. And it's in that afterward when the marriage—and the real luck of love— kicks in.

A successful financier I'll call Troy thought he was the luckiest guy in the world when he started dating a Victoria's Secret model. His friends were appropriately wide-eyed and jealous. Dating a gorgeous woman known for posing in a bra and panties could provide the ultimate opportunity for a Mick Jagger–like chance to swagger. *"I'm so lucky, I'm so lucky. . . ."*

The luck continued, or so it seemed, culminating in a yummy wedding much shared on social media. But then real life kicked in. It's a good bet that a guy who dates a knockout beautiful model (we'll call her Helen) is a type A, high-testosterone sort who likes to be the center of attention. Troy could strut all he wanted in the bedroom, but when they went out in public, he suddenly found himself regularly pushed into the background. Photographers wanted to get shots of Helen on the red carpet—and could he please step aside? There was always a flurry when they walked into a chic restaurant—but again, all eyes were on her, not him. He found himself resentful of how long it took her to get ready to go out, the amount she spent on clothes, and the fact that she seemed slightly more in love with herself than with him.

The luck ended with a very expensive divorce.

When you think about being lucky in love, you need to have a longer view than just the thrill of walking down the aisle. The person who is fun to date may not be the one who will make you feel loved (and lucky) in the good times and bad that come into everyone's life. The wedding industry may be the unluckiest thing that has happened to love. Expensive bands and flowers don't do anything for a happy marriage.

Once again, talent (in this case, the ability to be kind and forgiving) and hard work are at play in making luck. But what about the random chance of meeting your future mate in the first place? If you're single, finding the right person to marry can seem like an endless minefield. Helen Fisher, the biological anthropologist who has become one of the world's experts on love, met Barnaby and me one morning for breakfast to talk about dating and getting lucky in love. Blond and slim, Fisher has been at the love game for a long time, but she has the huge energy and glowing skin of someone half her age. And she's still excited by love.

"You're trying to win life's greatest prize—which is a life partner and a chance to send your DNA to the future," she said, munching on a healthy bowl of fresh fruit. "But going out on dates can feel like a job, and it takes work. You have to dress up and be charming and have clean hair."

Fisher is a research fellow at the Kinsey Institute and has an academic appointment at Rutgers University—but she currently gets a lot of attention for being the chief scientific advisor to the website Match.com. Everyone who talks to her wants to know how technology has changed love. And while she says that 40 percent of singles have dated somebody they met online, she's adamant that technology can't change love at all.

"The brain is powerfully built to find love, and anthropological studies tell us that 90 percent of any interaction is nonverbal. When you're with someone, the ancient human brain will click in and tell you if it's right," she said.

So despite being paid well by online dating sites, she says her first rule for getting lucky is to get out and connect in person. "I don't care whether you first meet at a church or a Starbucks or online— the only real algorithm is your own brain."

She shares Barry Schwartz's position that too many choices can undermine love. Stay online too long and you get overwhelmed. (There's always someone else a few clicks away!) She advises that you check out five to nine people on Match.com or any other match-making site, then stop and get to know *one* of them. "Go out there and be enthusiastic and interested. The more you get to know some-body, the more you like them," she said.

If you want to get lucky, you may need to expand your view of what you think you want. So, for example, Fisher has found that people on dating websites often give very specific outlines of the characteristics they need in a partner—and then connect with peo-ple who have completely different traits. It's a little like claiming that you want to watch BBC documentaries and then streaming ten old episodes of *Friends*. Are you sure you know what's going to make you happy? The algorithms on some of the dating apps are now taking into account what you do as well as what you say.

When asked about people who complain how difficult it is to meet someone special, Dr. Fisher just sighed. "We make our own luck by going to places where luck might happen. If you love opera, go to opera events. If you love art, go to events at the museum. If you care about money, go where the rich hang out. Eighty-seven percent of Americans will eventually marry, but you don't get there by staying home watching *Westworld*."

So what's the best place to meet a mate? When we talked about it later, Barnaby pointed out that luck comes more from the strength of the connections than from the power of the numbers. You're more likely to find love among the 125 people at a friend's wedding than among 20,000 fellow revelers at a football game. (If you want to connect to a potential partner, strike up a conversation over the dessert buffet rather than at the stadium hot dog stand.) Confidence, a positive mind-set, and an openness to possibility help make you lucky in love.

From his studies across many fields, Barnaby found that you're most likely to get lucky when you pay attention to where you'll find the best opportunities. And that means the best opportunities for *you*. Remember the idea Barnaby described earlier of ideal free distribution? Animals have a natural tendency to aggregate in certain areas where they're most likely to find food and mates. In human terms, that's called happy hour at a bar. They seem to know quite naturally where to gather relative to the resources available. If there's an area of thick vegetation good for grazing, you'll find lots of (say) deer there and fewer deer in the less-dense area across the field. That way there's plenty for everybody. Once too many deer are gathered in the same place, some will (reasonably enough) drift to another spot. Once again, there's enough for everyone.

It helps to remember that in the dating world, there's enough for everyone, too. Think about what advantages you have and what your peers are doing—and then you can reasonably figure out how to make your own luck. You can go to the bar where all the coolest, richest, and sexiest people hang out, because that's where you have the best chance of meeting a cool, rich, and sexy Mr. or Ms. Right. But if everyone else is gathering there, too, then you're all competing for the same, well, resources. Where there is more opportunity, there is a greater density of competitors. If you're the kind of person who can compete in that setting, then step right up and order a martini. But if you don't stand out amid the noise, maybe you have a better chance of getting lucky (in meeting someone, that is) at the quieter coffee shop down the block.

To be lucky in love, you need to know what you're aiming for—and that's not the same for everyone. If you want a very specific type of mate, demand and supply might not match. (Sorry, nothing is perfect.) To return to Barnaby's animal analogy for a moment, some get lucky by grazing on grass and others by browsing on trees—and setting the right target sets you up for subsequent luck. If you don't have the right target, you miss out on the luck.

Dr. Fisher herself got married once when she was young but jettisoned that relationship quickly and has never married again. She spent thirty years in a close, loving relationship with a man considerably older than she was, and after his death, she had several other involvements. Now she's attached to a new man and working out whether it's the perfect fit. In a little aside, she whispered that she likes him a lot, but they don't share all the same interests. Was the problem a deal-breaker—or just one of those things that you have to manage for a happy relationship?

Like everyone else, Dr. Fisher is trying to figure out what would make her feel lucky in love. She contends that we have evolved with three kinds of love: sex drive, romantic love, and attachment to a partner. All have a biological basis. The evolutionary reason for a sex drive is obvious, since evolution can't happen without it. Dr. Fisher said attachment is also an innate drive "that evolved so you can tolerate each other long enough to raise a child."

Ah, but what about romantic love, the stuff of myth and legend and Shakespeare's best plays? Dr. Fisher says it's also a basic drive. She and two colleagues once did an experiment where they put people who were intensely in love into fMRI scanners to study their brain function. They concluded that the neurochemical dopamine is closely connected to romantic love.

"There's a little factory in the base of the brain that makes dopamine, and it's right next to the regions that regulate thirst and hunger. Those are very basic drives—you don't get rid of them," Dr. Fisher told us.

Romantic love (all that dopamine!) may be an even more powerful drive than sex or attachment. Dr. Fisher pointed out that you don't kill yourself because somebody won't have sex with you—but the end of a great romance can lead to rage and anger and even suicide. Call it the Romeo and Juliet syndrome—"thus with a kiss I die."

In the throes of romantic love, you readily overlook the flaws of your partner because the brain creates a happy blur of positive illusion. When the romance dwindles, you notice more, and sometimes that's when you stop feeling so lucky. (Hello, Troy and his supermodel Helen.) Dr. Fisher thinks that maintaining some of those positive illusions—or at least focusing on what you like in the person rather than what you don't—is part of what keeps you feeling lucky into the attachment stage. Just ask Phoebe from Iowa.

The one little hitch to being lucky in love is that the three systems—romance, sex, and attachment—don't always point in the same direction. You can snuggle in bed next to the person to whom you're deeply attached and still feel a wild sex drive for somebody else. "There's always a committee meeting going on in your head," said Dr. Fisher.

Around the world and across all cultures, the seven-year itch turns out to be more like the four-year itch. Biology seems to have programmed couples to stay together long enough to raise a child out of infancy. And then evolution prefers that we have a new partner for genetic diversity. Yes, we can fight it, but as the poet Lord Byron railed in his epic *Don Juan*, "how the devil is it that fresh features / Have such a charm for us poor human creatures?"

A man I've known since he was a rakish bachelor is now happily married with two grown children, an expansive house in Santa Monica, and a ranch in Colorado. Did I say happily married? He had his first affair when his wife got pregnant with their oldest child, and since then he's had a new romance every couple of years. (I haven't kept up recently.)

He has maintained a charade of fidelity over the years, claiming he never wanted to hurt his wife. But everybody else knew what he was up to, and since his wife seems reasonably perceptive, best guess is that she likes her homes, her children, and her comfy life, and in the grand tradition of rich men's wives everywhere, she's happy to look the other way. She has the attachment part of her husband's love and won't worry where the sex drive wanders.

Is she lucky in love? I wouldn't trade places with her. Though she does have some excellent jewelry.

Thinking about Mick Jagger and Phoebe and my philandering friend, I wondered what scorecard made me so certain that Ron and I were lucky in love. On Dr. Fisher's scale, I could currently check romance, sex, *and* attachment—so three for three seemed as lucky as you get. But it was important to look at the time frame, too. Can you be lucky all the time? Over the years, we'd had small squabbles and big clashes and wasted weekends being angry instead of amorous. Our marriage wasn't always perfect. At weddings, I sometimes think that the best gift I could give the bride and groom is a note that reads: "You'll have some bad days!" But nobody wants to hear that. Maybe I could just slip a message inside the Cuisinart box saying that the real secret to luck in marriage is just deciding that you'll stay together, no matter what.

Barnaby and I had arranged to talk with Duke psychologist and behavioral economist Dan Ariely, famous for his research into the irrational ways that people behave. If you've ever spent twenty minutes online looking for the cheapest price on Rice Krispies and then gone out for a fancy dinner, you know what he means by irrational. With all Dr. Ariely's research, I wondered if he'd come up with any insights on the rational way to get lucky in love.

You bet he had.

"We have to get out of the mind-set of thinking you're looking for the best person in the world—because the best person in the world doesn't exist and looking is futile," he said bluntly. "At some point you say, 'This person is wonderful.' Maybe somebody out there is more wonderful, but I don't want to keep searching."

Uh-oh. Dr. Ariely is a much admired professor, but that sounded a lot like . . . settling. But Dr. Ariely was, of course, coming at this from a very rational perspective. He and Barnaby began discussing a classic example economists use that has been dubbed "the secretary problem" and is simply a way of looking at how you know when to stop any search. The formula is that an executive needs to hire an assistant, so he begins interviewing and looking for the right person.[1] He wants someone terrific—but every day that he doesn't have an assistant is a problem and comes with its own cost—nobody to answer the phone! The question is, when should he stop the search and hire someone, even if the person isn't perfect?

"The optimal solution is to figure out the distribution of people in the pool, and once you recognize it, take the first person who gets over that threshold," he told us. "The same is true for finding the right person to marry."

If you believe in true love, you may not want to sign on with Prince (or Princess) Okay when Prince Perfect may be just around the corner. But Dr. Ariely thinks having a plan is the best way to get lucky in love. Even in the most emotional of realms, you can't rely on your emotions. Following our instincts in love (or work or finance or buying Rice Krispies) doesn't always lead to the best rational choice. If you're single and want to get lucky in love, you can't just hope for love to land—you need a strategy. And hope is not a strategy, as one executive I know is fond of saying.

As we chatted, Dr. Ariely compared dating to investing in the stock market. You think you have a rational approach, but then something changes (the Dow is down by 200!), and you panic and let the emotions of a moment change your plan. "To be lucky in love or the stock market, you don't want to let your nature run the show," he said.

But then he stopped himself to point out one big difference between stocks and people. When you choose a stock, the stock doesn't change. But the moment you choose a person, the relationship alters. "You make luck when you decide that you're going to be here

---

1. Economists are apparently better at understanding offices than bedrooms—but the same process applies wherever you're looking. On the other hand, does anybody have secretaries anymore? Assistants? Maybe we should call it the Siri problem?

for a long time, so let's explore and figure out what works," said Dr. Ariely. "A relationship gets better when you invest in it. The commitment creates new opportunities."

To be lucky in love, you need to replace the squirm-inducing fear of settling with the exciting idea of investing. Put time and effort and trust and love into a person, and you get huge dividends. It occurred to me that Ron and I had followed that route—we were committed to each other and trusted the other one to hang around, no matter what. So we could explore and try things, cutting out the ones that didn't work and continuing with what did. "If we're going to be here for a long time, whatever I want for myself is also what I want for you," Dr. Ariely said. "And that's how you make luck. We can try out new things together and not worry that something won't work."

Staying isn't always the right choice. There are plenty of situations of emotional abuse or violence or alcoholism or other damaging behavior where the only way to get lucky is to leave. But in more benign circumstances, Dr. Ariely points out that it's not the choosing that matters so much as what you do once the choice is made.

Many behavioral psychologists have shown that once we make a decision, our brains kick in to prove that we've made the best choice. In various popular experiments, researchers have given volunteers small items such as a mug or a pen, and once it was officially theirs, they could trade it. But few did. Just possessing it made them like it more. And the same held for partners. In one survey of 1,100 people that Helen Fisher oversaw, 86 percent said that they would marry the same person over again.

Ariely offered the example of living in an apartment where you have a short-term lease that both you and the landlord have to keep agreeing to renew. "If you're deciding every day whether to extend the lease, you won't paint or buy flowers. You'll always be looking at other options," he said.

It was a good point on so many levels. When Ron and I were deciding whether we wanted to leave our suburban home and move to Manhattan, I suggested that we rent a small apartment and try it out. If we liked city life, we would take the next step. Ron didn't like the idea. He thought it would be a completely different experience if we bought a place and made it ours and felt committed.

And so that's what we did. We bought a tiny apartment that was in terrible shape and then lovingly renovated it. I chose the paint colors and the bathroom fixtures and the new kitchen cabinets, and Ron made sure the wiring was as he wanted it and the outlets were in the right places and . . . well, something about coaxial cable. I didn't have to understand everything. But the point is, after we invested our time and attention, we loved that little apartment way beyond reason.

I'm sure there are people who can get a short-term rental and still decide to paint and buy fresh flowers and recaulk the bathtub. But somehow it's easier when you know you'll be sticking around.

Barnaby suggested we get together with a professor named Paul Zak, who teaches at the Claremont Graduate University and started its Center for Neuroeconomics Studies. He also happens to appear on a lot of TV shows, where he's generally called Dr. Love.

How could I say no to Dr. Love?

As we waited in the lobby of the Cornell Club, Barnaby told me that Dr. Zak's research largely focused on how the neurochemical oxytocin was linked with trust, love, and morality. It sounded like a big role for a small molecule.

Then Barnaby leaned over and whispered that he should warn me that Dr. Love liked to . . .

Before he could finish, Dr. Love himself came in, and Barnaby introduced us.

"Hi, I like to hug," Dr. Zak said, practically finishing Barnaby's sentence.

Since he's tall and handsome, with the looks of an archetypal soap opera star, a hug seemed like a perfectly good greeting. But as we sat down, I asked him what that was all about.

"A hug releases oxytocin, which helps people open up," he said. "The first time I tried hugging everyone at a meeting, I found people smiled and shared a lot more with me."

I pointed out that the quick hug didn't really feel life changing.

Dr. Zak smiled. "Oxytocin is made in one second and lasts in the brain about twenty minutes."

Dr. Zak is on a mission to prove that our bodies know when we're lucky in love even if our conscious brains aren't quite so smart. For the ABC-TV show *The Bachelor*, he set up experiments for the 2016 season, checking the brain activity of bachelor Ben and six of the women he was meeting. The tests looked at how they reacted to each other's smells, the levels of oxytocin release, and physiological syncing—measured by heart rate variability and how closely their rhythms matched.

The experiments were done in a spic-and-span white room stocked with complicated-looking machines and test tubes and beakers filled with colored liquids—a set decorator's idea of a research lab. Some wondered if the experiments were as faux as the colored beakers. A bachelorette named Olivia emerged as the clear winner in all three tests—but Ben proposed to a woman named Lauren B.

in the end. Dr. Zak is convinced the research has validity, though *The Bachelor* may have been the wrong venue for showing it off.

The physiological responses that interest Dr. Zak definitely have a role in making us lucky in love. The ancient poets who thought of the heart as the source of love weren't completely wrong—our bodies send us love signals. Psychologists say that if you want somebody to get excited about you, do something scary with them on a first date—go rock climbing or midnight skiing, or take a spin on a roller coaster. The fancy name is "misattribution of arousal," meaning your brain gets mixed up about what is causing you to feel exhilarated. If you're on a roller coaster and screaming in excitement, your brain may attribute some of the thrill to the guy who's sitting next to you. Adventures get you aroused and make you feel connected to the other person.

I used to call a very close friend of mine whenever Ron and I hit a bump in our relationship, and she would repeatedly listen and give advice. But then she started to notice a pattern. One time when I was worried and wanted to talk, she refused to get concerned.

"You two will just have sex or take a hike or go to a museum and then everything will be okay again," she said.

It made me laugh so I repeated it to Ron, and I have to admit that it's been our mantra ever since. There's nothing that doesn't get better for us with sex, a hike, or a museum. Those happen to be things Ron and I like, anyway, and any couple can find their own lucky activities. All the neurochemicals released when you're doing something new (like a museum) or challenging (like a hike) help you bond. And sex does all of the above and more.

Dr. Zak met his own wife on a plane when he was sitting behind her and noticed that they were both served vegetarian meals. He leaned forward to chat her up and eventually moved to the empty seat next to her. Working on his PhD in economics at the time, he brought along a stack of papers in case there was a lull in the conversation.

"She was impressed by my big equations," he joked.

They've now been married for a couple of decades and have two teenage daughters, and Dr. Zak summed up marriage by noting that "you feel like murdering each other sometimes." He travels a lot and admits that he's had a lot of opportunities to stray. But he's passed them by because he's not convinced that being lucky in love in the Mick Jagger sense is always a good thing.

"If I get four women pregnant, I'm more successful evolutionarily, but if my wife finds out, she'll kick me out," he said. From a neurological perspective, the brain is an exquisite cost-benefit calculator, and he has decided that the bigger benefit is to stay. He gets to put all his attention on one person, build trust, and have the benefits for his kids of a secure foundation and his full efforts.

"If I put less weight on caring for my existing children, I could take advantage of some awesome-looking women," he said. "But I think I make myself luckier by suppressing the impulsiveness of the brain stem and relying on the prefrontal cortex to think it through."

So the first step to being lucky in love may be understanding that all choices are trade-offs. It may be that now that he is in his seventies, Mick Jagger wouldn't mind having a little less sex and a little more attachment. The happily attached Phoebe may just read a lot of romance novels to fill that missing niche. You can't have everything. But it helps to know that you don't have to search endlessly to get lucky in love. You just have to create the lucky situation you want—and maybe take a ride on a roller coaster.

CHAPTER TWELVE

Make Lucky Kids

Show children many paths. . . . Nudge them to work hard and take risks. . . . Help them take a positive view. . . . Let them know they can make their own luck.

O n a bright Sunday afternoon, I drove upstate for a friend's baby shower. The mom-to-be, pregnant with twins, was in her early forties, and the gifts arrayed in front of her weren't a surprise since she had registered for them. At her casual wedding some years earlier, she had shown no interest in fine china or crystal. But now she wanted to be sure that her babies would be swathed in organic cotton clothes and silky-soft blankets, that they would have Mozart music to keep them stimulated and electronic swings to keep them calm. An elegant bassinet, cocoon-shaped crib, and luxury stroller that looked like it belonged at Kensington Palace had all been carefully selected to give the little ones a lucky start.

We all want to do everything possible for our kids—and that's as it should be. But if luck occurs at the intersection of talent, hard work, and random chance, it wasn't clear to me how posh stuff made lucky kids. It could be that the biggest gift we ultimately give our children is teaching them how to make their own luck.

I was thinking about lucky kids early the next week as I wandered through the leafy campus of the Horace Mann School in the Bronx, New York. The kids here didn't all start in cocoon-shaped cribs, but most had well-resourced parents who valued education and cared that their kids got the best. Those on financial aid had parents who had read to them and nurtured them into enrichment programs and made sacrifices to help them flourish. Parents with the right values certainly gave them a head start—but what ultimately made for a lucky life?

Standing outside on a sunny sidewalk, I watched as a group of girls walked down a hill toward the athletic field. A security guard got discreetly out of his car as they crossed the street. At $45,000 a year, the school makes sure its kids are safe. But far more impressive than the guard was how the girls responded to him. Several waved as they walked by, and a couple called out, "Thank you, George!" He was a person, not an invisible presence. Being able to appreciate the people there to help them seemed like a good start on making luck.

Two girls in athletic shorts and Horace Mann T-shirts, lacrosse sticks tucked under their arms and long hair tied back to be practical, crossed the street. They were deeply engaged in conversation, and I wondered if they were talking about schoolwork or parties or the next lacrosse match. But my guesses weren't even close. As they passed close to me, I heard one say earnestly to the other, "Are you happy? Because remember, that's what really matters."

I smiled to myself. So there was the answer I needed, provided by a lacrosse-playing fourteen-year-old. Lucky kids are happy kids—and vice versa.

A few minutes later, I was in the light-filled office of Dr. Jessica Levenstein, head of the Horace Mann Upper Division. Dr. Levenstein started our conversation about lucky kids by telling me that the goal should always be a happy child. I smiled and told her the comment I'd heard from the lacrosse player. She nodded, obviously pleased. Her message was getting across.

But Dr. Levenstein has a different approach to happy kids than many administrators. With a PhD from Princeton and an expertise in Dante and Ovid, she's not the type to post smiley faces around the school. She sees happiness as much more complex than posh stuff and positive slogans—and believes it comes at least in part from curiosity and intellectual discovery. In her view, the luck children need "is the ability to recognize all the various paths open to them that could potentially lead to happiness."

Horace Mann regularly sends more seniors to Ivy League colleges than almost any other school in the country, but one of the great gifts Dr. Levenstein gives students is the ability to see beyond Princeton or Harvard and have a bigger view. When a sophomore approached her in a panic about an upcoming test, she tried to walk him through the thought experiment of what the impact would be of not doing as well as he'd hoped. Would he be disappointing his parents? Himself?

"Students often have the idea that there is one path to happiness, and if they veer off that path, the other alternative is misery," she said. Ambitious parents may want the child to get good grades so he can get into Harvard and get a job on Wall Street. "That may absolutely be the key to your happy life, but at sixteen, you don't know that yet. You also certainly don't know the other kinds of happy lives that you're not even considering. The challenge for all of us who work with students is to help expand their notions of what makes for happiness and a lucky life."

Dr. Levenstein sometimes invites back alums who've gone in original directions to talk to the students and show them that "there are possibilities that they can't even envision at this stage that may involve jobs they've never heard of in cities they don't know."

Encouraging students to think beyond Ivy League schools and Wall Street may sound like a high-class problem, but her point has a broader reach. Wherever they grow up, children often have a limited view of their possibilities. They see what their parents and friends are doing and little else. Maybe they can't imagine leaving their small town or getting a job at NASA instead of at the local Walmart. Parents and teachers make kids lucky by showing them opportunities and expanding their view.

So how do you do that? Dr. Levenstein thinks reading at home or in school can help. A work of fiction, she says, "can show children different ways to live. It gives them an understanding of the reality of other people's existence." The primary goal of an English class may be to teach students how to read and write at a sophisticated level, "but through works of fiction, we're showing students models for human behavior." I could think of a lot of books that set out to do that, but Dr. Levenstein surprised me by bringing up the Oedipus plays.

"Students don't identify with a child who is going to kill his father and sleep with his mother, but they do identify with a person who wants to make his own fate. They understand that idea of trying to wrest control of your own story," she said, proving why she's the educator and I'm not.

I thought how inspiring it would be to go back to high school and spend some time in Dr. Levenstein's class. Or pretty much any class at Horace Mann. And it wouldn't be a bad idea, because parents who can model the openness and flexibility of mind she teaches make their kids luckier.

Staying open to possibilities when your child's lucky future is on the line isn't easy. Even if you're now trying to make luck for yourself by seeing different opportunities and zigging when others zag, you might be (unwittingly) doing the opposite with your kids. There's a sense among parents that luck comes from control and a single path. Dr. Levenstein regularly fields calls from parents who want their child switched to a different teacher, often before the year has even begun. "They've decided there's only one teacher who can be beneficial, and without that, the year will be a disaster," she said. "If that's where the parent is, I don't see any happy way forward."

Whoops. I suspect we've all made a phone call like that. I did it when my younger son was going into fourth grade in the local public school. I'd heard from other moms on the sidelines at soccer practices that a teacher I'll call Mrs. W was a horror to be avoided. She had ruined many a fourth-grade year. So when Matt got assigned Mrs. W, I called the principal. Like Dr. Levenstein, she wouldn't change his class before it had even begun. She thought Matt and Mrs. W might be a good fit and encouraged me to give him a positive attitude about his teacher.

"How he approaches it could make all the difference," she said.

So I tried. And as a nice surprise for all of us, fourth grade turned out to be terrific. Mrs. W liked that Matt was smart, and she encouraged him in new directions. He still jokes about the day she took him out into the hallway with a pair of scissors and a piece of paper to show him how to cut. "You may be a genius in math and reading, but you never learned kindergarten skills," she told him. Fortunately, he laughed. They adored each other.[1]

Children (and adults) learn to make luck happen when they are encouraged to take any situation and make it work for themselves.

---

1. Matt later went to Horace Mann and had Dr. Levenstein as his English teacher. He was wonderfully inspired by her and has remained a huge fan. It's nice when we can learn from our kids, and Matt was the one who suggested I talk to "Dr. L" about luck.

You can't teach kids to make their own luck if they see life as something that befalls them. "If your immediate response is to try to figure out who you can blame, then you're always at the mercy of outside forces. People who see their lives as driven by their own actions are on a much happier path," Dr. Levenstein told me.

If a child comes home with a less-than-great result on a math test, a parent can immediately complain that the child has a bad teacher and life is unfair. Or she can say, "Let's look at this together and see what happened. I'm happy to help. Maybe you can prepare differently next time." Guess which child is on the path to a lucky future?

Horace Mann is one of those rare (and wonderful) schools where smart kids are celebrated and even considered cool. But Dr. Levenstein worries about parents who seem to tie affection to achievement. Lucky kids know they are loved for who they are and not just what they've done. It's fine to celebrate an A on a test or order up an ice-cream cake when your seventh-grader wins a science award. Hey, that's awesome! "But they shouldn't feel that your love for them is tied to that experience," said Dr. Levenstein.

Way, way back when I was in junior high, I came home from school with my very first report card. The school had tried an open approach (later abandoned) in which we picked our own classes and didn't get grades until the very end of ninth grade. So even though I was a smart kid, I'd never gotten to see an A. Now I had five of them neatly lined up.

My mom, who regularly judged her children by achievement, congratulated me. But I couldn't wait to show my intellectual (and soulful) dad how well I had done. When he got home that evening,

I waited excitedly until he was settled in his comfy chair in the den. Then I strode in and handed him the folded report card. He registered what it was but just put it in his lap and looked up at me.

"How did you do?" he asked.

"Open it and you'll see," I said smugly.

He shook his head. "I didn't ask how your teachers think you did. I want to know what you think and if you did the best you could."

I was taken aback. I stood there and pondered his question, then sputtered that I had worked hard and learned a lot and, yes, done the very best I could.

He handed the report card back to me without opening it, and there was a twinkle in his eyes. "Then I'm very proud of you," my dad said.

Of all the moments that happened to me as a kid, I'm amazed at how vivid that memory remains. Talking with Dr. Levenstein, I understood that it stayed with me because my dad was giving me permission to define for myself what it meant to be lucky in life. As long as I was happy with what I had done, he was, too. I got to decide what mattered.

When Dr. Levenstein talks about making luck for kids by helping them see many paths to happiness, she points out how important it is that parents recognize that flexibility and possibility in their own lives.

"There cannot be a moment where the parent voices to a child, 'I'm not doing what I want to do or living where I want to live, but I can't change it,'" she said, "because that communicates the idea of life as a straitjacket and that the decisions you make when young keep you locked up until retirement. I really object to that idea."

She grew up in New York with a dad who was a successful advertising executive—but quit to follow his passion of becoming a playwright. Dr. Levenstein's husband was a professor at Yale until a few years ago, when he decided he would rather be a writer than an academic. He left New Haven and is now passionate about the books he's researching and writing. He hopes they'll have an impact—and he is happy with his work and his life. It's a coincidence that Dr. Levenstein's dad and her husband have similar stories—but it's one she is eager to pass on.

"I hope that when my children grow up, they will keep exploring and never feel stuck in one place," she said. "I would like them to know there is endless opportunity at any age."

I would have liked to talk with Dr. Levenstein all day, but she had a school to run, so I thanked her and walked from the lovely campus back to the subway. Heading back to Manhattan, I heard her wisdom ringing as a mantra. Lucky kids are happy kids. And lucky kids know there are many paths to happiness.

Back home, I called Barnaby and told him about the conversation with Dr. Levenstein. He liked her positions. Letting children know there are many paths to a lucky life also gives them the freedom to try the unusual and fail—which may set them up for even more luck later.

"Ever hear of Traf-O-Data?" Barnaby asked me.

"Nope."

"It was a company that Bill Gates and Paul Allen started when they were still in high school. They had an idea to analyze traffic data by computer. It didn't go very far, but they later said it was what set them up to be successful with Microsoft."

"Nobody told them they should focus on studying for their SATs instead?"

"I guess not," Barnaby said with a laugh.

When you're as successful as Bill Gates, you can look back at anything your parents did and think it was right. Gates's father was the cofounder of a big law practice, and his mother served on numerous corporate and civic boards. His father has admitted that it wasn't easy dealing with Bill when he was prickly and stubborn at age twelve or thirteen. They insisted he try sports he didn't necessarily like, so he could see new possibilities and not just stick with the familiar. But ultimately they let him be who he was.

"I had a lot of energy and stubbornness about things that I wanted to do," Gates explained in an interview a few years ago. When he was in his last year of high school, young Bill was enthralled by computers and wanted to take a job in the new area—but it would take him away from his school. "I was amazed that my dad, after meeting with the headmaster and getting all the data, said, 'Yeah, that's something you can go and do.'"

You need to know (and trust) your own child to give that go-ahead when what they want to do seems to take them down an unconventional path. But expanding your view along with your child's can make both of you feel lucky.

I can't claim that I was always so open-minded to new opportunities when my sons were growing up, but I always tried. And (fortunately) it's those good moments that kids talk about later. One evening early in his senior year of high school, my older son, Zach, came into the kitchen just as I was starting to make dinner. He watched me cutting up some carrots, and I could tell there was something on his mind. He had been working on his college essays, and his usual confidence seemed to have seeped away. I felt a pang, realizing that the college application process can wear down even the strongest soul.

"Can I ask you something?" he asked, reaching for a carrot.

"Sure, what's up?"

He took a bite of the carrot and munched on it slowly. "What happens if I don't get in anywhere I apply?"

I could see the worry in his eyes, and I took a deep breath. It was hard to imagine my smart, hardworking son not having a college option for the next year. But who knew? The process was crazy, and anything could happen. If it did . . .

"That would be great!" I said. "You'll take a year off and travel or do research or find something exciting that you'd never try otherwise. You'll have a wonderful experience and then apply again. Honestly, I think it would be terrific for you."

"You mean that?" he asked.

"Definitely. It's just a different path to take, and you'd make it wonderful."

Zach took another bite of the carrot, said, "Thanks, Mom," and headed back to his room.

I didn't think much more about it, and the year to explore never happened, since he got accepted early to his first-choice school. But years later, Zach reported the kitchen-and-carrot conversation back to me. He (generously) said that my reply not only lifted some of the pressure but reminded him that there was more than one way to live a life. Swerving to take a different path than he planned could make him even luckier.

As Dr. Levenstein and Bill Gates Sr. pointed out, telling kids, "Yeah, that's something you can go and do," can free them to be themselves and discover their own path. It's a big step in making luck.

One downside of encouraging kids to be themselves is that at age eight or twelve or sixteen, they don't really know who they are. You can't be yourself when you're busy trying to be like everyone else.

One little six-year-old girl I know recently got her ears pierced, and when I asked her why, she told me that all her friends had pierced ears. Her mom agreed to a six-year-old's wearing earrings because she wanted her daughter to feel like part of the crowd.

Maybe that made her feel lucky the day she got her first gold studs. But in the long run? Probably not.

To be lucky, kids sometimes need to be willing to stand out from the crowd. I always marvel that Barnaby was homeschooled until college—but I think it's one reason he's been able to be so persistent in choosing his own paths and making his own luck. He never felt the pressure to conform to the kids in the cafeteria.

Now that he has two little daughters of his own, Barnaby and his wife, Michelle, are trying their own version of homeschooling—which includes tutors, specialized classes, city experiences, and scheduled times with Dad. Only 3 percent of American children are homeschooled, and since his daughter Mandarin is a precocious five-year-old (Jasmine is not yet two) and both parents work full-time, why not just put her in one of the city's elite schools?

"I think a custom-tailored program does better at cultivating a lucky child," Barnaby said. "Imagine running a race when you know you're fast, but there's only one size shoe to wear. Good teachers try to adjust the pace, but at the end of the day, nothing is as good as shoes that fit properly—or an individualized program."

Barnaby also worries that kids who are busy trying to fit in at school may be reluctant to ask questions. "Curiosity is a precursor for getting lucky in life," Barnaby said. "Children who can ask, 'Why not?' learn to see what others aren't seeing and imagine what they're not imagining."

When Mandarin took a school practice test, one of the questions had her pick items that could be used at the beach. She checked off a snowboard—and when it was marked wrong, she stood her ground. "It could be a snowboard, but it looks a lot like a surfboard," she insisted.

Barnaby grinned as he told me the story. "We like to think that we know the world better than a child does, but she might have the real answer in seeing the world slightly differently. Part of luck is encouraging that."

Children who go to a regular school can get an additional foundation for luck when their parents supplement the learning at home, encouraging the children to be curious and persistent and excited by new ideas.

Not every parent is raising a Barnaby or a Bill Gates or a Mandarin—and even if you are, it's not always clear how to balance structure and discipline with creativity and freedom. Do you make kids lucky by agreeing to what makes them happy in the moment (those pierced ears), or do you push them toward what might pay off later?

Barnaby suggested that one person who might have some insights into the question was the infamous Tiger Mom.

"Great idea!" I said.

Amy Chua is a professor at Yale Law School, an expert on ethnic conflict and globalization, and an admired teacher. But she became internationally famous as a mom. Her bestselling book *Battle Hymn of the Tiger Mother* aroused controversy around the world for her over-the-top parenting techniques. She reported that she made her two daughters practice piano and violin several hours a day, pushed them to be number one in every subject, and threw back a birthday card one of her daughters made because it didn't show enough effort.

At the very beginning of her book, she outlined the things she wouldn't let her daughters do. They included "attend a sleepover; have a playdate; be in a school play; complain about not being in a school play; watch TV or play computer games; choose their own extracurricular activities; get any grade less than an A."

But when Barnaby and I chatted with her one afternoon, she didn't sound so tough. "I just think parenting is so hard," Professor Chua said with a sigh. "Despite my strong voice and reputation, I'm actually very humbled, and I don't think there's an easy answer to this."

Chua has complicated ideas about making kids lucky. She told us that her Chinese family was (like many others) very superstitious, and the accepted wisdom was that she was a lucky person. Eight is a Chinese lucky number, and her birthday is on October 26—and yes, two plus six is eight. She started to realize that being told you're a lucky person builds on itself.

"If you're told you're lucky, you have the guts to take risks and make mistakes and still have the confidence to go ahead," she said. "Many things that children see as lucky are the result of massive amounts of preparation and investment. What's that adage about the harder I work, the luckier I get? If you could internalize for children the idea that if I work hard, I will have a good shot at something and seem lucky, it's actually very empowering."

Chua realized that ideas about controlling your own luck were even built into the Chinese superstitions. She told us about the "feng shui stuff" that prescribes certain orientations for a house as being lucky. "But if you're facing the wrong direction you can put up mirrors and reverse it, or cut a hole and let the good feng shui come," she said. "There's luck, but there are loopholes so you can also control your fate."

She passed that message along to her daughters. Whenever one of them complained about fate or things going wrong, "I would just immediately say, 'No, it's within your power to put this right and make yourself lucky.'"

It's a good bet that Professor Chua never called the principal at the high school to demand that her daughters be put in a different class. She just taught them to make any situation work. When her husband wanted to be more protective, she urged him to push the girls to take risks.

"It's easier to let your children be fragile and protect them, but I think that is just not a good way to go," she said. "A lot of children say, 'I'm not good at test taking' or 'I'm not good at math,' and if we indulge that, they never discover how much they can do."

However much she cared about achievement, Chua felt strongly that her children had to make their own success and luck. She opposes helicopter parenting, in which moms and dads swoop in to do their children's homework or try to save them from problems. "The parent can't just do it for the child—they have to earn the luck themselves," she said adamantly. "The world is tough out there, and children need to be nudged to try hard and believe in themselves."

Professor Chua knows that children are all different—and ironically, she wrote the book in part because she realized that what worked so well with her older daughter hit some bumps with the different (and more rebellious) personality of her younger child. But both girls landed at Harvard and remember their childhoods happily. Her older daughter, Sophia, appreciates that her parents were always on her side, and their high expectations told her "they had the confidence that I could do amazing things."

Lulu, who ultimately rebelled at the strain of hours spent practicing the violin, is now glad that her mom didn't give up on her. "If I did poorly in a test, she did not let me lie in bed and wallow. She'd tell me I needed to get up and study to get a better mark so I would feel better," she said.

While it first seemed to me that Jessica Levenstein and Amy Chua had very different ideas about making lucky kids, I was starting to see how much they had in common. Levenstein wanted the students at Horace Mann to see many paths to happiness, and Chua prescribed a single path for her own daughters. But Lulu's comment struck me because at the end of the day, she had learned not to blame anyone, to take responsibility, and to make her own luck (and good grades). Levenstein would surely approve of that.

Dr. Levenstein had told me that happiness isn't always tied to achievement—there are happy kids within each level of ability. Professor Chua had been less sure of that with her daughters—she thought success would make them happy. But now she was more aware that it was the process—the trying, the risk-taking, the believing in yourself—that makes you lucky.

Professor Chua told us that even though she's known for discipline, "I've looped back, I'm almost on the other side now. I think our children are overscripted, overcontrolled now. I can see how anxious their parents are, and I think we've taken a wrong turn somewhere. The goal is to make children strong in themselves."

But it's not really a contradiction at all, because she continues to believe that the strength and luck come when children "put the work in, have some control, and demonstrate to themselves that through their own volition they can accomplish something." We all want confident kids—but telling them how great they are doesn't really do much. They need to see how they can make luck happen themselves.

Given the controversies around her books and the attacks they've prompted, Chua could see herself as very lucky or very unlucky. "And I totally see myself as one of the luckiest people you know," she said brightly. That positive attitude is a key element in making more luck. "People like positive people, so projecting optimism and confidence and upbeatness as opposed to negativity is actually part of success," she said.

After we said good-bye, I thought of two posters I had seen at Horace Mann with phrases the students had contributed about what made for a healthy life. I had written them down, and I pulled out my notebook now and looked at the lines. They included:

Being comfortable in your community
Feeling you belong
A sense of peace and fulfillment
Positive self-concept
Being happy with yourself despite your flaws

It seemed to me that the students who had written those lines had a great start on a lucky life. Given the school they attended, they worked hard, which would lead to the cycle of confidence building and luck making that Amy Chua envisioned. But they were also being encouraged to have that positive, inquisitive spirit. Lucky kids understand that if they look for the good, they're likely to find it.

PART FOUR

THE OTHER SIDE OF LUCK

You never know what worse luck your bad luck has saved you from.

—*Cormac McCarthy*

CHAPTER THIRTEEN

Bad Luck: Why Your Worst Moment Can Be Your Luckiest

Take a broader view. . . . Imagine positive outcomes. . . . See bad luck as a chance for something good to happen. . . . Laugh a little.

After all the discussions I'd been having with Barnaby about the exciting paths for making good luck, one problem was starting to nag at me. Random bad stuff happens to people. You can recognize possibilities and grab at opportunities, you can work hard and proceed with passion and optimism, you can show unusual talent and even zig when others zag. But when illness strikes, a tragic accident occurs, or (too often in America) a mass shooter appears from nowhere, you can be buffeted by forces you can't control.

Barnaby agreed, but as always, he had a slightly different perspective. "Sometimes you need to have a bigger view to know what's good luck or bad luck," he said. Just that week at the Luck Lab, he had been talking with the renowned astrophysicist Piet Hut, who suggested to him that you can make good luck from bad moments by trying to step out of yourself and see the situation more broadly. Barnaby compared it to walking alone in the woods. The forest is thick all around you, so you can't see anything, and maybe it's scary. "But if you could pull back and have a big view from above, you'd feel differently. You'd see where you've come from and the many directions you can go. You wouldn't feel stuck and abandoned in that one spot. Seeing more will give you a greater sense of control."

You can't step outside your body in real life, but you can try to imagine the positive outcomes that might yet be. Or at least realize that they may be there even if you *can't* imagine them. What looks like terrible luck today could turn out to be great luck tomorrow.

It reminded me of the 1998 movie *Sliding Doors*, in which Gwyneth Paltrow plays a British woman named Helen who gets fired from her PR job one morning and rushes home. Going to the subway, she reaches the train just as the doors close in her face. The next train is delayed (more bad luck), so she leaves the station to hail a cab, and standing outside, she gets mugged (even more bad luck). With a slash on her head, she rushes to the hospital.

Not a lucky day, right? You might say that everything that could go wrong did. But then the movie backs up and shows another possibility for the day. In this case, the train doors are still open when Helen arrives and she gets on the train. Much better luck! Except when she arrives at her apartment, she finds her live-in boyfriend in bed with another woman.

In the rest of the movie, both scenarios continue to unfold. And beneath the romantic plotting is the bigger message that we never quite know how life will play out. Good luck can turn into bad—and vice versa. Discovering that your boyfriend is unfaithful could be bad luck—but what if it sets you up to meet someone better, kinder, and less fickle? Or to meet a tragic, unforeseen end?

We can't always predict how events will unfold, and if parallel universes exist, we don't yet have access to them. So all you can do is take the current event that has been handed to you and try to turn it into good luck rather than bad.

Back when I was running a big magazine, I called author Lee

Child one morning and asked if he would like to write a cover story for me. I admired Lee's vigorous writing and his wildly popular novels featuring tough-guy hero Jack Reacher. I thought he might be a nice match to interview the (then) famously recalcitrant actor Robert De Niro. Lee agreed, and a few days later, I got his report.

"I just finished, and I had a delightful time with Bob," he said in his plummy English accent. "It was a great interview and will be a terrific story."

I grinned. Reporters rarely had a delightful time with De Niro—or got to call him Bob.

"You're amazing!" I said.

"When you send Jack Reacher to do a job, he does it," Lee replied.

I laughed, and when we talked again, I discovered that Lee really was as determined as the fictional character he famously created. Lee became a writer only after he was fired from the television job in the UK that he had held for thirteen years. He expected to be there forever, but new management came in—and he couldn't believe his bad luck. He had a mortgage, a car loan, a daughter, and only a few months of savings in the bank. He was angry and frustrated and felt completely betrayed, but he channeled it all into finding his next opportunity.

"I'm a naturally belligerent person. Show me a challenge, and I'll beat it or die trying," he said.

So he created Jack Reacher, who got his steely resolve after he was downsized out of the Marines. Lee, and Jack, had the determination to turn bad luck to good. Lee later wrote a piece for me about how you move on after losing a job, and his advice was impressive.

"Try something. Anything. Sit back, take a breath, believe in yourself, identify your dream, and go for it 110%. Trust me, your motivation will never be as strong. And the chance might never come your way again," he wrote.

I loved his perspective that bad luck is a chance that has come your way—and might not again. When you're in the midst of it, you probably don't immediately see your bad luck as a good opportunity. Even if you're as talented as Lee Child, you don't know that you're going to become an internationally famous author and end up with Tom Cruise starring in the movie adaptations of your books.[1] It doesn't happen for everyone, of course, and sometimes losing a job is a disaster from which it's very difficult to recover. But if you have some cushion, a tough situation like losing a job can give you the opening to reassess what you really want. It may shake you out of your complacency and inspire you to take the risks and chances that can lead to unexpected good luck.

When I told Barnaby my theory about bad luck turning into opportunity, he quickly agreed and suggested we get in touch with Baroness Susan Greenfield.

"How could a baroness ever have bad luck?" I asked.

"She'll tell you," he said.

I soon found out that Baroness Greenfield of Ot Moor, in the County of Oxfordshire (really, don't you love the English?), got her title because of her work as a scientist studying brain physiology. She is what the English refer to as a life peer, which means you're

---

1. Having Cruise play Jack Reacher caused some controversy, since the character in the novels is described as a bruising six-foot-five and 220 pounds. At a reported five-seven, Cruise is . . . smaller. Child diplomatically explained that Cruise's big talent makes up for it.

not born into the House of Lords—you do something important to get there. Forget the whiff of rolling estates and visits with the Queen—this baroness has done impressive research into Alzheimer's disease and spent a lot of time hanging around test tubes.

Greenfield (we quickly dropped the title when we spoke) was the first woman to give an important series of talks called the Christmas Lectures at the Royal Institution of Great Britain, an organization started in 1799 as a center for scientific research and education. Amid great fanfare, she was appointed as the first woman director in 1998. Twelve years later, amid even greater fanfare, she was sent packing.

"A lot of rubbish was written in the press, and I felt like Margaret Thatcher in the last days of her government. It was a very unpleasant experience," she told us.

Some would suggest that Greenfield was a victim of old-fashioned sexism—the boys at the club didn't like her coming in and shaking things up. Barnaby remembered visiting her there once and described it as "a stuffy place with pictures on the walls of a lot of dead white men in dark suits, and there was Susan in a short red dress and shiny high-heeled leather boots. She was very independent and assertive and spirited in a nice way."

But maybe too spirited for the conservative boys. The Royal Institution claimed that a development program Greenfield had led—with full backing of the board—had resulted in a big debt and blamed the losses on her. Greenfield remembered getting the final phone call that her position was being declared redundant. That's a nice way of saying that they were throwing her out.

"I hung up and thought, 'What happens now?' That was my worst moment, staring into the abyss," she said. "But it was December

24th and my parents arrived, and I had to be all *Happy Christmas!* We were going out to the musical of *Chitty Chitty Bang Bang*, and I wouldn't ruin it. I can have a bloody-minded attitude when I try."

The Brits relish a good scandal, and after the "redundancy" went public, Greenfield knew she was landing smack in the midst of one. But she made herself stand tall and keep a sense of humor.

"When I was young and first going to parties with boys, I worried, 'What will they think of me?' And my mom said, 'Worry about what you will think of *them*.' She was a dancer and an iconoclast and gave me resilience and the perspective to see how absurd life can be."

Like most people who lose a job, Greenfield felt slightly unmoored. But she decided that "luck stems from having something you care about." She wasn't interested in what she calls "empty socializing," so she kept her priorities focused on work and continued to develop often-controversial ideas that she felt passionately about.

"I think my theory of Alzheimer's is right and everyone else's is wrong!" she said buoyantly. "You need something you believe in that strongly to knock on doors."[2]

She kept her energy high ("people draw from that and like that"), and within a few years, she was able to set up a biotech company that has her enormously excited. The Christmas when she left the Royal Institution and looked into the abyss has a very different resonance now.

"I didn't know it then, but that very unpleasant experience turned out to be very good luck. If it hadn't happened, I'd still be stuck in London hosting dinners. Instead I started my biotech company

---

2. Greenfield thinks that a peptide called AChE could be implicated in the cell death associated with Alzheimer's. The idea is not yet well accepted, but her company is looking to develop drugs that could intervene.

and wake up excited to get to work every day. I think of it as Cosmic Argos."

I hesitated, but I had to ask. "What's Cosmic Argos?"

"Argos. You know the Argos stores, right?"

I had to admit I didn't. She explained that they are hugely popular catalogue-based stores in the UK where you fill out an order form for what you want and then hand it to the clerk. You wait for a few minutes—and then the item you've requested is brought to you.

"So my friends and I joke about Cosmic Argos," she said with a laugh. "You put your thoughts out, and the right result is brought to you. I had what I thought was the worst reversal, and it turned out to be fantastic. If you do it right, Cosmic Argos has a plan for you."

After we hung up, I thought that Baroness Greenfield was one of the more delightful people I'd spoken to lately. But her Cosmic Argos wasn't anything magical. She had taken that worst moment and turned it around by her own determination and optimism and passion. You could probably throw any bad luck in her path and she would turn it to good fortune.

As I traveled around the country giving talks about my gratitude book, I was struck by how many people reached out to tell me about bad luck they had experienced—an illness, a tragedy, a death in the family. Over and over I heard how the difficult circumstance had made them pause to be more grateful and appreciate the good things that happened every day.

One young woman came up to me before a talk with a warm smile and a cheerful demeanor—and told me that she had been diagnosed with ovarian cancer a year earlier.

"I'm so sorry," I said, grabbing her hand in sympathy.

"Thanks. This should have been the worst year of my life, but there are so many moments where I feel very lucky."

Her eyes were shining, and she didn't let go of my hand. The treatments had been awful, she said, but she was now in remission. She went for a scan every two weeks and her sister always accompanied her, and they would go out for lunch and celebrate each time there was another good report. She also had a wonderful husband, always at her side.

"My children are only four and seven, and I want to be here for them. But right now I love them and we have fun every day—and I feel lucky for every moment we are together," she said.

Wow. I felt my eyes filling with tears. Being diagnosed with ovarian cancer had to count as one of the unluckiest events that could strike a young mom. But she counted herself lucky that it brought happy times with her sister, a deeper connection to her husband, and memory-making moments with her children.

I told her how much I admired her ability to find the bright side of a very dark story.

"It's the only way to get through," she said.

Luck, like gratitude, isn't dependent on events. It's what you do with the events and the perspective you take that matters.

A few days later, I was in Los Angeles and drove my rental car over to the Shutters hotel in Santa Monica. It's always been one of my favorite spots—situated at the edge of an enormous beach and so perfectly decorated that it looks like a movie set of an LA hotel rather than a real one. My friend Monica Holloway was waiting for me in the lobby, sitting in one of the deep sofas near a blazing fireplace. It was sixty-five degrees out, which is fireplace weather in Santa Monica.

"You look fabulous!" I said as she got up and gave me a hug.

"I'm too dressy for lunch," she said, tugging theatrically at her wide palazzo pants, which were as bold and creative as she is. "But I have to go to an Emmy Awards party directly from here."

When I first met Monica just a few years ago, I was slightly awed by her. She's blond and funny and has great wit mixed with equal parts warmth. Plus, I discovered she was married to Michael Price, one of the top producers at *The Simpsons*. I imagined her home life as something out of a sitcom. Two funny and talented people living in LA . . . roll the cameras!

But as we talked for many hours over lunch at the beautiful beachfront dining room at Shutters, I discovered that Monica's life was not nearly that simple. She and Michael had actually separated at one point when the perfect marriage of two funny people didn't feel so perfect. And yes, she seemed unusually fortunate now—but that was the result of serious effort to change her bad luck to good.

Monica spent her childhood in a small town in Ohio with a violent and abusive father. Her first job was driving a hearse to the airport to pick up dead bodies for a funeral home. She never felt safe until she left and got married. When she had a baby, she was determined to give him the fun, secure environment that she never had. But then her darling Wills was diagnosed with autism. She remembered an appointment with a neuropsychologist who told her that Wills would never read or drive or be independent.

"That was the worst moment," she said as we sipped our iced teas and made our way through the bread basket.

But from that worst moment came a hint of how life might get better. Monica said she was upset and frightened after that appointment, and she was in the car leaving the parking lot when a woman almost ran into them. "I started screaming at her and just let loose all the anger I was feeling. At one point I yelled, 'Shame on you for scaring my baby'—and in the backseat I heard Wills laughing and giggling. *He was laughing.*" He'd actually found her outburst funny!

Having grown up frightened as a child, Monica wanted a house full of laughter and openness. At first, it felt like a body blow to have an autistic child who was afraid of everything. "But because he was frightened, I got brave!" Monica said joyously, looking from our window table out to the beach. "I had to reassure Wills that the world was safe, so I had to make myself believe it, too."

And his giggles in the car that day made her realize that whatever disadvantage they started from, she might still be able to make luck happen.

"We *are* funny," Monica told me.

Wills is now in college, and he can read and drive and lives independently. I didn't think of this as a miracle story about curing autism, which is a complicated disease with many gradations. Other families who have been just as determined and loving and skillful as Monica and Michael have not had such fortunate results.

But the bigger issue to me was Monica's attitude—that she would find lucky outcomes in any misery. As we talked about that, she nodded ardently. She told me that she used to tally up the bad things in her life—an abusive father, an autistic son—and wonder about the cruel hand that she'd been dealt. But then she decided to turn that around.

"I can laugh about stuff now. What starts out seeming awful can end up being funny and even have a lucky side. Like the naked man in the shower."

"The naked man . . . ?"

"Haven't I told you about that?" asked Monica with a grin.

Her tally of bad events included a couple of bouts with skin cancer, which required surgery. But in typical Monica fashion, she was able to find the lucky side of those, too. ("I got a new nose in the deal and a new chin!" she said, describing the cosmetic surgery that followed.)

One of the surgeries took place at that challenging time in her life when she and her husband were separated. So instead of going home after surgery, she went to a plush hotel that specializes in such postoperative care.

"At about three-thirty in the morning, I heard the shower running in my bathroom. I was in a haze and I could hardly see, but I thought, 'This isn't right,'" she said. "So I got up and stumbled around and I saw a pile of men's clothing on the floor, like somebody had undressed there. It didn't make any sense. And then I went into the bathroom and there was a naked man in the shower."

Monica went screaming out of her room to get help. But announcing in the middle of the night that there's a naked man in your shower doesn't always bring the expected response. The people at the front desk calmly explained that it couldn't have happened—she must be hallucinating from the painkillers.

She wasn't hallucinating. Eventually, the unknown man who had mysteriously wandered past all security was taken away. But Monica didn't want to stay at the hotel another minute. Even though they were separated, she called her husband, Michael.

"He came over like the cavalry to be with me," she said. "I was wearing silk pajamas with polka dots, and my eyes and face were completely blown up, and we laughed so hard. I told him that I hadn't seen another naked man in nineteen years, and now that I'd had the chance, my eyes were so swollen I couldn't even see anything. We were both laughing, and he took me home. It bonded us again."

It occurred to me that Monica's willingness to laugh at the absurdities of life leads to luck. Most people would see having surgery, a swollen face, and a naked intruder in a hotel room as a series of unfortunate events. But if you can mix in a dose of laughter and use them to recharge your marriage, then maybe you're not a hapless victim after all. You give yourself some control over absurd events that seem to come from nowhere. You can take the bad circumstances and turn them around to make good luck from the unlikeliest sources—and the very worst moments.

When I got back to New York, I told Barnaby about my idea that luck didn't necessarily come in a straight path. As Monica and Susan Greenfield had shown me, sometimes it took the bad to lead to the good.

Barnaby took a sheet of paper and drew four or five inverted Vs in different sizes, making a mini-mountainscape. "I've been looking at something similar at the Luck Lab," he said. "We've been analyzing how companies can maximize their strategies for optimal gain. We call it 'local hill-climbing strategy.'"

That didn't sound nearly as interesting as a naked man in a shower, but I nodded, ready to hear more. The theory was that a company (or individual) wants to get to the highest possible peak and stay there for the longest possible time. If you've climbed one of those medium-sized hills and made it to the top, you have to decide if you want to try to stay where you are—or try to make it to the top of an even higher hill.

Barnaby pointed to the inverted Vs on his paper and put his finger at the apex of one of his medium-sized hills. "If you want to get from here to here"—he moved his finger to one of the taller hills—"then you have to climb down first. There's no direct path from peak to peak. So to optimize your luck, you might have to pass through a valley."

Transitions are never easy. If you want something more than you have, you often need to risk your current situation to get it. Is it better to stay put on that medium-sized hill or try to make luck by reaching the bigger mountain? Those questions crop up in our personal lives, too.

I thought of my college friend Lia, who had been married for a long time and had a couple of lovely grown-up kids. To outside observers, she was puttering along quite well, and you could say she was sitting on the top of one of those medium-sized hills. But she wasn't completely happy and felt her life lacked the romance and passion and adventure she still wanted. Getting that would require moving to a different hill and starting the climb all over again.

And that's what she did. In what had to be the worst year of her life, Lia separated from her husband and then managed to pull off an amicable divorce. She ended up in a small apartment with a few pieces of furniture and a lot of uncertainty. But she was willing to take the risk to reach the goal she wanted. Now a couple of years have passed, and she and a new love are over-the-moon happy and planning their future together—the one she imagined. Her kids are understanding, and her ex-husband remains her friend. She's on her way to the peak of that much bigger hill that she wanted—real happiness.

A lot of people thought Lia was a little crazy to leave that previous hill (aka her longtime marriage). Who knew how it would end up? The immediate future looked glum. But making luck sometimes requires a willingness to climb down and go into the valley. You endure the worst moment (or year) of your life in order to go for the luckier one.

"You have to know what you're after and what you're willing to risk," Barnaby said. "When you're seeking that highest peak, you take a lot of chances."

Companies are often in a similar position. To change and get to the higher peak, they have to go through that valley—which in corporate terms can mean a lower stock price or reduced profits. I mentioned to Barnaby that I'd been watching a movie on Netflix the previous night, and we discussed how that company had gone through big changes.

"Things got worse before they got better," Barnaby said.

Netflix started as a DVD-by-mail business (remember those days?) and managed to put Blockbuster out of business. It was definitely on the top of one medium-sized heap. But CEO Reed Hastings looked around and realized he could make greater luck on the bigger hill of streaming video. Great idea—except once he moved away from the mail-only model and began experimenting with some controversial pricing strategies, the company was widely attacked. At one point in 2011, the Netflix stock price plunged 80 percent.

Hastings turned that worst moment into a lucky future. If you've binge-watched shows like *House of Cards,* you know the company figured out an entirely new approach. They started making their own great programs—and that made great luck, too. They climbed out of the valley and onto a new peak. The stock price is up a few hundred percent since that worst moment.

Reed Hastings probably had some sleepless nights when the company was in its worst moments. Many entrepreneurs and CEOs have struggled through such uncertain transitions. But it also occurred to me that there is a big emotional difference between climbing down from your perch in search of something better, as Hastings and my friend Lia did—and being pushed, as happened to Monica and Susan Greenfield. In the former situation, you start with a sense of control and an awareness of the risks. But when the worst moments come unbidden, you have a greater struggle. Suddenly you're in the valley, and you never planned to be there. All you can do is realize where you are and decide which hill you want to start climbing.

Barnaby told me that at his Luck Lab, he had been talking about the hill-climbing strategy with astrophysicist Piet Hut, the same person who described the value of trying to see a situation more broadly. Hut said that if you pull back and imagine looking at yourself from a distance, you can see all the hills around you.

Hut should know about seeing things from a distance—he has an asteroid named after him.[3] He also knows about turning worst moments into lucky ones, because he's had his share of both. At age thirty-two, he was the youngest person to be made a full professor at the Institute for Advanced Study and was considered a superstar. He came up with a breakthrough formula for measuring the movement of stars and developed the world's fastest (at the time) supercomputer to simulate the behavior of galaxies. But fifteen years after giving him tenure, IAS claimed that Hut the superstar was more like a supernova—the kind that burns out. They filed a suit in court to force him to resign. The complaint against him said, among other things, that he had "failed to develop into an outstanding astrophysicist, much less a leader in the field." Ouch. Talk about a worst moment.

---

3. Asteroid 17031 Piethut, in case you want to check it out. Hut has also done work on how to keep asteroids from hitting Earth—definitely a way of making luck for all of us.

But to be fair, this hadn't come totally out of the blue for Hut. He had become interested in Eastern philosophy, and instead of devoting himself to straight astrophysics, he was, as Barnaby explained, "looking at how Eastern contemplative traditions affect Western science." You might say that Hut was trying to stay on the top of one hill while looking longingly over at another.

The case was eventually settled out of court, with Hut agreeing to move out of the astrophysics department. His work didn't fit into any of the four divisions at the institute, so they created a new interdisciplinary department that was essentially just for him. And that's when the worst moment started to turn into a lucky one.

"It turned out even luckier than he could have imagined," Barnaby said. "He runs his own research area. He can hire anyone without a lengthy vetting process and make his own decisions and create his own activities. If he wants to host yoga camps on the lawn, he can. He has the ultimate in academic freedom."

Instead of hosting yoga camps, Hut has been using the extraordinary freedom to look at big issues like the origins of life and order. He has helped put together a hundred-million-dollar consortium in Japan to look into these questions and launched a new organization in New York City called YHouse with a stated mission to understand the nature of awareness and the interface between science and technology and civil discourse. If that sounds like a mouthful, Barnaby explained that there are complex concepts to consider as robots play a bigger and bigger role in our lives—like whether robots can have emotions and who is accountable when a robot does something wrong.

"These are topics being mulled by the biggest technology companies in the world right now, and Piet has become an international leader in this kind of science, completely in a class by himself,"

Barnaby said. "He never could have done all this from his previous position."

The worst moment for Piet Hut led to the lucky opportunity he wanted to pursue his real passions. And his search to understand the most basic questions about life and meaning could make all of us luckier, too.

Whether you're pursuing robots, romance, or a new job, bad luck isn't always what it seems. Sometimes it's just the impetus you need to make the good luck happen.

CHAPTER FOURTEEN

The Ambulance in Your Backyard

Worry about the right things. . . . Stop looking for trouble. . . .
Understand what you can control. . . . Listen to your doctor
and not your neighbor. . . . Be willing to do nothing.

Barnaby arrived for our Wednesday meeting one rainy day obsessing about staying healthy. Since he has two little daughters, germs were part of the game. One person in his family got a cold and passed it to the next and the next—an endless loop that the parents of many preschoolers know well.

"I don't have time to be sick!" he said, echoing the worry of busy people everywhere.

Illnesses (big and small) can seem like the ultimate bad luck that is out of our control. I told Barnaby about a slim forty-five-year-old woman I met who ran marathons and never smoked and was diagnosed with advanced-stage lung cancer. It seemed shocking and random. How could you possibly explain it?

Ultimately, there probably *is* a way to explain it—researchers continue closing in on more and more discoveries of the genetic and biological underpinnings of disease. But until science has a firmer grasp of them, most of us are frightened by the seeming randomness of how disease strikes. A healthy nonsmoker getting lung cancer? How can you control the bad luck that seems uncontrollable? As we look for causes of the unknown, we're not that far removed from the ancient Roman poet Lucretius, who thought people got sickened by "seeds" in the air, and ancient Greeks like Hippocrates, who blamed an imbalance of the four humors. Some early Chinese physicians thought illness came from spirits who had been angered, and even now many religions believe in divine causes and cures.

Instead of focusing on what you don't know and can't control, you can make luck by concentrating on the health issues you *can* influence. A study led by researchers at the Harvard School of Public Health found that well over a million people in the United States die prematurely every year because they're overweight, smoke, or have high blood pressure. All those early deaths are preventable. Smoking alone accounts for a stunning one in five deaths. Losing weight or tossing away your cigarettes isn't easy—but if you want to increase your luck of a full and healthy life, it's one of the best approaches.

"People think about health as just another lottery," Barnaby said. "But more often they put themselves on the path of killing themselves and then blame bad luck. A key to luck is to get yourself on a good path, and then worry about the right things."

We spend a lot of time worrying about the wrong things—and we get a lot of help with that. Shark attacks worry you? Well, of course. Steven Spielberg's 1975 movie *Jaws* grossed some $260 million in the United States alone, and the Discovery Channel launched its annual Shark Week programming in 1988. It's now the longest-running cable television event in history. Discovery even tossed in a "mockumentary" one year, suggesting that a prehistoric shark called the megalodon had survived and gobbled up a pleasure boat and its crew. The channel has an online feature that lists twenty ways to avoid a shark attack. So if you want to get lucky in the water, you won't swim with a bleeding cut, you'll avoid shiny jewelry and brightly colored swimwear, and you'll stay out of the water if you have an uneven tan, which may resemble the color variations found on fish.

Got all that? Oh, and don't wear a wet suit on a surfboard because it can make you look like a tasty seal.

The irony of all this is that, according to the Centers for Disease Control and Prevention, only about one person a year in the United States dies from a shark attack. But about ten people die *every day* of unintentional drowning. Take off the wet suit because you're worried about sharks, and you may increase your risk of drowning. (A wet suit increases your buoyancy.) And if you really want to get lucky in life, you can frolic happily on the beach and not worry about either sharks or drowning—as long as you remember to stick to the speed limit when you're driving home. Close to a hundred Americans die every day in traffic accidents. That's *one hundred*. Every day. Want to get lucky? Put on a seat belt.

You increase your luck when you focus on real facts, not stirred-up fears. One doctor I know told me about a patient who came to his office in November 2014 asking questions about how to avoid being struck down by Ebola. The outbreak in West Africa was very real, but she hadn't been to West Africa. She didn't know anybody who had been to West Africa. The only people who had contracted the disease in the United States were two nurses who treated Ebola patients from other countries.

"A handful of people who got the disease in Africa were being treated in US hospitals and they were all over the news," he said, "so I told her to turn off the TV and take a flu shot." His advice was clearly the best way to increase her health-luck in the next few months, since tens of thousands of people die every year from influenza. But she declined the flu shot. "She said it had made her friend Mabel sick," said the doctor with a little shake of his head.

Psychologists talk about heuristics, meaning the mental short-cuts we use to make decisions. Looking at statistics, facts, and optimal answers is often very complicated, so we resort to simpler methods. The comment of a friend, a story on the news, or a vague intuition becomes enough to influence what we think. The problem is that we may use the heuristic that works in one situation to solve another, and sometimes they lead to the wrong conclusions.

It's more exciting to talk about sharks than seat belts and more dramatic to worry about Ebola than flu, but it's a good idea to dig a little deeper (and try some serious reasoning) in questions around health. The doctor's recommendation is going to make you luckier than Mabel's. He has seen hundreds of patients before and after flu shots and has a real basis for his advice. But Mabel's anecdotal story hits your emotional buttons and becomes the one that you remember. In this case, though, following the heuristic of what's familiar and comfortable is not necessarily the best idea.

My husband is an extremely busy doctor with a sterling reputation and an overdevotion to his patients, and when my sons were little, they got used to his coming home late from the hospital. Running to greet him in their fluffy pajamas, the boys would throw their arms around him and ask, "Did you save any lives today, Daddy?"

Ron is an internist, so his regular day isn't an episode of *Grey's Anatomy*. His office is filled with ordinary people, not bleeding patients needing emergency heart transplants (by doctors who are otherwise having sex in the supply room). But recently one of those ordinary people, whom I'll call Lucy, came in with a bad headache. She was stressed at work, and it would have been reasonable for any internist, particularly one as busy as Ron, to dash off a prescription for migraine medicine or suggest she de-stress with yoga. But she outlined her symptoms clearly, and some combination of experience and instinct told him there was a bigger problem. He sent her down the hall for an MRI. Within an hour, he had studied the scan, seen a brain aneurysm that was beginning to rupture, and had her in the hospital. Another hour and the bleeding into the brain (called a subarachnoid hemorrhage) could have been fatal.

"So you saved her life," I said with a smile when Ron told me the story that night. "We should tell the boys. They'd be proud."

Ron is an unusually good diagnostician, and I shuddered to think what would have happened if Lucy had visited a different internist. Some 30,000 people suffer from a ruptured brain aneurysm every year, and about 40 percent die. Of those who survive, more than two-thirds have permanent disabilities. With a different outcome, Lucy's friends might have talked about it as one of those tragic events—something you can't prevent. She had just been horribly unlucky.

Instead, she's perfectly fine.

So how do you make yourself one of the lucky ones in this situation? You want to know what's going on, but demanding more tests isn't necessarily the solution. According to the Brain Aneurysm Foundation, only about 1 percent of the patients who come to an emergency room with a severe headache have a subarachnoid hemorrhage. In a doctor's office, the number would be even lower. More than 99 percent of the time, a doctor would be right to mention meditation rather than an MRI. He might give you Excedrin and say to call if the headache gets worse.

For Lucy, of course, that would have been too late. It helped that patient and doctor knew each other well enough to talk it through and realize that something seemed far from normal. Both of them communicating and being involved made the difference.

At another time, Ron recognized a rare heart condition, and he saved a third patient by diagnosing an impending stroke. So from my vantage, the best way to get lucky with your health is to make sure Ron is your doctor. But that may not be practical. (And sorry, he no longer sees new patients.)

Finding the right doctor can improve your luck, but Dr. Kevin Jones, a much-respected researcher at the Huntsman Cancer Institute in Salt Lake City, says you have to play a role in making your own luck, too. When I called him one morning to talk about how doctors make decisions, he told me that medical choices aren't always clear-cut, so it's important to encourage the right conversation between the doctor and patient, much as happened with Lucy.

"The big challenge of medicine is letting patients see how much uncertainty there is," he said. "This can be very unsettling, and some patients like a doctor who is brimming with confidence and claims to know exactly what is wrong. But the way doctors think about things is different from how they communicate to patients."

He pointed out that doctors essentially think in lists. If, like Lucy, you go to a doctor with a bad headache, he's going to run through in his mind the many different things it's likely to be. He'll probably settle on what's most likely—such as a migraine. But if you tell him it's the worst headache you've ever had in your life, he might think again. That's where you play the role in making your own luck. You have to be the partner in your own health care.

"It's what we call a 'differential diagnosis,'" explained Dr. Jones. "We'll try a treatment aimed at what is number one on the list, but if it's not working or there's reason to look further, maybe we need to move on to number two." The line of questions you can ask to improve your luck, said Dr. Jones is "What are the other possibilities you've considered? Is this really a slam-dunk-easy diagnosis, or is there any other treatment you thought about?"

That level of openness can be challenging on both sides, but Dr. Jones thinks it leads to more lucky outcomes. Some doctors go for swagger, he said, and "an air of certainty is great as long as it works, but when it doesn't, you have the patient wondering what happened. Did I do something wrong? Is my doctor an idiot? When really the most likely scenario is that it's just the next thing on the list."

As a bone cancer surgeon who specializes in treating rare cancers called sarcomas in children and adults, Dr. Jones knows that by the time people come to him, they have seen many other doctors and are feeling somewhat overwhelmed. Patients often run to many doctors for second and third and fourth opinions, hoping to improve their chance of a lucky result. But Dr. Jones thinks you can just ask any physician "where they stand on the range of opinions in the field and whether they're conservative or aggressive. When it comes to cancer, I cut wide and take large margins. There are other people in my field of sarcoma surgery who try to cut as close as they can to tumors. You don't have to get three different opinions—you can ask the doctor his philosophy and how it stacks up against others."[1]

A few days later, I happened to be with a friend in the office of a doctor on the Upper West Side of Manhattan. It was a private office associated with NewYork-Presbyterian Hospital, and while we waited for the doctor to come into the examining room, we noticed

---

1. Dr. Jones is never the first doctor to look at a problem, and getting a second set of eyes on anything serious can be a good idea—just because anyone can miss something.

a poster hanging on the wall with five questions patients should ask. The basics were:

✦ Do I really need this test or procedure?
✦ What are the risks?
✦ Are there simpler, safer options?
✦ What happens if I don't do anything?
✦ How much does it cost?

The questions were simple and straightforward, and it struck me that by opening the kind of patient-doctor conversations Dr. Jones advised, they could help produce luckier outcomes. I was surprised to note that the poster put the emphasis on *challenging* procedures rather than asking for more of them. One of the best hospitals in the country was reminding us that when it comes to health, more interventions don't necessarily increase your life or your luck. In medicine right now, that's a huge change and a new direction.

Doing some investigating later, I discovered that the poster was even more important than I had realized—because overtesting often leads to very unlucky outcomes. Researchers have given us new technologies and an alphabet soup of ways to look inside the human body—X-ray, ultrasound, CAT, PET, MRI, NMR, MR spectroscopy . . . the list goes on. Most people figure that the more probing and looking and testing they do, the luckier they'll get. But the exact opposite might be true.

It comes down to the maxim that mothers have repeated to their children for generations—if you look for trouble, you'll probably find it. In medicine, that means that if the doctor looks for a problem even when there aren't any symptoms, there's a good chance he'll land on some suspicious finding. Uncertainty may lead to another test and then another one and perhaps an invasive procedure just to be sure—and whoops, there's a complication. Now you really *are* sick, since secondary infections, misdiagnoses, and adverse reactions can kill you. I came across articles in several esteemed medical journals showing that some of the most popular tests—like standard screenings for heart disease and prostate cancer—often do more harm than good. As an article in *JAMA Internal Medicine* pointed out, "No test (not even a non-invasive one) is benign, and often less is more."

Excessive tests and procedures waste some $200 billion every year in the United States. Let's forget money for the moment, because focusing on cost makes too many people figure that if they can afford it, they might as well do it. But it could be that all they're doing is buying themselves a greater chance of bad luck.

A few years ago, a well-known sports medicine doctor named James Andrews wondered whether MRI scans are overused and misinterpreted. Dr. Andrews knows a thing or two about treating athletes—back in 1985 he did arthroscopic surgery on baseball pitcher Roger Clemens, who went on to win seven Cy Young Awards. (Clemens also publicly credited Dr. Andrews with saving his career.) Other sports stars including Michael Jordan, Tom Brady, Peyton Manning, and Drew Brees have also been his patients.

As an experiment, Dr. Andrews did MRI scans on thirty-one professional baseball pitchers in 2011. A pitcher's luck depends on how well his arm functions—and Dr. Andrews found that twenty-seven of the pitchers had rotator cuff damage and twenty-eight had abnormal shoulder cartilage. But here's the kicker. Every one of the athletes was perfectly healthy and pitching just fine. Doing surgery would be the unluckiest thing they could do.

"If you want an excuse to operate on a pitcher's throwing shoulder, just get an MRI," he said.

Other doctors have pointed out that scans almost always turn up something abnormal. "It is very rare for an MRI to come back with the words 'normal study.' I can't tell you the last time I've seen it," said Christopher DiGiovanni, an orthopedic surgeon now at Massachusetts General Hospital.

It's not just the highly sensitive MRI that causes unlucky interventions. Other studies have suggested that scans of a normal runner's knees will regularly turn up ripped cartilage and torn ligaments even if the person is in no pain. Put a heart monitor on someone for long enough (as many cardiologists now do) and there will be occasional periods of fast heartbeats. But if there are no symptoms, should you treat these perceived problems?

Once you get started looking and treating, it's very hard to say no. One recent study found that in a single year, 25 to 42 percent of Medicare patients are subjected to a needless treatment. All this is more than theoretical, since there's a good chance you or someone you know has been through the experience. It happened to me twice. Once a doctor convinced me to get a mammogram even though I was not yet forty. "Why wait?" he asked. (I later discovered I would have been luckier to wait.) The test found a tiny something that the doctor was sure was benign—"but we should do a biopsy anyway." So I went to the hospital early one morning and put on a blue gown and paper slippers and sat freezing in the waiting room for an hour while my husband kept his arm protectively around me.

Then I was led to the surgical suite and attacked by a scalpel. Of course it was fine. Given how young I was, the odds of a false positive on that mammogram far outweighed the likelihood of a real finding. So there was nothing wrong at all—except the surgeon cut a little more than she should have for the biopsy and it took many months for my body to return to normal.

Then a few years ago, another doctor recommended a scan "just as a double triple check" for what seemed to me a perfectly normal symptom. Again I agreed, because how do you say no? The scan was fine—but turned up an incidental finding of a little thingie. And if there's a little thingie, a doctor wants to follow it up. So there were more tests. Follow-ups for several months. I finally asked the radiologist if she had ever seen this kind of thingie turn to something more dangerous, and she said, "I haven't in my experience, but that doesn't mean it's impossible." Her experience included more than thirty years, so I decided enough was enough. But then my doctor (shockingly) suggested surgery. "Nothing seems wrong, but I can do it in a morning, and then you'll know it's gone," he said. This time I did say no—as loudly as I could. I switched doctors. I didn't do any more scans. I am fine and healthy.

I happen to be one of the least medically anxious people you'll ever meet, so I got through both of these incidents without too much trouble. But it made me realize how intervention leads to intervention—and the pursuit of good health can lead to bad luck. It's estimated that more than 200,000 people die every year from hospital mistakes. So if you want to stay lucky, you don't do an unnecessary surgery. You stay out of a hospital unless you really need one, and if you do have to be admitted, don't linger there longer than absolutely necessary.

———————

Most of us aren't very good at assessing risks, and statistics are more likely to scare us than lead us in a lucky direction. But after I spent one morning reading up on Bayes' theorem, I finally understood why tests sometimes cause more problems than they solve. Reverend Thomas Bayes came up with the complicated mathematical formula back in the 1700s, but math aside, it essentially says that the probabilities of events change as you get more specific information.

Let's say there's a fatal disease that strikes 1 in 1,000 people in your demographic. The test to find out if you have it is 90 percent accurate (which means only 10 percent false positives), and it's 100 percent accurate if you do have the disease. Since it's cheap and easy and you're anxious, you go ahead with it. A couple of days later, the doctor calls and in hushed tones tells you the bad news. Your test was positive. You hang up the phone reeling. Given the odds, you assume you have a 90 percent chance of facing a swift and awful death.

But don't book that final around-the-world cruise just yet, because the truth is that the odds are on your side. You're luckier than you realize.[2]

Here's where Bayes' theorem comes in. Let's give the test to 1,000 people and put all those who get a positive result onto that cruise.

———————

2. Doctors also get confused by these kind of statistical problems. In one study, doctors were told that the probability of breast cancer is 1 percent for a woman at age forty who participates in routine screening, and the cancer will be found 80 percent of the time. There is also a false positive rate of 9.6 percent. If a patient has a positive mammography, what's the likelihood she has breast cancer? Most doctors said between 70 and 80 percent. If you play out the numbers as above, you see it's under 8 percent. In screening 1,000 women, there would be 10 found who have cancer and 96 found who are false positive. Once again, think of those 101 people on the cruise ship, and you understand.

Since the disease strikes 1 in 1,000 and the test is 100 percent accurate in finding the disease if you do have it, the 1 genuinely stricken person will have a positive result. Send her to the ship. But remember the test is 90 percent accurate overall, so it will also return 10 percent false positives. Ten percent of 1,000 is 100—which means all those people will have a positive test, too. We now have another 100 people to go on that cruise.

Your test was positive, so you're one of the people on the ship. Now look around. There are 101 folks there—and *only 1* is actually sick. Feeling a little more confident? Instead of a 90 percent likelihood of the awful disease, you have a *less than 1 percent* chance.

Pretty cool, isn't it?

The big variable is how many people have the disease to start with. If the disease is common, there will be a lot more people on that ship from the group that actually is sick, and so your odds aren't quite as good. The probabilities may change when you look by age or location or gender—and that explains why a mammogram on a woman under forty is so much more likely to have a false positive than a real finding of cancer. There just aren't that many women who have the disease at that age, so the cruise is filled with false positives and very few actual cases.

Whenever medical panels recommend against certain tests—like mammograms on women below a certain age—it's because the panels see that the dangers of false positives far outweigh the bigger benefits. But inevitably, the one person on that cruise who did have the disease announces that her life was saved, so why would we ever change the policy? Reasonable arguments can be made on both sides. Activists will claim that the government is looking only to cut costs at the expense of health. But maybe the opposite is true. Maybe we increase our health and luck when we cut costs and stop looking for problems that don't necessarily exist with the prevalence that we imagined. Sometimes doing too much means our luck sails away.

No matter how careful you are, the world is still filled with viruses and pathogens and tree roots to trip over, and there's a good chance that one of them will get you. When that happens, you make yourself luckier by knowing what to expect and how to prepare.

Barnaby told me that a few years ago, his mother was very ill and needed attention quickly. They were in Philadelphia at the time and quite near the excellent Hospital of the University of Pennsylvania—so he packed his mom into the car and got her to the emergency room. He knew it was an excellent teaching hospital that could handle complex situations, but he wasn't prepared for the scene he encountered.

"The ER waiting room was packed, and there were people screaming in pain and a few were lying on the linoleum floor. One woman was crying that her chest hurt and she was afraid of dying," Barnaby said, shaking his head at the memory. "When we signed in, the person at the desk said they tried to see people as quickly as possible—and the wait was currently four hours."

Barnaby called a friend who had previously been an anesthesiologist at the hospital to see if she could help. "She just sighed and said, 'This is the situation in many emergency rooms in America, Barnaby. I'm sorry.'" But Barnaby is never deterred. He called his own doctor and described the situation, and the doctor realized it was urgent enough to intervene. They were moved to the front of the line.

Waiting times in emergency rooms vary around the country, and the worst situation is often if you have an injury or broken bone.

You're in pain and want something done *now*—but in terms of triage, you're low on the list. You don't die from a sprained ankle. According to the website ProPublica, in most parts of the country, if you go to an ER with a broken bone, you'll spend an average of an hour or so before you even receive pain meds.[3]

Having a relationship with a primary care physician can increase your luck after an injury or when you're deciding if you need an ER. Over the years, I've heard my husband on the phone late at night with patients probably hundreds of times, calmly assessing a situation and advising the panicked person on next steps to take. If you don't have a primary care physician now, finding one is an easy way to increase your luck. Sure, most doctors see a lot of patients, and some studies have questioned whether an annual physical really improves health. But that regular visit does give you a connection to a doctor who can coordinate your care and make the call to the emergency room if necessary to get you admitted. In the lucky-in-health sweepstakes, that counts for a lot.

Barnaby and I gave a call to Dr. Neha Vapiwala, advisory dean at the Perelman School of Medicine and director of the residency program there, to talk about how to make luck inside a hospital. Most of the better hospitals in the country are now putting safety practices in place—and trying to change the dismal fact that medical mistakes are now the third leading cause of death in the country. That's pretty stunning. Only cancer and heart disease kill more people than medical mistakes. Dr. Vapiwala suggested that you increase the likelihood of a lucky outcome if you have someone who

---

3. The website ProPublica has an "ER Wait Watcher" that outlines how long you're likely to hang around an ER in your area before you're seen—and then until you're admitted or sent home. The longest waits are in Maryland and the District of Columbia.

can hang around the hospital with you, be your advocate, and keep an eye on things.

"Don't assume that everyone else knows what's going on and therefore you shouldn't ask a question," she said. "There are many mistakes that can get made, so you want to trust but verify."

I thought about a story a young doctor named Britney told me. A friend of hers had been hospitalized for early complications from a pregnancy. One night a nurse woke her up at midnight saying that it was time to take her pills. "My friend said, 'Are you sure? I've been here a week and I never get medicine in the middle of the night.' The nurse insisted, but my friend wouldn't take it." Britney shook her head. "It was midnight and she'd been woken up and was drowsy but she still managed to question it! How many people could do that?" It was good that she did—because sure enough, the nurse had brought the medicine to the wrong patient.

"She was there trying to save her pregnancy, so imagine the consequences if she'd taken drugs that weren't even for her," Britney said.

When she told me the story, Britney herself was pregnant—and knowing too much about the ins and outs of hospitals had made her somewhat panicked about her own delivery. She had decided to have a doula with her, just so there could be one more person asking questions and making sure no mistakes were made.

I mentioned the story to Dr. Vapiwala, who quickly agreed that you make your own luck by staying involved with your care. "You should have the comfort level to talk to the doctors and nurses treating you," she said. "Some people are afraid to antagonize the team— just like they don't want to upset the waiter who is bringing their food." But the outcomes here are more significant than an overdone burger or a soggy salad. Dr. Vapiwala suggested that you need to be able to find a tone of questioning without negativity, and the team treating you needs to be able to hear it.

After we hung up, I came across a new study out of Israel that looked at how doctors and nurses dealt with the fragile, vulnerable babies in an intensive care unit. Using simulated scenarios, the researchers found that when a parent said something rude, the doctors and nurses made more errors and their skills deteriorated. They weren't being vindictive—they knew they were being evaluated—but their performance slipped anyway. The authors of the study concluded that the rude comments distracted the doctors and nurses and drew their cognitive resources from the work they needed to do.

"We are all human beings, we are affected by rudeness," said one of the authors of the study.

So the conclusion from all this is that if you want to get lucky during a hospitalization, you need to take charge of your own care, make sure someone is advocating for you, ask questions but not in a negative way, and avoid rudeness that can have negative repercussions.

Too complicated? Nobody said getting lucky was easy.

Making your own luck in health is a lot easier if money isn't a problem. Reading up on the subject, I found several studies showing that the richest 1 percent of Americans live up to fifteen years longer than the poorest 1 percent. That's a fairly stunning gap. This pattern isn't new—having money has led to longer life for at least a couple of centuries.

The standard explanation is that if you have money, you can get the best doctors and the best care. Or more important, you can see a doctor at all. One series of reports found that low-income

Americans don't go to doctors because they can't afford them—leading to worse outcomes.[4] But it's more complicated than that. A study published in *JAMA* found that poorer Americans have a dramatically different life expectancy depending on where they live. It starts to seem that health care interventions make a difference, but far more important to longevity are individual behaviors. People who abuse drugs and alcohol die sooner. People who exercise, don't smoke, and stay within a normal weight range live longer.

Sure, you can blame your health problems on bad genes, but most studies now estimate that only about 25 percent of the variation in longevity is caused by genetic factors. Whatever your income level and family background, you can make luck in health by the choices you make. And the choices have to be rational—not based on the latest trends or pseudoscience. One man I know keeps to a careful gluten-free and meat-free diet (he doesn't have an actual gluten allergy—he just thinks it's better), but he also drinks about five glasses of wine a night. I've tried to tell him that there's actual evidence showing excessive alcohol can cause harm and almost nothing that says meat and gluten will do you in. He thinks he's making himself luckier—but I'm not so sure.

Trying to make yourself luckier in health matters can take many forms. Barnaby has an enormously wealthy friend who lives in one of the largest townhouses in Manhattan and also has several other homes around the world. He's used to controlling a lot of things in his life, and so he has spent some time figuring out how to get lucky in health.

"He decided he could increase his luck by having a fully outfitted

---

4. In the UK and Canada, where there are single-payer systems for health care, this isn't the case.

ambulance at each of his homes," Barnaby told me. "In some circumstances, your luck depends on how fast you can be treated, and this was his insurance that he would always get immediate attention."

Okay, that made sense. The rest of us couldn't afford our own ambulances, but we could use his example to make a plan for how to get to a hospital in an emergency. My home in Connecticut is in a fairly remote area, at least an hour from any highly skilled hospital, so it inspired me to think about what I would do if something happened.

Barnaby told me that his friend got the ambulances and hired staff to attend to them. I liked this story as a quirky example of how unconventional thinking can reduce risk and create luck. But then came a twist. On one particular day at his home in the Caribbean, the businessman decided to test out his system. He raced over to the ambulance, which was right there waiting for him, and he was ushered into the back. All was working as planned! The driver got behind the wheel and hit the ignition—but nothing happened. The car wouldn't start. It turned out that the driver, bored from all the hours of sitting around, had been listening to a soccer game on the car radio all day. The battery was dead.

Barnaby and I laughed about the story. You can try hard to make yourself lucky in health issues by taking control of what you can— but you still can't foresee everything.[5]

On a Friday night in the midst of thinking about luck and health, I went to Broadway to see the new musical *Groundhog Day*.[6] The

---

5. Though the battery was dead, Barnaby's friend remains very much alive and healthy.

6. One way I've made myself lucky over the years is by a decision to write about theater—which keeps me getting press tickets.

audience was packed with critics and reporters (the show was about to officially open), so it was an important night. The show, based on the popular movie, was terrific, and by intermission, it was clear that lead actor Andy Karl was the breakout star of the season. He was handsome and funny and perfect in the role. The audience loved him. I loved him.

The fast-paced show required lots of physical exertion from Karl, but he made it seem effortless. Then toward the end of the show, he was dashing across the stage, did a leap, and landed wrong. He fell, and his knee gave out. He crawled off the stage. The show stopped, and the curtain came down. The stage manager asked if there was a doctor in the house.

It turned out that Karl had badly injured his knee. But after twenty minutes or so, he decided to finish. The curtain came up again with the star center stage, and barely able to walk, Karl leaned on scenery and a makeshift cane. His face was contorted with pain, but he kept singing and charming. By coincidence, the lyrics of one of the songs included the lines "I'm here, and I'm fine," and the audience roared approval.

At the end, the audience jumped up cheering for him, and Karl looked out to the standing ovation, tears streaming down his face. He wasn't just the new star of Broadway—he was an inspiration. We all face challenges, and sometimes all you can do is to keep going and trying to make the best of whatever situation you have.

Leaving the theater, I thought of an Arabic-speaking friend of mine, who had told me that there wasn't a word in his language for "accident." "The word we would use is *hadit*, which means more 'incident' or 'event,'" he said. *Hadit* was a good way to think about that night. Getting injured was just one of those events that happens and can't be anticipated. Karl had done everything right to prepare—he was in great shape (with the muscles to prove it) and had probably done that leap a hundred times in rehearsal.

When an incident occurs—whether a busted knee or an unexpected diagnosis—we still have a role in how our luck unfolds. We can give up and bemoan the fates and the bad timing. Or we can decide to face whatever happens with a firm determination to make our own luck and a decision that the show (and life) must go on.

CHAPTER FIFTEEN

How to Get Lucky in a Disaster (Natural or Otherwise)

Get all the information you can. . . . Take time to prepare (even if you feel silly). . . . Engage your higher brain. . . . Avoid wishful thinking.

Spending a warm May weekend on campus for my college reunion, I slipped away from the socializing one afternoon and sat in the back of a classroom as a young professor of geology named Maureen Long talked about earthquakes. And tsunamis. And other problems related to natural disasters. I left thinking I should have been a geology major—which clearly shows what a good teacher she is.

When I saw Barnaby the next week, I mentioned that her lecture had inspired me to think about who survives natural disasters and who doesn't. Was it simply random chance, or did the survivors do something right to prepare? There had to be a way to increase your luck in these unluckiest of situations.

Earthquakes, tornadoes, hurricanes, tsunamis, and other natural disasters seem shocking each time they occur, but they happen fairly regularly.[1] Airplane crashes aren't exactly "natural," but they seem to fit in the same category. How do you become the person who walks away unharmed?

"It's such a good question," Barnaby said, "and I've thought about

---

1. They recently seem to be occurring with greater frequency and force.

it a lot because my mother was once the earthquake planner for the state of Alaska."

I gave a little laugh—I had yet to find a topic that Barnaby didn't have some experience with. He explained that his mom had trained in arts and design and knew nothing about seismic science, but she was spirited and entrepreneurial and got the Alaska job anyway. She learned the science quickly and tried to raise earthquake awareness through programs in schools and public brochures. But she was stymied at every turn by powerful people who owned land and property in vulnerable spots—and didn't want the topic discussed.

"Alaska is on the Ring of Fire—which is basically the most earthquake-prone set of plates in the world," Barnaby told me. A great earthquake that struck on Good Friday of 1964 was the most powerful in the history of America and the second-most powerful ever recorded in the world (9.2 on the Richter scale). Given Alaska's sparse population, casualties were limited, though more than a hundred people died in the tsunamis that followed.

"There was extensive damage in downtown Anchorage, but just a few hours after the quake, an influential property developer named Wally Hickel announced he would rebuild," Barnaby said. "Geologists urged him not to, but he put up a luxury hotel, anyway."[2]

Maybe it's not so surprising that a developer/politician who puts his name on buildings values his own profits—and ignores long-term consequences. When he eventually ran for office, people liked Hickel's promises of prosperity and he became governor. His legacy of supporting business may seem less reasonable if another earthquake sweeps through.

---

2. Hickel's Hotel Captain Cook is still standing and very popular. It has three towers and 550 guest rooms and inspired more building in the area.

"Anybody who wants to be lucky when visiting Anchorage should be careful about staying in hotels built on questionable land," Barnaby advised.

When it comes to natural disasters, we're not very good at thinking ahead. I couldn't find a single review of Hickel's hotel on TripAdvisor that mentioned earthquakes. And why would anyone really think of that? If you want to play the odds, you figure that a big one isn't going to strike just when you're spending a night in Anchorage before your Alaskan cruise.

But eventually the odds can go against you. A geophysicist named Mary Lou Zoback spent years trying to get the city of San Francisco to pay more attention to the earthquake readiness of its buildings, but like Barnaby's mom, she came up against real estate interests worried about property values. "Eventually they realized there was some grassroots interest in the safety of buildings," she told us.

The San Francisco earthquake of 1906 killed some 3,000 people, and more than a hundred years later, Zoback pointed out that some of the most popular spots in the city (like the marina and the financial district) are built in sensitive areas. During an earthquake, the buildings on top of them could be vulnerable.

But better luck may be on the way. Laws have passed that require people to buttress older structures, and all the new building taking place in San Francisco (and there's a lot of it) has to be earthquake resistant.

Thoroughly intrigued now by how you could stay lucky in an earthquake, I gave a call to the professor I'd met at my reunion, Maureen Long, and told her how much I'd enjoyed her talk to alums.

"Oh, that makes me happy," she said. "It's such an exciting subject to understand."

As warm on the phone as she had been in person, she told me

that she decided to become a geophysicist when she was in eighth grade and took the standard course on earth science. She was captivated by plate tectonics, the study of the underlying structures of the earth. "I thought it was the coolest thing I'd ever heard of," she said.

The movement of the plates leads to earthquakes and volcanoes, but Professor Long pointed out that they may have a lucky side, too. Other planets like Mars and Venus don't have plate tectonics, and there's the possibility that over millions and tens of millions of years, they contribute to our planet's habitability.

"We're trying to understand what it is about the Earth that leads to this very specific behavior, with the plates moving around and the oceanic crust getting recycled back into the mantle and building continents," she said. "The fact that the Earth can exchange material between its interior and its oceans over millions of years might play a role in regulating the very long-term carbon cycle of the planet. It speaks to a lot of fundamental questions about what allowed life to develop."

That did sound pretty cool. And lucky, too. But on a shorter-term basis, the plate shiftings mean earthquakes are a lot more common than you think. There are about fifteen magnitude 7 earthquakes a year—and you don't want to be around when one hits. Many of them happen far away from people and infrastructure, so we don't hear about them on the evening news. But then comes one like the 2010 Haiti earthquake, which killed well over 100,000 people (some estimates go much higher) and offered a devastating reminder that poor infrastructure and a complete lack of preparedness can lead to very, very bad luck.

Tragedy often hits unexpectedly, but sometimes there are warning signals that can give you time to prepare. The earthquake that rumbled under the Indian Ocean in 2004 was a magnitude 9 (the third largest ever recorded) and unleashed a devastating tsunami. The first waves—really walls of water—that ravaged the coast of Thailand came quickly. Vacationers lolling on the beaches were submerged in the swirling water, and there was no obvious way to prepare to be lucky. But across the ocean, waves continued to propagate, and tens of thousands of fatalities occurred in places far away, many hours later. "You need systems in place ahead of time so people can be warned and evacuate," said Professor Long. Without these systems, the tsunami killed some 250,000 people in fourteen countries.

Scientists can't yet predict where and when an earthquake will occur, but there are other ways to get warnings.[3] "You can sometimes get thirty, forty, or fifty seconds of warning, which doesn't sound like a lot—but it means you can shut down the nuclear reactor and get the subway trains out of the tunnel. It's a very exciting innovation." The systems exist in Japan and are being developed in California and the Pacific Northwest. The advance notice means you might get lucky enough to move to a doorframe or duck under a table and avoid falling debris.

Widespread luck in natural disasters often requires a carefully prepared official plan—like early warning systems and safer building codes. But when the governments don't do enough, the rest of us are left on our own. We have to figure out the steps that will make us lucky even when others aren't.

Barnaby suggested we talk to Laurence Gonzales, who has been writing about dangerous situations for years. He's looked at everything

---

3. Professor Long explained that the initial waves from an earthquake—called the P-waves—travel faster than the surface waves, which are the damaging ones. "In places where you have a lot of instruments and can get the data very rapidly, you can sense the P-waves and put out a warning," she said.

from wilderness accidents to plane crashes, trying to understand who survives and who doesn't. In a long conversation with him, we discovered that when it comes to disaster preparedness, Gonzales is a do-everything kind of guy. He told us that he and his wife had been at a doctor's office the previous day when a fire alarm went off. She was writing a check at the reception desk "and she didn't even hesitate. She dropped her checkbook, walked over to me, and we went straight to the exit and out. Was it a false alarm? It usually is. But if an alarm goes off, you leave the building. Otherwise why have a fire alarm?"

It's a good point, but most of us *don't* leave the building the moment we hear an alarm. We hesitate, we try to get more information, we see what everybody else is doing. Our instinct is to believe that everything is okay. Many years ago, my husband and I were asleep in our suburban home with our (then) very young children down the hall. At about three A.M., the burglar alarm sounded and the phone rang immediately, with our alarm company calling to check. My husband reached for the phone. "False alarm," he said groggily, and he gave the code that said all was well.

He hung up, and I looked at him in shock.

"Why did you do that?" I asked.

He got out of bed and, in his boxer shorts, went downstairs to look for intruders. I'm not sure what he would have done if he found one. Fortunately it *was* a false alarm, but we have talked about that night often.

The psychoanalyst Stephen Grosz wouldn't have been surprised. In his book *The Examined Life*, he points out how difficult it is for us to break our usual patterns. My husband is competent and self-sufficient, and those traits usually work out well. They are his instinctive fallback. He had never encountered an alarm in our home that *wasn't* set off by mistake. But hearing an alarm in the middle of the night, he might have done better to try shutting off his natural instincts. Grosz said that in one nightclub fire, some people went to pay their checks before leaving and others died because they tried to leave through the door they entered. Oftentimes people simply linger too long—they may smell the smoke, but they wait to see the flames. "We resist change. Committing ourselves to a small change, even one that is unmistakably in our best interest, is often more frightening than ignoring a dangerous situation," he said.

Laurence Gonzales pointed out that we create mental models that let us acclimatize to almost anything. He described how his little granddaughter first saw a garbage truck when she was not yet two years old, and she was scared and excited as it roared by. But once she had seen the truck enough times, she stopped noticing it. "She incorporated it into a model that allows her to proceed through life efficiently," he told us.

As a grown-up, you can't live happily—or make yourself lucky—if you're stunned or scared by every event. You acclimatize. You recognize that not everything needs your attention. But sometimes you become so comfortable that you don't realize when you're facing danger. Gonzales told us that on the Gulf Coast of Texas, where he grew up, people would have hurricane parties. "You didn't get out of town or go into a big building to protect yourself—you ordered a bunch of booze and had your friends over," he said. Before one very big hurricane some years ago, the sheriff headed over to a row of apartment houses on a Galveston beach to warn people that the storm was coming and they needed to leave. One group that was partying on a fifth-floor balcony called back, "Hey, don't sweat it, we do this every year"—and they just laughed and waved.

"The storm surf in that hurricane was thirty-five feet, and it killed all those people," Gonzales told us. "This is the classic story of how mental models can undermine us."

If you're accustomed to hurricanes and fire alarms and garbage trucks that don't lead to problems, how do you know when you've hit the one that's different? Gonzales thinks that lucky people are those who are more alert to warning flags and have less tolerance for close shaves.

"I've been a pilot most of my life, flying airplanes, and my motto is that I'd rather be on the ground wishing I were in the air than in the air wishing I were on the ground," he said. When he rented a plane, his rule of thumb was that if he found three things wrong with it, he would reject it, figuring that there were even more problems that he hadn't yet found.

I could see how setting up parameters ahead of time might work in all sorts of situations. Instead of falling into the mode of assuming all is well, you have guidelines that kick in, and your rational brain would have to purposefully override them. However smoothly our lives normally go, we are often teetering on the edge of unrecognized disaster, and Gonzales thinks we make ourselves lucky by "cultivating an attitude of a little more humility and suspicion."

When a system is complex, the likelihood of catastrophic failure is extremely high. Gonzales calls it the dinner party paradox. Imagine that you've made a reservation at a very popular restaurant where your entire party has to arrive exactly on time or you don't get the table. You have reliable friends who are 90 percent likely to be on time. The question is, How many friends can you invite before you're pretty much assured of not having dinner?

Your first instinct (like mine) is probably—invite as many as you want! My friends are 90 percent reliable! But doing the math gives a surprising answer. Once you have more than six people, the reservation is probably doomed and you'll end up having to catch a burger at the local diner.[4]

"Now, take a system like a DC-10 aircraft, which has 250,000 parts, or the space shuttle, with significantly more," said Gonzales. "Even if you manufacture each part to 99.9 percent reliability, do the arithmetic and there comes a level of complexity beyond which a catastrophic failure is absolutely certain."

When those big disasters happen, our instincts kick in and usually lead to a dramatic response. There's the oft-discussed fight-or-flight syndrome and what some neuroscientists call the "rage circuit" (think what happens when you hit your thumb with a hammer). But to be the lucky survivor, you sometimes have to fight against all those instincts. "If you can bring your higher brain, your logical brain, into the picture, then you can start to manage these automatic responses in a way that's going to be useful," Gonzales said.

I asked Gonzales how you can engage that higher brain, and he suggested activities that are "patterned, rhythmic, repeated, and directed toward some goal." Knitting seems to fit the list, as does sharpening knives or playing a musical instrument or a game of pool. "They all have a linear step-by-step engagement of the thinking brain that has a calming effect, because it engages the neocortex and helps you dominate your emotional responses," said Gonzales.

In the middle of a disaster, you're not going to start knitting to get yourself under control. But Gonzales thinks that if you've trained

---

4. Each person is 90 percent reliable, so if two people are coming, the odds of one of them being late is 90 percent times 90 percent, or an 81 percent likelihood. With another person, you multiply by 90 percent again. Once you keep multiplying, you're okay through six people, and with the next person, you're down to a 47 percent chance that they'll all arrive on time—less than half. Get ready for the diner.

your nervous system ahead of time with those calming activities, you have a better chance of getting through. "Part of the process of righting yourself in an emergency is believing that it's possible," he said.

A couple of years ago, my husband built an enormous deck on our country house. It took all summer, hours and hours each weekend, and he got great satisfaction in the methodical work of situating each plank and pounding it into place. Don't ask me—I didn't understand it at all. But now it occurred to me that in his real life as a doctor, Ron is faced by daily crises and emergencies. He needs that higher-brain ability to cope with them rationally and unemotionally, and maybe building a deck or playing the piano (which he also does) helps with that. If so, it's fine with me. The deck looks great.

Finding a way to get the rational mind working and engaged in an emergency can make all the difference between emerging as one of the lucky ones or not. Gonzales said that when he and his wife check into a hotel room, they immediately walk down the hall to the exit stairway to familiarize themselves with what they would do if they had to crawl out in a smoky fire.

"That sounds a little excessive," I said. "You travel a lot, and hotel fires are pretty rare. Is it really worth your time?"

"You have to think about the risk-reward loop. What do I gain, and what do I lose? If there's a fire and I don't get out, I'm dead. In going down the hall to find the exit, I'm just using a few minutes of my precious TV-watching time."

Okay, fair enough. But after we hung up, I thought that we also shouldn't fool ourselves into thinking we can control (or predict) every disaster. By its very nature, a disaster is unexpected, and the lucky people will be those who keep their wits and higher brain function no matter what happens. You can check the emergency exits everyplace you go, but if there's a disaster during your hotel stay, it's probably going to be something completely unexpected. Instead of turning on the TV, maybe you could use the extra time to prepare your brain by knitting. At least you get a sweater out of it.

When a cool head meets a hot disaster, there can be unexpected success. That was the case in early 2009 when a US Airways flight leaving LaGuardia Airport was hit by a flock of geese a few minutes after takeoff. Both engines went out, and pilot Chesley Sullenberger determined he couldn't get back to the airport in time. Without a lot of options—and with absolutely no *good* options—he decided to land the plane on the Hudson River in New York City.

Birds get sucked into plane turbines all the time, but it's exceedingly rare for the engine to be damaged. If it does happen, the pilot can just make a routine landing with one engine. For a double bird strike to disable *both* engines goes to whatever category is well beyond exceedingly rare. Nobody could possibly plan (or train) for an incident as unexpected as losing two engines at 2,800 feet over the densely populated Manhattan Island. Sullenberger had to respond instantly.

In the midst of the unforeseen, you do best if you can stay calm, call on your experience and knowledge, and look for a familiar pattern. As a retired US Air pilot named John Wiley put it at the time, "You take the picture you've got and you turn it into one that you recognize. You visualize the river like it's just another runway."

Sullenberger landed flight 1549 on the river near the middle of Manhattan. The crew led the passengers off the plane and onto the floating wings to await the rescue boats that quickly arrived. A police helicopter with trained divers hovered above for anyone who jumped in panic into the icy water.

All 155 people on board survived. Television reporters around the world called it the "Miracle on the Hudson," and Sullenberger became an immediate hero—he got calls from two presidents and a standing ovation at the Super Bowl. A Clint Eastwood–directed movie about his heroics called *Sully,* starring Tom Hanks as the calm and reticent pilot, got top reviews and earned more than $200 million at the box office. But it was the mayor of Sully's small hometown of Danville, California, who summed it up.

"He had two minutes to make a decision. I can't even say my name that fast," said Mayor Newell Arnerich.

Plane disasters always get attention because they are both unusual and terrifying. They make us feel out of control. But the triumph mixed with disaster in this case was even more compelling. It reminded us that any crisis may have a random cause (birds, really?), but the luck of survival depends on the same talent and hard work that defines luck in other circumstances. The right person can control the randomness of a crisis and produce a lucky result. Sullenberger had been flying for forty years, but what ultimately mattered was what he did in the 208 seconds from bird strike to water landing. Sometimes you make luck over a lifetime. In a crisis, you make it in a few seconds.

If you're not a pilot but want to stay lucky when you're flying, the good news is that luck is already on your side. I came across a very amusing (in my view) app called Am I Going Down?, which lets you put in the flight details of your next trip and then uses official data from various transportation boards to tell you the likelihood of a crash. The app developer came up with the program to help his wife with her fear of flying. His idea was that if you're worried about flying, you don't need to take sleeping pills—you should just "take the truth." So, for example, if you're flying on a British Airways 747-400 from London to New York, the app says you have a one in nine million chance of going down. You could take the flight every day for the next 25,000 or so years without a problem. Still need that Xanax?

When I chatted about this with Barnaby, he told me that he had once been on a small Cessna when the engine cut out at a few thousand feet. There was an ominous quiet in the cabin, and looking out the window, he could see the single propeller had stopped cold. His heart seemed to stop cold, too. Fortunately, the pilot was able to restart the engine.

The good news is that most plane crashes aren't fatal. In one study of commercial crashes involving about 53,000 people, some 98 percent survived. (Admittedly, a small Cessna may not do as well.) If you are in a crash, is there a way to make luck? In 2013, scientists and test pilots purposely crashed a Boeing 727 filled with sensors and test dummies in the Mexican desert. They found that the back of the plane is the safest place to be. About 78 percent of the passengers in the back section would have survived, while those in the first dozen rows didn't do as well. (Being in the middle of the plane—over the wings—was, well, in the middle.) The researchers did offer the caveat that a different kind of crash (i.e., tail first) would have a different outcome.

The overall chances of death on a commercial flight are 1 in 4.7 million, so Barnaby pointed out that anytime he gets a nifty first-class upgrade, he intends to keep it. Going to the back of the plane doesn't do very much to improve those already excellent odds. You can make yourself luckier by wearing your seat belt and, if there's an unexpected landing, bracing for impact (as passengers did on Sully's flight). If you're really serious about increasing luck on a plane, you might want to bring a face mask or a large bottle of Purell, since the biggest danger on a flight may be from the germs you pick up.

With millions of people hopscotching daily all over the country and the world, we do better than ever at sharing ideas and innovations, but we have also created a giant mixing pot of viruses and bacteria. Most germs put you in bed for a day or two, but Barnaby reminded me that "some like Ebola virus or flesh-eating bacteria are outright deadly. What concerns epidemiologists is that sooner or later there will be a pathogen that wipes out half a billion people or more before they can find a way to stop it."

With that unsettling thought in mind, we gave a call to Pardis Sabeti, a brilliant scientist and mathematician whom Barnaby knew from their days at Oxford. She first gained academic fame when she was in her mid-twenties for breakthroughs linking changes in DNA structures to better methods of fighting disease. She's now a full professor at Harvard—and is known around Cambridge for Rollerblading to classes and singing in an alternative-rock band.

When Ebola hit West Africa in 2014, Dr. Sabeti led a group that used genomic sequencing to figure out how the deadly disease was being transmitted—and better ways to identify and treat it. The disease was terrifying. There was no vaccine or drug to fight it. People were dying quickly.

Dr. Sabeti told us that she put three mottoes on the board for her team during the outbreak—and they could be guidelines for anyone looking to stay lucky (and healthy) during a major outbreak. They were:

1. Safety first
2. No wishful thinking
3. Prioritize

"The only way to avoid bad luck is to recognize that it can happen," Dr. Sabeti said. "We've had plagues in the past and you have to be very respectful of the power of darkness. Not underestimating the potential for bad things to happen is one of the best ways to avoid them."

To Dr. Sabeti, safety first meant thinking about how to mitigate risk while moving forward. Prioritizing became crucial because "you want to figure out what you can do that will add value, rather than getting on your horse and riding off in all directions."

In the context of any crisis, wishful thinking may be the most dangerous problem of all. The guys who were partying as the hurricane came in and the people who stayed at the nightclub as the fire broke out were all victims of wishful thinking. *Nothing bad can happen because it hasn't before.* During the Ebola outbreak, Dr. Sabeti became frustrated with policy makers whose approach was "maybe it won't spread to Sierra Leone, or maybe it won't come to America. Magical or wishful thinking isn't the way to make a decision."

One way to create good luck in a crisis is to avoid bad luck—and that requires clear-sighted planning. "Some people think that if you get an insurance policy, you're willing something bad to happen, but it's really quite the opposite. You batten down the hatches so that you can relax. If you've thought about the worst-case scenario, you're prepared for everything. In the context of this outbreak, I would see people working from the premise that the virus wouldn't mutate. Much better to say, 'Maybe it will mutate—and then what?'"

Dr. Sabeti believes you make luck in a crisis by being neither complacent nor alarmist. She found herself telling people over and over, "Don't be scared, be prepared." At one point early in the Ebola outbreak, before any cases had come to America, she was giving a talk at a conference of Harvard's biggest donors. "I told all these billionaires to go out and get a bunch of canned products that would allow them to stay inside for twenty-one days. I didn't say it to make them panic and go crazy, but let's say in an ideal world you have twenty-one days of canned food at home, the outbreak gets resolved quickly, and you give the food to the homeless. Isn't that better than if you wait, wait, wait, thinking everything will be okay—and then it's not okay? Then you have scenes like in the movies where people are punching each other in grocery stores."

During an outbreak, Dr. Sabeti thinks that more information brings more luck. It's true on a global scale, where shared findings usually lead to better public health outcomes. And it's also true for an individual. If you understand what's going on, you can take reasonable steps and avoid mass hysteria. She's currently trying to create a global outbreak surveillance system, starting with an app that Harvard students can use when they have an infection. They input their symptoms and get information about what might be wrong. An individual diagnosis is hard to make in infectious disease—"99 percent of the time you have no idea what it is, but just hope it's not lethal," she said—but when it's a shared event with multiple samplings, the signal-to-noise ratio improves. There's more chance of recognizing the start of an outbreak.

"You want a system that's comfortable for people so that they can immediately leverage it in a crisis scenario," she said. "It's like the kidnap training I got when I was traveling—"

"You got kidnap training?" I asked, interrupting her in surprise.

"Yes, several times. In the middle of a crisis your field of vision narrows and you lose your logical stance. Everything goes very dark. You want to have everything at your fingertips before you even start.

The key to luck and survival is understanding what you can control and what you can't and so avoiding the panic."

However good you are at grabbing the opportunities to make a lucky life, some things can happen to throw you off. Illness, death, and political upheaval (or kidnapping) can upend the best-laid plans. Things change, often unexpectedly. As the author Joan Didion wrote shortly after her husband collapsed in their living room from a massive heart attack:

> *Life changes fast.*
> *Life changes in the instant.*
> *You sit down to dinner and life as you know it ends.*

Didion was struck by the ordinariness of tragedy. "Confronted with sudden disaster we all focus on how unremarkable the circumstances were in which the unthinkable occurred," she said. Tragedy can come from the clear blue sky—often literally. The morning of September 11, 2001, was clear and cloudless, and people often describe the sunshine of that morning with a kind of awe—as if there should have been some greater warning, some black clouds and thunderstorms, before the planes struck the World Trade Center and the Pentagon.

For Dr. Sabeti, personal disaster also came on the day of a cloudless sky. Soon after the Ebola crisis, she was invited to give the opening talk at a conference of world leaders—the kind of event where politicians and celebrities and Silicon Valley stars and global leaders all gather. You can imagine Ashton Kutcher and the president of Mexico jamming with Senator Cory Booker and a high-tech

CEO. In the mornings they hear smart talks and in the afternoons engage with one another in sports activities that Dr. Sabeti described as "insane and way too risky."

Being a keynote speaker at this kind of gathering is a big deal, and Dr. Sabeti prepared for the day with an hour and a half of stretching and handstands "and other crazy stuff." Her talk was extremely well received, and everyone was busy discussing it afterward and gathering around her. "People started weighing in on what I should do for the afternoon," she said. Her original plan for rope climbing got shunted aside when she discovered a participant the previous year had shattered an ankle. So she switched to an ATV tour when she was told it was the safest option.

"Somehow in this context I just took it on face value and didn't ask a lot of very specific questions about safety," she said. "Little did I know that even though we were on a road, it was on the side of a two-hundred-foot drop. Basically the driver lost control and jumped out and we went over a cliff."

Thrown from the ATV, she was smashed against boulders that crushed her pelvis and knees and caused head injuries. Dr. Sabeti was flown from Montana to a trauma center in Seattle, where she went through twenty-five hours of surgery in four days. "Doctors said I had a 5 to 8 percent chance of survival. Most people with this kind of multiple trauma die. I'm one of the luckiest of the unluckiest."

Given her experience in dealing with crises and disaster, Dr. Sabeti has played and replayed her own accident in her mind. Even in an unforeseeable situation, she thinks preparation helps—she was in such good shape that her tissue regenerated quickly, and her body was resilient enough to survive daily blood transfusions.

"I have forty plates in my body, and I suffered a serious concussion where I couldn't read for four months. My vision changed, and

I have chronic vertigo. Most people in my condition never go back to work," she said. But she is back in her lab, and though it took many months, she is again bubbling with ideas that she cares about.

After any disaster—an earthquake or a hurricane, a plane crash or an Ebola outbreak or a devastating accident—the survivors don't just pick up their lives where they left off. They are forever changed. They are stunned by the random chance that left them living and also slightly overwhelmed to realize that their own actions contributed to their fate. In the unluckiest of circumstances, they found a way to emerge as one of the lucky survivors. It is scary and sobering. Dr. Sabeti's physical struggles may never go away. But she will continue making luck for herself and others.

Nobody wants to be in an earthquake or a hurricane, and not a lot of good comes from hotel fires or airplane crashes or devastating accidents. Being one of the lucky survivors can feel very random. But a willingness to prepare, think calmly, and involve your higher brain can give you the very narrow, lucky edge that just might make the difference.

PART FIVE

THE BIG PICTURE

Anything's possible in human nature. Love.
Madness. Hope. Infinite joy.

—Arundhati Roy, *The God of Small Things*

CHAPTER SIXTEEN

The Lucky Path: Find Your Compass

Know that you have many possibilities. . . . Navigate with a compass, not a map. . . . Change the song with the next note you play.

Barnaby came back from his Luck Lab one day excited about how far we'd come. He was confident that we had uncovered the ways to create lucky opportunities on many fronts. But for the next step, he was thinking about what luck meant in a larger context.

"The big question we have left is what makes a lucky life," he said. "We've figured out all the ingredients that go into it, but now you have to put them together in the right way."

The ingredients we had lined up included generating more luck for yourself in all sorts of ways—success in your career, confidence with your kids, energy in your love life, and an ability to turn bad days into good ones. All that gives you a sense of control over the possibilities ahead. But as you put all those lucky pieces together, what do they add up to in the bigger sense?

"It's a little bit like baking," Barnaby said. "You have the salt and the flour and the water, but how you blend them together makes all the difference. You can end up with a loaf of white bread or a fancy challah. You have to know which you prefer and what you're trying to make."

Barnaby didn't strike me as either a white bread or a challah guy—more like whole wheat with raisins and poppy seeds (or something equally unusual and interesting). But the point was fair enough. In luck and life, if you don't know where you're going, you're probably not going to get there.

A few years earlier, Barnaby was investigating the expansive topic of meaning and purpose in life, and he did a study of students on college campuses. He wanted to find out how college would help them reach their larger life goals. But he quickly realized that most of the students didn't *have* larger life goals.

"They lacked a bigger picture of what would matter to them in life," Barnaby said. Students he met on campuses across the country spoke vaguely about their post-graduation future, but when he asked for specifics about the jobs they imagined, he got a lot of uncomfortable pauses and answers along the lines of "anything I can get" or "something that pays a lot."[1] The lack of clarity wasn't just about their careers. Barnaby said he would have been happy if someone said he wanted to get married and have a house by the sea or hoped to return to his hometown and help his ailing parents. Anything that suggested a deeper reflection on life and ultimate goals.

"It's hard enough turning an aspiration to reality when you *have* an aspiration. To make luck you have to think ahead and have a sense of what matters to you. Otherwise you just wind up wherever the river takes you," he said.

"I think that's called going with the flow," I said with a laugh.

"But you need to put yourself in the right place before luck can find you," Barnaby said earnestly. "What you aim for has a big bearing on where you end up."

Most of us understand that we can't control everything. When

---

1. The only notable exception was students headed for professional schools like medicine or architecture, where lots of preplanning had been required.

we asked people in our survey about elements in their own life that had led to luck, "planning my life and career carefully" landed in dead last place. Well over half the people in our survey thought their luck increased if they tried a new direction when a previous one wasn't working. The largest percentage (64 percent) thought they got lucky by being curious and seeking new opportunities.

But Barnaby was pointing out an important subtlety. Our respondents were completely right that you can't plan everything and have to be open to new opportunities. The ability to recognize those possibilities (often when others don't) lets you make luck. And that's the tricky part. You need a context in order to see what's around you.

To go back to Barnaby's baking metaphor, you probably have flour and water and salt in your kitchen, but without some goal that involves making or eating or selling bread, those ingredients will just sit there. Once you take out the KitchenAid and start making that bread, your view of everything else changes. You see the possibilities that can make the lucky magic happen. The packages of dried fruit and raisins and chocolate bits that have been tucked away (unnoticed) in your cabinet for months suddenly take on new potential. You open them up, mix them in, and create a wonderful new loaf. When you win the blue ribbon at the county fair, you can modestly attribute it to the random chance of what happened to be in your cabinet. But it's more accurate to think of it as planned serendipity. You hadn't decided ahead on that particular result, but once you got on the right (bread-making) path, you were alert to opportunities and saw what others couldn't.

What's true for baking bread is also true for . . . building an airline. Barnaby had recently met Tony Fernandes, the entrepreneur who founded the no-frills airline AirAsia. As they spoke, Fernandes modestly attributed his success to serendipity. He told Barnaby that he had been thinking about how to create a low-cost way to fly for the more than half of Asians who never got on a plane. He was looking for the right entry point. After the tragedy of September 11, 2001, the costs for leasing planes dropped dramatically, so it was much easier to get into the business. As he said—serendipity.

Or maybe not.

"I don't know what you were doing in late 2001, but I was here and it didn't occur to me to buy an airline," I said when Barnaby told me the story.

"Yes, it's nice that he attributes his success to serendipity, but he had been setting up his plan and was waiting for the right moment. When it occurred, he saw the opportunity and captured the luck. It has made him a billionaire."[2]

When I was very young, I saw life as a series of tests to pass—and I unconsciously figured that I just had to keep working hard and getting As to end up with a lucky life. But at some point in my mid-twenties, I realized that life wasn't the same as school at all. Instead of a steady path of courses and exams leading to the triumph of a cap and gown, I now had endless opportunities for jobs and love affairs and adventures that could lead—anywhere.

Looking back at my own experience, I can understand why the college students Barnaby interviewed seemed so vague. The path of success for middle-class kids is laid out very clearly: Do well in school, score high on your SATs, get into college. But then you graduate. And

---

2. Fernandes managed to meet with the prime minister of Malaysia to talk about buying a government-owned airline that was going bankrupt. When he got the go-ahead, he mortgaged his house and scraped together the money. Within a year, he had erased the debt and brought low-cost flying to people who'd never had it before.

part of growing up is making the discovery that you need to pick your own path and make your own luck.

Barnaby pointed out that our sense of what matters—and what makes a lucky life—changes over the years. When you were in high school, winning a track meet probably seemed like the most important thing in the world, but now the first-place trophy is probably tucked away in the back of a closet. A few years later, you might have spent months obsessing about having the perfect wedding, but now that you're raising four kids and two dogs, you can't remember why that one day seemed to matter so much.

The trophy and the wedding may both be part of a lucky life, but a single event (of any sort) brings luck only when it fits into a broader picture. So, for example, getting the starring role in a movie when you're just a kid could seem like the luckiest thing in the world. Lindsay Lohan surely felt that way when she starred in her first Disney movie at age twelve and had a quick streak of hits that made her a teen sensation before she was old enough to drive. How lucky is that! The years of drug abuse and rehab that followed would suggest it wasn't very lucky for her at all.

But Lohan is barely in her early thirties now, so she may turn those bad years around and move forward. (Drew Barrymore did it after similar early circumstances.) She was on a lucky path and fell off. She can get back on it or choose a different path or figure out what, in a greater sense, would make a lucky life for her.

The even younger actress Emma Watson got her first professional acting role playing Hermione Granger in the blockbuster Harry Potter movies. Uh-oh. After Lohan, we all knew what happened to young stars. But Emma stayed sane. She took time to make other movies, graduate from Brown University, and become an international advocate for women's rights. Oh, and she got certified as a yoga teacher and meditates so that she can "always be at home with myself." Starring in *Freaky Friday* or *Harry Potter* is just an event. Whether you turn it into a lucky life or a disaster depends on what you do with it—the path you follow, the next step you take.

It made me think of the great jazz musician Miles Davis, who used to say that there's no such thing as a wrong note in jazz—it's the next note you play that makes it right or wrong. He could have said that there's no such thing as a right note, either. You can start with something wonderful and turn it sour, or start with the flattest sound and make it sing. Being able to play a riff on any note—that's called jazz. It's also called what makes you lucky in life.

Part of the thrill of a jazz club is hearing one musician play off the next, picking up on what the other person has done and making it different and bigger and maybe greater. What ultimately matters is how it all fits together.

Those paths to luck are sometimes checkered, and we seem to (unconsciously) believe that life should even out. When something good happens to a person who has been struggling, we sigh in relief and say, "You deserved it." And when we hear about a celebrity facing troubles, we sympathize but aren't completely surprised. It just makes them more human. Nobody can have everything.

I was thinking about lucky paths—and how you get on and off them—when I got a call from Prince Talal of Jordan, who was visiting New York and suggested we get together. Because we are involved in the same international organization, we have gotten to know each other over the years. I always liked talking to him because he is deeply intellectual and grasps the subtleties of life.

So meeting him for coffee at the St. Regis hotel sounded like a good idea.

Prince Talal is the grandson of one king and the nephew of another, and as we sat down, it occurred to me that it hadn't been very difficult for him to get on a lucky path. A prince—by definition—is born lucky. Maybe luck doesn't fall from the sky, but it certainly gets sprinkled down from the gene pool. Even though he was dressed casually (slim jeans and a James Perse T-shirt, if you must know), there was a regal air about him that he seems never to lose.

He graciously asked about my work, and so we started talking about luck. He made a few thoughtful comments about the need to make choices and create your own destiny. I fiddled with my coffee cup and finally asked if a prince—a guy who has been called "Your Royal Highness" his whole life—could understand the concept of making your own luck.

"Of course I can," he said, furrowing his thick eyebrows.

"Some people would say that you didn't have to make your luck—it was handed to you," I said carefully.

His searing eyes made it clear that he wasn't falling for the journalistic fallback of "some people would say . . ."

"Is that what you think?" he asked.

I cleared my throat. I sipped some water. "You tell me," I said.

And so he did.

Luck was handed to him? Maybe not entirely. When Prince Talal was sixteen, he went waterskiing one day in the Gulf of Aqaba in the Red Sea. The driver of the boat got too close to a jetty, and Talal smashed into it with full force. With massive internal injuries, he spent eight months at the Methodist Hospital in Houston, where he wavered on the brink of death and lost half his liver and a portion of his lung.

"Eight months in the hospital?" I asked.

"When you're in that situation, you have no bigger view," he said. "You just get through each day."

Royal blood or not, he couldn't expect anyone else to save him. For eight months, he pushed through. He survived. He left the hospital, graduated from the Royal Military Academy in the UK, and returned to being fearless. Ten years after the jetty accident and just six months after his marriage to the beautiful Princess Ghida, he had a second big blow when he was diagnosed with cancer (non-Hodgkin's lymphoma). It's possible that the medications he took after the first injury led to the cancer or at least complicated the problem. So began another round of hospitalizations and extensive treatments.[3]

"At that age, all you want to do is live, and you put all your energy into it," he said.

As he talked, I realized why making luck had become such a compelling topic to me. Because everyone—whoever you are and wherever you start—has to play by its rules. Random events happen, and you have the choice of how to handle them. The hard work and resilience and determination and persistence that you put in at that point give you the lucky life (or not). Prince Talal was not giving in or giving up. He pushed through for a second time. And kept

---

3. Prince Talal's family circumstances certainly allowed him to get the excellent care that was not readily available in the region. His wife later became the chairman of the board of the King Hussein Cancer Center in Jordan and has helped turn it into an internationally esteemed facility. When I spoke to her, she said that she is determined to make sure that everybody in the region gets the same quality of care her husband did. "I had the privilege to travel to the States when my husband had cancer. And I care deeply that other wives, other mothers, other sisters, have the same possibility for hope that I did. Their tears are the same as my tears, and their love is the same as my love," she told me.

pushing to remake his life and body. He got back on the path he had earlier chosen, continued his military career, and climbed to the top ranks. He has the straightest posture you've ever seen (I felt like I was slouching even when I wasn't) and a never-quit defiance in his bearing.

"I heard that you run marathons now," I said.

His eyebrows unfurrowed, and he gave a little smile. "I don't always like it, but the best choice is to keep going," he said in his elegant British accent.

Today Prince Talal is strong and fit, with muscles layered on his slim frame. (Yes, I noticed.) You get that by hard work, not luck.

"I take my duty and responsibility seriously," he told me.

When I first met Prince Talal at an event some years earlier, I saw him as privileged and fortunate and existing in a lucky circle of elites that I could only begin to imagine. He was elegantly bedecked in gold cuff links and a pocket square and an English-tailored suit so perfectly cut it could draw blood. I didn't know about his accident or cancer or the real tenacity it takes to keep going when your life has been turned upside down. It had taken me until now to understand that whether you're a prince or a king, you're not guaranteed a life of happiness. Like everyone else, you make your luck happen. Prince Talal got himself on the lucky path by knowing that whatever gifts he had been born with could easily be taken away. When you fight to make a lucky future for yourself and your family, you have the best chance of getting one.

When I next saw Barnaby, I told him about the conversation. It struck me that when you're looking from the outside, it's very easy to misjudge the source of luck. Was I right about the prince's fortitude in creating his luck (well beyond family and title), or had I just fallen for his royal charm?

"No, you're right," Barnaby said, nodding thoughtfully. "You don't get lucky by a single event—even if it's the conditions of your birth." Coming from royalty is like starring young in a popular movie. You can end up being a Lindsay Lohan or an Emma Watson.

"In creating a lucky life, everything is contingent on so many other things that are happening. Wherever you start, you end up with a big chain of causal structures that can each lead to luck," Barnaby said.

Dealing with circumstances as they come up—putting each link into place—is one way to increase your luck. But trying to *predict* what will happen doesn't necessarily increase your luck at all. Each day, millions or billions of possibilities are swirling around you, and the slightest change in one or another can lead to a new and unexpected outcome. Scientists call this "chaos theory." It was first described by the mathematician and meteorologist Edward Norton Lorenz after he used a computer model to make a weather prediction—and the prediction turned out completely wrong. Lorenz ultimately concluded that a tiny (really, really tiny) deviation in the first number he input to the model changed everything afterward.[4] This might have been the most elaborate explanation ever created for getting a weather forecast wrong.

Lorenz went on to show that a small variance in an initial condition keeps multiplying and changes everything that happens afterward. He offered the now much-cited image of a butterfly flapping its wings in Brazil setting off a tornado in Texas. The butterfly stirs

---

4. He had input 0.506 and said later he should have used 0.506127.

enough molecules to change the atmosphere just a little bit. The change gets bigger and bigger and moves across the world, and before you know it, the unstable air leads to that tornado ripping through a fancy neighborhood in Texas. Maybe it upends the house of a former president, who has to be rescued from the ruins.

"Why did this happen? What did I do wrong?" he asks.

What he did wrong in life might be a long list or a short one, but it has nothing at all to do with the tornado or the wreckage or the fact that the former president is now homeless.

Sound fanciful? As often happens, a science fiction writer got there before the scientists. In his short story "A Sound of Thunder," author Ray Bradbury envisioned a group of hunters traveling back to the time of the dinosaurs. All has been arranged so that they don't disrupt history (for example, they can shoot a dinosaur only when it is about to die anyway). But after their journey, they return to their own time again and discover the present has indeed changed. The recent election had ended with a different winner. One of the hunters notices a crushed butterfly on his boot—and realizes that the death of the butterfly all that time ago initiated enough changes that an election turned out differently.

I tentatively asked Barnaby if he thought that chaos theory put *our* theory of making luck into question. If a butterfly flapping its wings or crushed beneath a boot can influence tornadoes and elections, how can we expect to be in control of our own lives and luck?

Barnaby sat forward eagerly. "Whenever you hear people talk about the butterfly effect, you have to remember that there are thousands or millions of other things also going on. There are so many butterflies flapping their wings! Each one may have a downstream effect—but you have lots of chances along the way to affect things and make changes."

I smiled. Of course! Even if that butterfly is (in some way) causing the storm, you have the chance to build a tornado-proof house, or you can choose to live in an area where bad weather doesn't happen.

"The worst thing is to feel that you can't control anything and being afraid to try. Then you're left at the mercy of butterflies. Or other people," Barnaby said. "You don't want to be the fool waiting for things to happen and saying that whatever is good is good and whatever is bad is bad and there's nothing you can do. The butterfly creates the tornado only if nobody does anything along the way."

"I love that attitude!" I admitted with a big grin.

Passionate about the topic, Barnaby started talking a little faster. "We all have so many chances to change things. The cards you're dealt aren't the ones you have to play with all along. You get to swap them out and decide which ones to hold on to and which to throw away."

He had been reading that morning about the Three Fates of antiquity—the goddesses in Greek and Roman mythology who were often depicted in art as spinning the threads of life. They decided when life started and ended, but they didn't control everything that happened along the way.

Many religions that followed have a similar concept that some things are determined but much remains in our control. "Fate is what will happen if you don't do anything, but destiny is your potential and requires your action along the way," Barnaby said. It reminded me of the old joke about the man who prayed every day to win the lottery. The drawing came and went, and he didn't win. So he prayed some more. Another lottery and another and he still didn't win.

"God, I'm a good man. I'm devout and ethical. Why can't you let me win the lottery? What more do you want from me?" he asked in frustration.

"Maybe you can help me out and at least buy a ticket," God replied.

Barnaby laughed. "Benjamin Franklin would like that. I think he had the line that God helps those who help themselves."

I checked, and Sophocles first said something like that back in about 400 BC, and Euripides and Ovid had versions of it, too. Seventeenth-century French and English philosophers made it popular ("Help thyself and God will help thee," said priest and poet George Herbert),[5] and then Franklin brought it to America. In other words, the idea that luck comes to those who make it for themselves has deep roots in both poetry and religion.

Barnaby pointed out that whatever your religious beliefs, whether you believe in destiny or Fates or free will, the greatest regret most people have comes from looking back and feeling that they didn't quite do enough to reach their potential. Lucky people are those who are willing to put themselves on the line, be a little fearless, and give their all to achieve a goal. It's better to have tried and failed than never to have tried at all.

"If you ran in the Olympics and didn't win the gold medal, at least you ran in the Olympics," Barnaby said. "The bigger regret and unhappiness comes if you didn't try out and you always wonder what might have been."

Avoiding those regrets means having an aim and knowing what will ultimately make you feel lucky. That doesn't mean you have to get on a single path and stay there—but you do have to know where

---

5. If you think everything sounds better in French, there's the lyrical line from Jean de La Fontaine, *Aide-toi et le ciel t'aidera,* or *Help yourself and heaven will help you.*

you're headed. I mentioned to Barnaby that I had just come across a comment from Joi Ito, the entrepreneur and head of the MIT Media Lab, suggesting that it was better to navigate through life with a compass rather than a map. I liked the image, and it struck me as exactly the way to get lucky. With a compass, you need to know the general direction you want to go—and then stay alert as you follow the twists and turns of your own path. A map (or Google Maps) gives you a rigid route to follow, and as you trudge along, you may miss the turns that lead to luck.

"Sure, I've worked with Joi," Barnaby said (of course he had!). "He's a genius and often talks about the incredible speed of change in the technology world. What's interesting is that as things move faster and faster, that compass image becomes even more relevant." To make luck in a quickly changing world, you need a general idea where you're headed, but you also need to be able to stay flexible and make turns. Going in the right direction doesn't necessarily mean following the dotted line on your GPS. If everyone else is going on that path, you might want to choose a different one.

Navigating with a compass requires you to be a bit more fearless, but it brings those lucky opportunities that Joi Ito surmised. My very athletic husband and I often take long hikes in the woods, and he is definitely a compass kind of guy. He knows where he's headed, but he wants to make his own route to get there. One day recently we were hiking on a pretty trail, and since I was worried about protruding roots, loose stones, and darting snakes, I kept my head down and stared at my feet for every step. I didn't really know where we were headed—I just followed behind him, thinking only about the next step.

"Did you see that magnificent hawk?" Ron asked, turning back to me as we neared the top of the steep climb.

"Nope."

"It was circling right above us as we passed through that big band of white pines."

"White pines?" I asked.

"Yes, right after the waterfall."

"What waterfall?"

While I looked only at the tops of my boots, Ron had perfected the skill of watching the path while looking forward and upward and all around—which is where lucky sightings are made. He'd had experiences that I had missed, because if you keep your head down as you walk through life (either literally or metaphorically), you miss the opportunity to make yourself lucky. If you have an idea where you're headed and the confidence that (one way or another) you'll get there, then you can reach the top of the mountain—and still pause to see the magnificent hawk.

Getting on one path and then switching to another when the time is right may be the best formula for creating luck over the whole arc of your life. But most of us are slightly myopic about the future. We have situations to deal with every day—problems that need solving, jobs that are demanding, and children who need snacks or homework help or midnight comforting. We feel lucky enough if we handle those immediate concerns. Like the college students Barnaby met (focused on their immediate concerns, like classes, beer, and football games), we know the future will come—but we figure it will take care of itself.

"It's like the exchange in *Alice's Adventures in Wonderland* between Alice and the Cheshire Cat," Barnaby said. "Alice wants to go to amazing places, but she doesn't know exactly where, so the cat replies that she will ultimately get somewhere if she simply walks long enough."

It's a funny line, but it's also what most of us do—just keep walking and figure life will happen, good or bad. People intent on making luck ignore the Cheshire Cat's advice and know ahead of time the amazing place where they want to end up. As Barnaby put it, they make plans and stick to them, and if the plan fails, they try something else and something else until they succeed in weaving past life's inevitable setbacks.

Barnaby had just come back from a conference in California where he met several impressive people who had made luck over the whole arc of their lives by knowing when it was time to go in a new direction. One of them was Sherry Lansing, the former president of production at 20th Century Fox and CEO of Paramount Pictures.

"How cool that you met her—she was always one of my role models!" I said. Lansing had made luck for herself at a time when it wasn't easy for women to do that. She was the first woman to head a Hollywood studio and had a long string of successes, including movies like *Fatal Attraction* and *Titanic*. She was an inspiration to all of us who followed her—and was known for being creative and kind and beautiful.

"She's still all that—including beautiful," Barnaby said. "In fact, she's radiant. She walks into a room and you can feel the glow."

"I hope you told her that," I said.

When she was sixty, Lansing had done the unexpected and walked away from her glamorous Hollywood life. People were shocked. Nobody gives up the bright lights and power unless they have to. But Lansing was determined to move on.

"Even if you love what you do, you need to know when it is time to let go and take a new path," she told Barnaby. Then offering a bit of advice, she added, "Change keeps you young, so never stop changing."

Figuring that you don't make a lucky life by repeating yourself, she got involved in projects to fight cancer and revamp public education. Now, ten years later, the joy she once found in making movies is directed in new ways. And apparently it is making her happy—and radiant.

At that same conference, Barnaby spent some time talking with his friend Arianna Huffington, who started her eponymous *Huffington Post* from nothing and eventually sold it to AOL for $315 million. Like Lansing, she implicitly understood that part of the lucky-life equation involves switching paths at the right moment.

The very determined Huffington had been on many paths in her life—author, activist, wife of a congressman, candidate for governor of California, conservative, and liberal. But *The Huffington Post* gave her global recognition. She told Barnaby that she got used to working eighteen-hour days—one sure way to make luck. But then one April afternoon, she collapsed at her desk from exhaustion, and as she fell down, her head clipped the corner of her desk, breaking her cheekbone. Her next memory was of being on the floor in a pool of blood and thinking, *Is this what success looks like?*

Like Lansing, Huffington decided that it was time to focus on something that would give a different meaning to her life.

"I used to walk down the street either talking on my phone or looking at messages. Then one day I looked around near where I live in SoHo and saw a most beautiful building. I asked my friend when it went up and she said, 'In 1929.'" I wondered what else I had been missing." It occurred to Huffington that if we're not paying attention, we sometimes miss the little things—like beautiful architecture—that make us feel lucky. And maybe we also miss the big things, like building blocks for a healthy life.

"I had become so used to being exhausted that it took that episode of falling on the floor for me to look at my life and reevaluate," she said. Rounding out her financial success with a kind of spiritual and emotional good luck, she left *The Huffington Post* to get on a new path of spreading health and wellness and balance through a company that she named Thrive Global. She has even been on a campaign to encourage people to get more sleep—maybe luck comes with our good dreams.

The idea of making luck by switching paths suddenly seemed to be in the air. Victor Nee, the Cornell professor we had taken a walk with through Central Park a few months earlier, got back in touch with Barnaby to tell him about the progress he was making in his study of tech firms. He had found that one indicator of success was how quickly a company could "rewire."

"In tech, the ground is constantly shifting, and what was hot six months ago is old news today," he said. "The critical skill becomes the ability to reinterpret the core strengths of a new market." A key was an update on what he had previously described to us as knowledge spillover. Whatever new path you took, you could use the knowledge you had gained in one situation to create success and luck in another unrelated situation.

You don't have to be a tech genius or a media mogul to see the value of rewiring. Barnaby pointed out that most of us do it naturally throughout our lives. "You go from being a successful college student to having a career or being a parent," he said. "There are different junctures where you take different turns to make a new form of luck."

Remember the inverted Vs that Barnaby drew once to show me the hills and valleys we all face in our lives? Now he reminded me that part of climbing up and making luck in one area of life is climbing down again. You can try jumping from peak to peak, but a lucky life also includes those times in between the highs.

Making a lucky life means appreciating where you are now—but still looking ahead for new opportunities. As life changes, you need the courage to look for new challenges and find luck in new places.

That seemed like a good start for making a lucky life. But as it turns out, there's one more thing you need. And we were about to discover it.

CHAPTER SEVENTEEN

The Lucky Attitude: Believe That You Can Make Luck

Believe you are lucky. . . . Treat triumph and disaster the same. . . . Look for the joy.

Walking down the street one day, I realized that after all the time Barnaby and I had spent investigating luck, I was feeling luckier. I had been encouraging myself to recognize opportunities, make thoughtful moves, and persist when others quit. I was exhilarated by the idea that you have more control over all aspects of your life than you sometimes realize. No matter who you are, luck isn't a given—you have to make it happen for yourself.

But I was still intrigued by Barnaby's question of what—in the grander view—made a lucky life.

So the next time we met, I decided to turn the question on him.

"What is a lucky life?" I asked.

"Realizing your dreams and potentials, I suppose," Barnaby said. Then he looked at me and laughed. "Quick answer, but unsatisfying, right?"

"Right," I agreed. "Try it this way. Who's your role model for a lucky life? Somebody you would trade places with right now."

He looked off into the distance for a couple of minutes, and I could practically see his brain ticking through various possibilities. I sipped iced tea. I waited. Finally I mentioned a couple of extremely wealthy people whom he had been hanging out with recently—flying on their planes, visiting their private islands, having meetings in their enormous townhouses. Barnaby knows a lot of billionaires, since he has advised many of them on how to make the greatest impact with their philanthropy. If you're looking for people who've had a lucky life, they seemed a reasonable place to begin.

"I like them and admire what they can do in the world with their resources," Barnaby said, "but as individuals they struggle just like the rest of us." He mentioned that one had gone through a couple of divorces and another was having difficulties with a grown child. "They've been very successful in some ways, but have they made a luckier life overall? I don't really know."

"And you're not willing to trade in your wife and daughters to find out?"

"Definitely not!" he said with a laugh. "I'm already lucky there!"

The last question in our national survey asked: "Do you think of yourself as a lucky person?" Some 67 percent of people said yes, and 33 percent said no. Barnaby and I wondered if specific factors made some people feel luckier than others. So he analyzed the data, looking for demographic differences, and he couldn't find any. No matter where you lived, how much money you made, whether you were male or female, married or not, your chances of calling yourself a lucky person were about the same.

So if outside events didn't influence your perception of being lucky, could it be that what made you lucky was simply . . . thinking you are lucky? Your own attitude and optimism and sense of hope could ultimately define whether you had a lucky life.

I was pondering the idea the next evening, as I sipped rosé at a wine tasting organized by a friend of my husband, a gregariously charming doctor named Michael Nochomovitz. The room was packed with interesting people, and toward the end of the evening, I met a scientist named Jonathan Stamler, who had flown in from Cleveland for the occasion. When I told him I was investigating luck, he immediately responded.

"I do lab research—so I know all about luck!" he said.

Stamler was funny and smart and (I later discovered) world renowned for a discovery he had made related to protein function in cells. He immediately told me about a friend and colleague of his who recently won the Nobel Prize and thought that luck played a real role in science. Not the random-chance kind of luck—a very different shade.

"He's brilliant, and a lot of great researchers want to work in his lab," Stamler told me excitedly. "When he interviews them, he'll talk to them a long time and then the last question he asks is 'Are you lucky?' If someone says no, they don't get hired—no matter how good they are."

"Is that the Napoleon theory?" I asked—noting that as the great emperor waged wars, he supposedly said, "I'd rather have generals who are lucky than good."[1]

Stamler smiled. "It's subtler than that. In research it's important to *believe* that you're lucky. Any discovery requires creativity and openness and a willingness to try the unexpected. You need a positive attitude and a belief that you can find something innovative. If you don't *think* you're lucky, you won't *be* lucky."

Now I smiled, too. If some of the top scientists in the country

---

1. Some version of that comment is often attributed to Napoleon, but the actual source is hard to pin down. I did find in his writings the comment that "war is composed of nothing but accidents. . . . There is but one favorable moment, the great art is to seize it." I like that because it fits right in with what we've been saying about seeing opportunity and then making luck happen.

recognized that the right outlook was necessary to be lucky in the lab, then we were on to something important.

Looking around the room, I realized that a positive attitude could make luck for just about anyone. As if to prove it, a pretty young woman named Victoria James came over to refill our wineglasses. With her youthful face and gentle style, she might have been easy to overlook.

"A lot of people still mistake me for the coat check girl," she said with a sweet smile.

But she was actually a big star in the food world—the youngest woman ever to become a certified sommelier. She had written a book about rosé wine and had a big reputation in some of the city's best restaurants. Now barely in her mid-twenties, she spent her time traveling around the world tasting wine, and she oversaw the buying and selling of expensive bottles for the Michelin-starred restaurant where we were gathered.

"Do you believe you're lucky?" I asked as she joined our conversation.

"You have to believe that in this business!" she said. She laughingly admitted that she once tried growing Pinot Noir grapes in a pot on her fire escape. The venture didn't quite work out, but when you believe in yourself, the circles of a lucky life spiral in many directions. She now has a boyfriend who makes an award-winning California rosé (from grapes grown in real soil).

Becoming a wine expert may sound like a la-di-da ambition, not the path to a lucky life for the rest of us down-to-earth types. But Victoria seemed sensible and pragmatic and far from haut monde.

"I got my first job as a waitress when I was thirteen," she said. She found the one diner near her home that would look the other way at underage labor—"the kind of place where a lot of the waitresses were named Flo."

A few years later when she needed money for college, she realized that bartenders earned more than waitresses. "But I knew nothing about wine or liquor, so I decided to learn," she said. She took classes, made friends in the field, studied and tasted endlessly. Newly passionate about wine and knowing it was a field dominated by arrogant older men, she made flash cards with 20,000 entries before taking her sommelier exam.

She believed in her own lucky future. And so she made one happen. It never bothered her that she might not be welcome in the fancy inner circles of wine connoisseurs. She was determined. She had a positive attitude. She made her luck.

When she walked away again, I marveled to Dr. Stamler about how far talent could take you when coupled with determination and the belief that you could become lucky.

"Do you think you'll win a Nobel Prize like your friend did?" I asked. He looked startled at the question. (I was just being provocative, but I later discovered through confidential sources that his name was regularly in the running.)

"There's a lot that goes into winning," he said. An important breakthrough worthy of international acclaim was just the start. You also had to play the proper academic politics, get people on your side, and believe in yourself enough to get other people to believe, too. The early-morning call that came from the Swedish Academy was always depicted as a complete surprise—but it rarely came from out of the blue. Most of the recipients had worked very hard to make the good luck come their way.

Sipping my rosé, I realized that whether you want to be a

scientist or sommelier or win the Nobel Prize, the answer to "Are you a lucky person?" should always be yes. Because the very first step to a lucky life is a positive attitude. It's not mystical or preordained—it's just that the more you believe you can make your own luck, the more you will do exactly that. You make a lucky life by believing that you deserve to be lucky.

A few days later, Barnaby and I continued to talk about what makes a lucky life, and he told me about Dr. George Vaillant, a psychiatrist and professor he knew who spent decades contemplating the ingredients for a good life. It wasn't theoretical—Vaillant oversaw the famous Harvard study that tracked hundreds of men (yes, they were all men in those days) from the time they were college sophomores in 1938 until the end of their lives. One of the longest-running studies ever done, it looked at what made people happy and healthy.

"Essentially they were trying to uncover the ingredients for a lucky life," Barnaby said. "George always told me that the answer was very clear. When people looked back, it wasn't fame or wealth or high achievement that made them happy—it was the quality of their relationships."

The study had gone for seventy-five years—and it was continuing.[2]

"George said that he could give the conclusion of the study in just five words."

"Which were . . . ?"

"Happiness is love. Full stop."

---

2. Dr. Vaillant is retired now and battling illness, and the research continues under a new director, Robert Waldinger. Some 1,300 children of the original participants (girls included!) have agreed to be part of the ongoing study.

I laughed. "And that was just from studying men."

Dr. Vaillant found that a person's happiness with his relationships at age fifty was a better predictor of health at age eighty than more obvious markers like cholesterol. The relationships didn't have to be all hearts and flowers and Hallmark cards—after all, any romance has arguments and difficulties—but the definition of a good relationship turned out to be one where you could count on another person to be there for you. Relationships beyond romantic ones were important, too. An ability to make friends, talk to people, and get others on your side all contributed to long-term happiness and luck.

I went back and read some of the many papers and books Dr. Vaillant had written about the study. He had concluded that many of the things we would usually consider as luck makers in life— social class, parental success, religion—don't make much difference. Above a certain level, intelligence doesn't enter into the equation, nor does political ideology. (Though the most liberal men had the best sex lives. No explanation for why that would be.) What really mattered was positive emotions. Dr. Vaillant insisted that feelings like love, hope, and joy aren't just nice—they are essential for a lucky life and the survival of our species.

"We need to bring our positive emotions to conscious attention, and we must not disdain to study them with our science," he said.

Seven decades of study said that if you want to feel lucky and live a good life, then get happy. Look for the positive. And don't be embarrassed to share it.

When I talked about it more with Barnaby, he pointed out that the concept of our beliefs shaping our luck and destiny has deep spiritual and philosophical roots. Barnaby's career in philanthropy had given him the extraordinary opportunity to meet and travel with some important religious and social leaders, including Nelson

Mandela, the Dalai Lama, Chief Rabbi Jonathan Sacks, Pastor Rick Warren, and Archbishop Desmond Tutu. "What each of them told me in one way or another was that we all filter events through our own views—we have a template for how we perceive the world. And certain personal outlooks are going to yield more success than others."

We can make luck on both personal and global levels by changing our thinking—that template we have in our head. So, for example, a hundred years ago, Mahatma Gandhi taught the value of countering oppression with nonviolent protest rather than violence. Gandhi believed that our outlooks and attitudes create the future that we make for ourselves and others.

"His belief was that your thoughts become your actions, your actions become your habits, and your habits become your destiny," Barnaby said. "So there's really a direct line from the beliefs you start with to the destiny you create for yourself."

I nodded. It was nice to hear him quote Gandhi, since a few months earlier I had done a project with Mahatma Gandhi's grandson Arun Gandhi. Now in his eighties, Arun is devoted to spreading the messages of love and hope that he learned from his grandfather when he lived with him on his ashram as a teenager. Arun believes what his grandfather told him then, that you need to "be the change you wish to see in the world." Whatever the circumstances you face, you make luck for yourself and others by living with hope and expectation. You choose the favorable future you want and then live as if it had already occurred.

A positive attitude has many dimensions—and believing in your own good fortune doesn't mean that you have sunshine every day. But it does mean that you have a bigger perspective. Gandhi spent many of those days (and weeks and years) in jail, but he turned them to luck with the passion and conviction that he could shape a better future.

Barnaby pointed out that people with a negative outlook sometimes prevent bad things from happening by being wary and suspicious. "But avoiding bad luck isn't enough in this world anymore," he said. "You need optimism to create good luck and find a hopeful way forward."

Now that we were on that subject of creating a lucky destiny, Barnaby asked if I'd like to meet Deepak Chopra, the spiritualist and New Age guru, whom he had recently gotten to know. Barnaby and I had talked about him earlier, and I was intrigued that Barnaby, the serious science guy, was so inspired by some of Chopra's ideas. Now Barnaby explained that Chopra's concept of a lucky life included discovering your own talents and giving yourself the freedom to find your own path. Chopra brought the New Agey platitudes about karma down to earth by saying that if you try to bring happiness and success to others, you are setting the stage for luck to flow back to you.

So on a rainy afternoon, Barnaby and I went to the downtown haven known as Deepak's Homebase. We waited in his cozy office, and Deepak arrived exactly on time, looking relaxed and surprisingly stylish in black pants and a black shirt with a red quilted Patagonia vest and red sneakers. His black eyeglasses were studded with rhinestones, and he had a silver bracelet on one arm and a red Fitbit on the other. He looked like the Elton John of gurus, but he was also perceptive and thoughtful and original. I liked him immediately. He was completely unruffled when we asked his view on what it meant in a grander sense to lead a lucky life. (It's possible that when you're

Deepak Chopra, "What is the meaning of life?" is the kind of question you get asked every day.)

"I think it's we who give meaning and purpose based on our current state of awareness," he said. "As human beings, we create constructs that we call reality, but all we can really have is experience."

To show what he meant, he pulled out his phone and found a video someone had sent him earlier in the day of a baby playing with a colorful spinning toy. The baby batted at the toy excitedly, not really understanding what it was but filled with awe.

"What is experience?" Deepak asked rhetorically. Then pointing to the video, he said, "This is experience—joy, curiosity, wonder, timelessness, spontaneity, and playfulness. He has no sense of me and other. It is just awareness experiencing itself."

Deepak told us that he was very interested in the idea of flow. Psychologists often use "flow" to describe what happens when artists or musicians (or anyone else) get so fully involved in a creative process that time disappears and they become one with their work. Deepak saw it in an even more expansive sense—"when you are in the moment and spontaneous and you have no regrets, no anticipation, no sense of a self separated from what you are doing."

We've all had those moments when time flies by, and instead of thinking and worrying, we just feel content. Was that the basis for a lucky life?

"There is an aliveness to flow and therefore a joy," Deepak said. "Maybe that's ultimately what people are seeking—whether they try to find it through Tantric sex or biofeedback or Rumi's poetry or virtual reality or invented reality."

"Or for some, watching money flow," Barnaby joked.

Whatever approach you choose, if you can find joys in the moment and garner the feeling that what you are doing is exactly what you *want* to be doing, then perhaps you've found the ultimate luck of existence.

"Given the options, how do you personally get into a state of flow?" I asked Deepak.

He shrugged. "I spend a lot of time just walking the street by myself or in meditation or writing. I think we all want to get to the peace that comes from joy and lightness and effortless spontaneity."

Deepak pointed out that many of us get caught up in our own formulations of what is right and wrong, but "one person's wonderful experience may not be another's. Humans are paradoxical creatures and become sanctimonious and self-righteous about their version of what is good or lucky."

I told Deepak that I sometimes wished I had studied astrophysics so I could have a bigger view of the universe and all the elements that went into a lucky life. But he shook his head and told me that wasn't how I would find it.

"The latest model has two trillion galaxies, seven hundred sextillion stars, and trillions and trillions and trillions of planets. Earth would not be one grain of sand on all the seashores of this model," he said.

And yet the experiences we have every day are all that we can hold on to. Deepak agreed that we make ourselves (and the world) luckier when we look for the positive and try to replace negative thoughts with more positive, constructive ones. He had written before that moods follow thoughts, and it doesn't help to indulge your gloom. Once you are sunk in anxiety, it's hard to lift yourself up. If you reinforce good moods, you have a better chance of creating flow, luck, and a sense of joy.

When we left, I told Barnaby how much I had liked meeting Deepak. Effortlessly charismatic, he has made a lucky life by trying to help others understand the world better, and I could see why he had such a huge following. He was willing to think in ways that challenged our conventional wisdom.

"He seemed to be saying that with our thoughts and actions, we can shape our world and our own happiness," Barnaby said.

"And in that happiness is our lucky life," I suggested.

"Exactly," Barnaby agreed. "You're in charge of your own actions and also your outlook. You determine whether you look at events through a positive or a negative lens. You get to decide whether the outcomes that arise from your interactions with the world are lucky or not."

When I was in my early twenties, I met a man named Tom who was savvy and clever and incredibly hardworking. He'd had early successes and seemed destined for a huge career. Some years older than me, he was ending a marriage that had been wrong from the start and had left his huge home in suburban Maryland for a tiny studio apartment in Manhattan. When I visited one evening, he perched on the edge of the bed (there was no place else to sit) and mentioned that one of the closets in his suburban house was slightly bigger than his new apartment.

"But I don't really need anything more than this," he said calmly. "Why would I? That big closet and big house didn't make me happy, and here I have everything I want. I feel very lucky."

At the time the comment left me slightly bewildered. Tom was one of the most driven people I knew, so surely he wanted more than a studio apartment. And yet he seemed serene and sincere as he looked around and announced his contentment. Only now did I understand his reflection in its true light—as one of the secrets to making a lucky life. Tom had plenty of persistence and ambition and creative energy. But he implicitly understood that everyone makes mistakes and is subject to random fates, and he would never let either interfere with his optimistic spirit. Tom would find the positive in whatever he had and whatever he achieved.

Perhaps more than anything else, the ability to find the good in any situation is the definition of what makes a lucky life.

Tom and I stayed close friends over the years, and he let me know when he became one of the chief officers at a major investment bank. I joined him one day for lunch at his private dining room on the executive floor of the tall building where he worked. From our table for two, we looked out over a vast river view that included the Statue of Liberty. All of the world seemed—literally and figuratively—to be at his feet.

"You've always been able to find the good, but now you don't have to look too hard," I said, gesturing toward the window.

He gave a modest shrug. "Good and bad things happen in life, and you can't get too swayed by one or the other." He mentioned that he had always been inspired by the Rudyard Kipling poem about keeping your head when all about you are losing theirs and blaming it on you.

I nodded, since he had quoted his favorite lines from that poem to me many times over the years. "'If you can meet with Triumph and Disaster / And treat those two impostors just the same,'" I recited.

He looked surprised—and then laughed. "I guess I've been saying that for a while. But it *is* very important to treat triumph and disaster the same. You do your best to make luck in life, but whatever happens, all that's really in your control is your attitude."

As if to test his theory, his wildly successful investment bank imploded a few years later.[3] Tom was devastated. He wasn't sure of his next move and felt like he was wandering in the wilderness. But he eventually landed a top spot at another major financial institution. When I joined him for lunch there one day, the views from his new private dining room were even more spectacular.

"You've landed well," I said as a uniformed waiter glided in and out.

Tom was as down-to-earth as always. "You already know my position on treating triumph and disaster the same," he said with a smile.

Tom was a great lesson to me that whatever happens, you get to decide whether you see your life as lucky or not. He held the same philosophy whether in a heavenly dining empyrean or an earthbound studio apartment. He coupled a positive attitude with focused ambition—and then accepted whatever new challenges came his way.

A few days after the conversation with Deepak Chopra, I was in a taxicab on the way to the airport for a quick business trip. I usually have my head buried in my phone (who doesn't?) when I have spare moments, but I had been thinking so much about luck and noticing the world around me that I decided to put it away and just look out the window.

There was no traffic at seven A.M., and the taxi zipped along. The morning was chilly and the blue sky mostly hidden by thick gray

---

3. Tom was a top executive at Lehman Brothers, and in 2008, when one financial institution after another was saved by the US government, Lehman was allowed to fail. The reasons it was singled out have never been completely clear. Many believe that its closing led to the global financial crisis.

clouds. But as I kept looking, I saw a halo of sun behind one of the clouds lighting up a patch of sky so it appeared like the image of a divine presence in an early Renaissance painting. A moment later, the sun burst free of the cloud entirely, and suddenly the narrow river we were passing lit up in a brilliant display of reflected sparkles. The shimmering light shot off in all directions. The scene was breathtaking—and then a cloud appeared again and it was gone.

As we continued to drive, the usually loud and ferocious New York City seemed quiet and vulnerable. Without the bustle of people and cars, the cityscape looked fragile, the bridges and buildings no sturdier than a child's play set. I had been lucky to see the sun's fireworks—lucky because I had looked. But I knew that random chance could change my day, too. A meteor could fall from the sky, the fragile bridge could fall, the lives we have all put so carefully together could be revealed to be built on sand and paste. There was nothing I could do about randomness other than to be prepared for it.

Still looking out the window, I realized that we can't control everything in life, but we can control more than we think. We choose our opportunities, our outlook, and our general life pathways. At the end of the day, what is life except the people we love and the experiences we share with them? We build a lucky life through the joy we find for ourselves and others. We learn to treat triumph and disaster the same and make luck from whatever is in front of us.

Luck is not a moment in time but the lifetime of moments we make. I didn't create the sunshine on the water, but I allowed myself to look up and appreciate it. We can all keep finding more of that sunshine. And every time we do, we are making our luck.

Acknowledgments

In writing this book, Barnaby and I learned how much you need other people to help make luck. We are very grateful to Alice Martell, who is a terrific agent as well as a friend, advisor, and cheerleader. Jill Schwartzman is the editor every writer wants—smart and insightful and able to make every chapter a little better than it started. Our warmest thanks to the team at Dutton, including Amanda Walker, Carrie Swetonic, Liza Cassity, Becky Odell, Elina Vaysbeyn, Alice Dalrymple, and Marya Pasciuto, as well as Ivan Held, Christine Ball, and John Parsley. Thanks also to Marlene Ryan for help with logistics, to the wonderfully helpful librarians at the Yale Club, and to all our friends who have shared our excitement about learning to make luck.

Researching this book was a great joy. We interviewed dozens of people and spoke to experts in many fields, and we learned something from everyone we met. We are grateful to all of them. We've told many of their stories in these pages, so you already know the names—but extra special thanks for their time and openness to Martin Seligman, Susan Greenfield, Dan Ariely, Paul Zak, Helen Fisher, Arianna Huffington, Leonard Mlodinow, Josh Groban, Sherry Lansing, Doug Wick, Henry Jarecki, Bob Mankoff, and Deepak Chopra.

Many people shared their wisdom and added immeasurably to our own thought processes, even if their ideas weren't mentioned explicitly. Our warmest thanks to Krista Tippett, Steve Mariotti, Howard Gardner, Bill Drayton, Mark Gerson, Dan Goldstein, Michael Mauboussin, Seth Godin, Stephen Kosslyn, Duncan Watts, Stanley Goldstein, Robert Frank, Tom Scott, Pina Templeton, Monica Seles, John Sculley, Andy Arluk, Paul Irving, Rick Von Feldt, Pun-Yin, Lynne Flynn, Charlotte Lee, Isaiah Kacyvenski, Marty Marcus, Gail Marcus, Patty Neger, and Reb and Amy Rebele.

Barnaby's ideas on luck and risk have been developing for many years, and he has been shaped by conversations with great thinkers, including Ernst Mayr, Jonathan Sacks, Martin Nowak, John Krebs, Richard Dawkins, John Cacioppo, Jeff Epstein, Howard Nussbaum, Piet Hut, David Krakauer, John Bogle, John Templeton, Leon Cooperman, Freeman Dyson, Matthew Bishop, John Brockman, Joi Ito, Ned Phelps, Linda Stone, Je Hyuk Lee, Judea Pearl, Michael Shermer, and Nolan Bushnell. The journey would not have been the same without their ideas and inspiration.

We both spend a lot of time at our laptops, working and thinking, but it means everything to look up at the end of the day and and be surrounded by our terrific families. Very big hugs to our amazing children who bring us joy and make us smile every day. And to our spouses—my husband, Ron, and Barnaby's wife, Michelle—we love you and thank you. You make us understand what it means to be lucky in love.

Notes

Chapter One: Prepare to Be Lucky

The French microbiologist Louis Pasteur saved millions of lives in the nineteenth century (and into today) when he figured out the process for pasteurizing milk and later created a vaccine against rabies. One of the first people to understand how germs cause disease, he refuted (incorrect) scientific ideas that had been around since Aristotle. To those who marveled at his breakthroughs, he famously pointed out that "luck favors the prepared mind." And indeed, his discoveries came only after years of complex experiments in his labs in Strasbourg and Lille, France. With his very extensive preparation, he had a nice run of making luck for himself and millions of others.

Chapter Three: Pick the Statistic You Want to Be

The birthday party problem is a *problem* only because our minds don't naturally understand exponents and statistics. The question is: How many people do you need for it to be likely that two of them will have the same birthday? It turns out that once you have 23 people in a room, there's a fifty-fifty chance of two of them having the same birthday. With 70 people, there's a 99.9 percent chance.

The first stumbling block is that when you think of two people in a room having the same birthday, you immediately think of someone having *your* birthday. In that room of 23 people, you would compare yourself to the other 22 partygoers to see if someone shared your birthday (you to person A, you to person B, you to person C . . .). But that's a very different problem! Leave yourself out of it, because maybe the guy next to you has the same birthday as the girl across the room. If you make all *those* comparisons (Person A to person B, person A to person C, person B to person C. . .), there are 253 chances to make a match.

Mathematicians say that the simplest (well, maybe) approach is to flip the problem around and look at the people who do *not* share a birthday. Since there are 365 days in a year (without February 29), the probability of person A *not* sharing a birthday with person B is 364/365 (or 99.7 percent). We've already said that in that room of 23, there are 253 comparisons, so the equation becomes $(364/365)^{253}$. With a good calculator, you'll find there's a 49.95 chance that all 253 comparisons contain no matches. That means there's a 50.05 percent chance that there *is* a match. Bravo! You've now proved that with 23 people, the odds of two people sharing a birthday are better than even! You can do the same math with 70 people and find out that the likelihood has soared to 99.9 percent. Getting to 100 percent is a different story. For that, you need 366 people.

Chapter Four: Skate to Where the Puck Will Be

The Gretzky conversation is adapted from his autobiography, *Gretzky: An Autobiography* (HarperCollins Publishers Canada, 1990).

According to the Nielsen numbers from 2016, Americans spend an average of 4 hours and 31 minutes per day watching television, with another 58 minutes on DVD or Blu-ray. They average 1 hour and 39 minutes with apps/web on their smartphones and 31 minutes with apps/web on a tablet. The numbers are dramatically different for those in the age groups from twelve to seventeen and even from eighteen to twenty-four, who watch half as much TV but spend almost twice as much time on their phone apps.

The *New York Times* analysis that only 20 percent of Americans live more than a couple of hours' drive from their moms appeared in *The Upshot*,

December 23, 2015, by Quoctrung Bui and Claire Cain Miller. People of lower income and education tend to stay closest to home, perhaps because their extended family can offer support such as child care and elder care, which can be expensive and isn't supported by the government. Their difficulties in moving restricts their luck-making potential.

The Facebook series of introductions is described in *The Facebook Effect* by David Kirkpatrick (Simon & Schuster, 2010).

Ideal free distribution is the principle that organisms will distribute themselves in ways that correspond with the prevalence of opportunities or resources. Out in the wild, resource-rich areas will attract and sustain larger populations than resource-sparse areas. When a landscape has different localized conditions, the organisms (whether plants or animals or men looking for dates) will not be spread in a uniform way.

Chapter Six: Zig When Others Zag

For James Watson, pushing the boundaries led to a Nobel Prize—but it also led to controversy. Comments he made about intelligence and race in 2007 caused such dissension that he was dropped from the boards of companies and forced to retire from at least one academic position. He eventually felt like such a pariah that he put his Nobel Prize up for auction at Christie's because, he said at the time, "no one really wants to admit I exist." A Russian billionaire paid more than $4 million to buy the medal—and then returned it to Dr. Watson, saying, "His award for the discovery of DNA structure must belong to him."

The British television shows that preceded *American Idol* included *Popstars* and *Making the Band*. Mike Darnell admired *Making the Band* and thought the most interesting part of it was the auditions—so he was excited about *American Idol* because it was essentially all auditions.

The British biologists P. M. Driver and D. A. Humphries, who studied animal behavior, wrote the book *Protean Behaviour: The Biology of Unpredictability* (Oxford University Press, 1988), from which this information is adapted.

Psychologist Stanley Milgram got wide attention for research he did in 1967 sending packages to 160 people in Omaha, Nebraska, and asking them to forward it to someone they knew personally—on the way to its getting to a particular stockbrocker in Boston. Though the project had serious flaws, Milgram concluded that the average package went through five intermediate hands (so six degrees first to last). But the idea wasn't completely original. Hungarian author Frigyes Karinthy published a story in 1929 that presented the idea that any two of the (then) 1.5 billion people in the world could be connected through five links. This concept has had many iterations. In 1999, three guys appeared on *The Daily Show* with Jon Stewart to explain how everyone in Hollywood was connected by having worked on a movie (or worked with someone who worked on a movie) with actor Kevin Bacon. *Six Degrees of Kevin Bacon* later became a book and a board game and the theme for a TV show. While Bacon first tried to distance himself from the idea, he eventually embraced it. (How could he not? He's zero degrees from Kevin Bacon.)

Chapter Seven: The Power of Persistence and Passion

The research Daniel Kahneman used was initially done to analyze the impacts of higher education. But he looked closely at the data to pull his own interesting conclusions and describes them in his award-winning book *Thinking, Fast and Slow* (Farrar, Straus and Giroux, 2011).

Given the startling number of cartoons that got submitted to Bob Mankoff each week, you could be rejected and still get lucky—by appearing in one of the books of rejected *New Yorker* cartoons. One favorite is *The*

Rejection Collection: Cartoons You Never Saw, and Never Will See, in The New Yorker (Gallery Books, 2006). It was so popular that a second volume of *The Rejection Collection* followed, this one subtitled *The Cream of the Crap* (Gallery Books, 2007). Meantime *New Yorker* cartoonist Sam Gross says he has numbered every cartoon he has submitted to the magazine over the last decades, and he now has more than 12,000 rejections.

Dr. Martin Seligman did his earliest research in how helplessness develops. He eventually turned the subject around to study how you can develop positive views and wrote an important book in the field, *Learned Optimism* (Alfred A. Knopf, 1991). His ideas on positive psychology continued to be well outlined in numerous books, including *Authentic Happiness: Using the New Positive Psychology to Realize Your Potential for Lasting Fulfillment* (Free Press, 2002) and *Flourish: A Visionary New Understanding of Happiness and Well-being* (Free Press, 2011).

Chapter Eight: How Many Eggs in Your Basket? (And How Many Baskets?)

The Fred Smith story is told in the book *Changing How the World Does Business: FedEx's Incredible Journey to Success—The Inside Story* by Roger Frock (Berrett-Koehler Publishers, 2006). Frock is a former senior vice-president of operations at FedEx and the guy who had the conversation with Smith after that blackjack weekend.

Chapter Nine: The Lucky Break That Really Counts

The lucky penny problem is an example of the power of multipliers. If you're just adding a penny every day, you need longer than 27,000 years to get to that ten million dollars. But doubling an amount changes it quickly. You start off slowly, and the first week, the penny goes from 1 cent to 2 cents, 4, 8, 16, 32, 64 cents. Not very satisfying. But here's what the whole chart would look if you take the challenge in the month of March.

March 1: $0.01
March 2: $0.02
March 3: $0.04
March 4: $0.08
March 5: $0.16
March 6: $0.32
March 7: $0.64
March 8: $1.28
March 9: $2.56
March 10: $5.12
March 11: $10.24
March 12: $20.48
March 13: $40.96
March 14: $81.92
March 15: $163.84
March 16: $327.68
March 17: $655.36
March 18: $1,310.72
March 19: $2,621.44
March 20: $5,242.88
March 21: $10,485.76
March 22: $20,971.52
March 23: $41,943.04
March 24: $83,886.08
March 25: $167,772.16
March 26: $335,544.32
March 27: $671,088.64
March 28: $1,342,177.28
March 29: $2,684,354.56

March 30: $5,368,709.12
March 31: $10,737,418.24

You would be better doing this game in March (31 days) instead of February (28 days)—because as the chart shows, there would be a difference of more than nine million dollars. Once the numbers start getting big, they get big very fast. Of course, if you know anybody who is offering this in real life and not just theory, please give us a call.

The geographic breakdown of MacArthur fellows is very interesting. The most populous states in the United States are currently (in order) California, Texas, Florida, and New York. In terms of where winners were born, Florida and Texas are far down the list, and the numbers drop even more for winners living in those two states at the time of the award. New York, which is fourth in overall population, is number one for both where winners were born and where they lived at the time of the award.

Chapter Eleven: Get Lucky in Love

Helen Fisher's study on dopamine was published in 2005 in the *Journal of Comparative Neurology* (493: 58–62). The article was called "Romantic Love: An fMRI Study of a Neural Mechanism for Mate Choice." She conducted the research with Arthur Aron at the department of psychology at the State University of New York at Stony Brook and Lucy Brown, from the departments of neurology and neuroscience at Albert Einstein College of Medicine in New York.

Chapter Fourteen: The Ambulance in Your Backyard

The Harvard School of Public Health study was published in 2009 in the online journal *PLOS*. It was led by researchers form the Harvard School of Public Health and collaborators from the University of Toronto and the University of Washington.

Information on shark attacks and other animal-caused fatalities in the United States between 2001 and 2013 is from the CDC's Wonder database.

Quotes from Dr. James Andrews and Dr. Christopher DiGiovanni are from the article "Sports Medicine Said to Overuse M.R.I.'s" by Gina Kolata, which appeared in *The New York Times* on October 28, 2011.

Bayes' theorem is stated mathematically as the following equation:

$$P(A/B) = \frac{P(B/A)P(A)}{P(B)}$$

Where *A* and *B* are events and $P(B) \neq 0$.

- P(A) and P(B) are the probabilities of observing *A* and *B* without regard to each other.
- P(A/B), a conditional probability, is the probability of observing event *A* given that *B* is true.
- P(B/A) is the probability of observing event *B* given that *A* is true.

Okay, that's a little confusing. But the math works, and the basic point is that you have to understand the probabilities of different kinds of events before you can make an accurate prediction. That's why, in the example we gave, a positive medical test that's 90 percent accurate could still mean that you have only a 1 percent chance of having the disease.

The studies on American health care were reported in the UK medical journal *The Lancet*. Another study, in the April 2016 issue of *JAMA*, showed the differences in longevity based on where people live within the United States. The poor in big cities tended to have life-spans closest to their middle-class neighbors.

Estimates that 25 percent of longevity comes from genes are reported in the article "Human Longevity: Genetics or Lifestyle? It Takes Two to Tango" by Giuseppe Passarino, Francesco De Rango, and Alberto Montesanto, published in 2016 in *Immunity & Ageing*.

Many of the billionaires in Silicon Valley are now sinking huge sums of money into projects looking for ways to increase life-span. Google put a billion dollars into the launch of a company called Calico (short for California Life Company) dedicated to research into interventions that slow aging and counteract age-related diseases. Numerous well-funded biotech start-ups and research labs are also studying how to make us all lucky enough to live longer (and healthier).

Chapter Fifteen: How to Get Lucky in a Disaster (Natural or Otherwise)

Quote from Stephen Grosz from *The Examined Life: How We Lose and Find Ourselves* (W. W. Norton, 2013).

Quote from pilot John Wiley (and information about flight 1549 being "extremely rare") from *Popular Mechanics* article "What Went Right: Flight 1549 Airbus A-320's Ditch into the Hudson," September 30, 2009.

In a study of 568 commercial crashes between 1983 and 2000, involving 53,487 passengers, 52,207 survived. This was reported in "Survivability of Accidents Involving Part 121 U.S. Air Carrier Operations, 1983 Through 2000," a safety report issued by the National Transportation Safety Board, March 2001.

Joan Didion quote from her book *The Year of Magical Thinking* (Alfred A. Knopf, 2005).

Chapter Sixteen: The Lucky Path: Find Your Compass

Joi Ito quote from the book *Whiplash: How to Survive Our Faster Future*, written with Jeff Howe (Grand Central Publishing, 2016).

Chapter Seventeen: The Lucky Attitude: Believe That You Can Make Luck

More insights by George Vaillant can be found in his book *Spiritual Evolution* (Harmony Books, 2008).

Deepak's Homebase where we visited him is inside ABC Carpet & Home, the gorgeous store on East 19th Street and Broadway in Manhattan. Some of Deepak Chopra's ideas here are summarized from his book *The Seven Spiritual Laws of Success: A Practical Guide to the Fulfillment of Your Dreams* (New World Library, 1994).

About the Authors

Janice Kaplan has enjoyed wide success as a magazine editor, television producer, writer, and journalist. The former editor in chief of *Parade* magazine, she is the author of thirteen popular books, including the *New York Times* bestseller *The Gratitude Diaries,* which received international praise. She has appeared regularly on network television shows and lives in New York City and Kent, Connecticut.

Barnaby Marsh is an expert on risk-taking. As a Rhodes scholar at Oxford, he did pioneering research on decision-making in complex situations. He has worked with leaders of major corporations, foundations, and philanthropists, and he continues his academic research at both the Program for Evolutionary Dynamics at Harvard and the Institute for Advanced Study in Princeton. He lives in New York City.